DR. ABRAVANEL'S ANTI-CRAVING WEIGHT LOSS DIET

DR. ABRAVANEL'S ANTI-CRAVING WEIGHT LOSS DIET

BASED ON THE 8-WEEK SKINNY SCHOOL® PROGRAM

ELLIOT D. ABRAVANEL, M.D.
AND
ELIZABETH A. KING

BANTAM BOOKS
NEW YORK • TORONTO • LONDON • SYDNEY • AUCKLAND

This or any other diet or fitness program should be
followed only under a doctor's supervision.

DR. ABRAVANEL'S ANTI-CRAVING WEIGHT LOSS DIET
A Bantam Book / February 1990

Library of Congress Cataloging-in-Publication Data

Abravanel, Elliot D.
  Dr. Abravanel's anti-craving weight loss diet : based on the revolutionary
skinny school program / Elliot D. Abravanel and Elizabeth A. King.
      p.   cm.
  Includes bibliographical references.
  ISBN 0-553-05771-5
  1. Reducing diets. 2. Reducing diets—Recipes. I. King, Elizabeth A.
II. Title.   III. Title: Doctor Abravanel's anti-craving weight loss diet.   IV. Title:
Anti-craving weight loss diet.
RM222.2.A26   1990
613.2'6—dc20
                                                                    89-18120
                                                                       CIP

Published simultaneously in the United States and Canada

Bantam Books are published by Bantam Books, a division of Bantam Doubleday
Dell Publishing Group, Inc. Its trademark, consisting of the words "Bantam
Books" and the portrayal of a rooster, is Registered in U.S. Patent and Trademark
Office and in other countries. Marca Registrada. Bantam Books, 666 Fifth Avenue,
New York, New York 10103.

PRINTED IN THE UNITED STATES OF AMERICA

BG   0 9 8 7 6 5 4 3 2 1

This book is dedicated to the memory of Dr. Murry Buxbaum. His insight that all cravings could be cured was the inspiration for all that we now know at Skinny School.

And to the memory of Grace Bechtold, editor and friend.

ACKNOWLEDGMENTS

Our gratitude to Marta Cossia Cortinez, who not only manages the Los Angeles Skinny Schools with great expertise, but has contributed to the Skinny School program in so many ways, year after year.

Thanks also to the Skinny School nurses in our Los Angeles Skinny Schools: Mona Oropeza, June Mead, Delia Matute, Yolanda Martinez, Lucy Ortega, Shannon Mead, Alicia Gonzales, and Yvonne Borroto. Your attention to our patients and their cravings has helped make this book possible. Thanks also to Lana Denning of Body Type Services, for her diligence while we wrote this book.

Thanks to Dr. Alaric Arenander for sharing his knowledge of the neuroglial brain.

Our appreciation goes also to the physicians and nurses across the country who are using the Skinny School program in their own practices. Through your skill and practice the program will continue to grow.

Finally, we want to share our appreciation of all the Skinny School patients who have candidly revealed their cravings and followed the program to cure them. Thank you for sharing your experiences. Your histories will help the readers of this book know that all cravings can be cured.

CONTENTS

FIGURES

INTRODUCTION

This probably isn't the first diet book you've ever bought (with a mixture of hope and dread). By now you must know very well which foods are good for you and which ones are deadly. You certainly know which foods pile up the pounds, and I'm sure you don't expect this book, uniquely among all the others, to suggest that it's possible to eat chocolate and french fries and the skin off the chicken and still lose weight.

So why *do* you need this book? Isn't it because so far, though you do *know* what foods you should avoid to lose weight, you haven't been able to stay away from them as much as you wish you could? This is the problem with diets, all diets. Knowledge doesn't confer *ability*. Losing weight doesn't depend on knowing, but on *doing*, or, rather, not doing. On being able *not* to eat what you shouldn't.

Of course, it's not just losing weight but all sorts of good-health practices that depend on your ability to resist something you know isn't in your best interest. Good health involves *not* smoking, *not* overeating, *not* drinking too much, *not* lying around watching TV and putting off your exercise, *not* getting too stressed. And yet, though we all know this, few of us are able to resist unhealthy temptations.

As a physician, I have given decades of thought to the particularly human question of why we do things we know aren't good for us. Why *do* we so often overeat? Animals never do—unless they live with people. For that matter, why do we drink? Why does anyone smoke? Why take dangerous drugs? Why act in so many strange ways that put health and peace of mind at so much risk—ways we fully *know* are bad for us?

The strange propensity we share as human beings, to act at times against our best interests, can make the practice of medicine frustrating and maddening. When doctors experience "burnout," this is usually the reason. We physicians can understand it when our patients do something harmful out of ignorance. But if we have let them know that something is bad, yet they keep right on, it's easy to become frustrated, or to blame ourselves—which is no fun either.

We even do the same things ourselves—look how long it took doctors themselves to quit smoking. But instead of just sighing and saying "I guess that's just the way people are," I've made a twenty-year study of what, actually, is going on, in order to find the root of the problem.

THE MOMENT WHEN DIETS FAIL

Weight control is my special interest, so I focused my study on one particular application of this problem: why we eat foods we know aren't good for us. And the answer, in turn, has led to my Skinny School program, and a complete cure for food cravings.

Let's think for a moment about what happens when a diet fails. Let's say you know for certain that corn chips are something you really *shouldn't* be eating. You know that if you eat one, you'll eat the whole bag. You're quite aware that they are unhealthy and/or fattening. The corn's okay, maybe, but the chips have too much grease, too much salt. You know this, yet you keep on somehow *wanting* those corn chips, and eating them—not all the time, perhaps, but at certain key moments which fully undermine your ultimate dieting success.

In your mind, even while you're munching away, you know it's a mistake. So why do you do it? Why does anyone? Why do *I* sometimes? Why don't you or I or any of us have the ability to change immediately, *right now*, drop corn chips (or chocolate or french fries or greasy hamburgers or whatever) from our diet, and start living totally on those "good" foods—like salad and broiled fish?

COMPU-NONSENSE

If you were a computer, you'd calculate the best diet for happiness and long life, and just follow it. There have been hundreds of diet books that have been written as if you *were* a computer and could follow logical advice without lapses or those awful moments of totally demoralized overeating. But I can't help wondering if those writers were living in the same world with the rest of us.

Anyway, suppose you've read some book, decided to go on the diet, and said good-bye to corn chips forever. Fine. But just at the moment when you've been *really good* for three days, and find yourself alone in your kitchen with a headache, a gnawing feeling in your stomach, and a set of diet-subverting thought-habits in your head (such as, "I take care of everybody, nobody takes care of me, and I need those corn chips")—plus those damn corn chips themselves—the book skips out and leaves you on your own. The subtext is, if you can't follow the writer's *excellent* advice at this difficult moment, that's *your* problem.

IT TAKES MORE THAN JUST SMARTS

Why a diet book doesn't help much at this point is one question; but a deeper question is, why do we *need* help in following diet advice we *know* would be good for us? Or any kind of advice? There are cravings for many other things besides food, things which aren't fattening but are much worse. Humans crave many things—drugs and cigarettes come to mind—which won't make you fat but will kill you. Why does anyone use these known killers?

Why *does* anyone still smoke? You'd think one surgeon general's warning would be enough. "Oh, you say it causes cancer? Sure, I'll stop right away." Many people have stopped smoking, of course—but why hasn't everyone? Some people are just starting to smoke now! Don't you wonder about this?

Why *doesn't* everyone wear seat belts, cut back on their drinking, get enough rest, and reduce their cholesterol? Why *do* teenagers have sex without protection? Why do patients not take their high blood pressure medication? Why do people consume harmful drugs as if they were exempt from all the laws of nature and man?

Are we all crazy, or what?

WELL, ARE WE?

This book is about the answer to that question. No, we're not all crazy, even if we do seem to act that way. On the contrary, there is a very good reason for all these cravings—the craving for foods that aren't on any diet as well as the craving for alcohol, cigarettes, drugs, and even certain dangerous actions.

The reason is this: behind every craving is a built-in, biological drive to experience a *particular feeling*. That feeling we're searching for is so strongly programmed into our makeup, and so strongly supported by our genetic heritage, that it is impossible to do without it.

Make no mistake, neither food nor drugs nor alcohol can actually create the feeling in you that you are searching for. But these substances work their spell on you by creating a feeling that resembles or mimics the feeling you actually need. They create a compelling illusion—and unless you know a reliable way to make yourself actually have that feeling, you will not be able to give up creating the illusion. You won't be able to stop eating the food (or taking the drug or the drink, or smoking the cigarette, or gambling) that makes you almost believe the illusion that you are getting what you want. This illusion is what all cravings are about.

UNRAVELING THE MYSTERY OF CRAVINGS

In the pages of this book we are going to unravel the mystery of all cravings. We'll look mainly at food cravings, because twenty years of practice and experience with my Skinny School program has made that my field of expertise. But what applies to cravings for food actually applies to every craving—that is, to every strong, irresistible desire for anything that you know is not good for you, no matter what it may be.

To understand the entire picture of cravings, and especially to understand how they can be cured, we'll need to look at these main areas:

1. We'll start by seeing what cravings actually are, and how they work to destroy every diet. This is the subject of Chapter 1, The Reality of Cravings.
2. Next, we'll determine what the feeling is that you are looking for when you eat a food that you crave. This is the subject of Chapter 2, What Cravings Are For.
3. We'll see how you can get the feeling you're searching for (it's actually a global feeling of complete inner peace, tranquillity, and power which I call the ''M-State'') *without* eating foods that destroy your diet. You'll find this in Chapter 3, The M-State: The Feeling You're Looking For.
4. We'll look at the effects (on our bodies and minds) of the particular foods that destroy diets—''craving foods''—and see how they work to mimic or create an illusion of the M-State you're really looking for.

   We'll make a detailed comparison between the *real* M-State, which is truly pleasurable as well as totally healthful, and the *fake* M-State created by craving foods, which is incomplete (even in the ''pleasure'' it provides), and ultimately destructive. We'll take a case history of a typical Skinny School patient, so you can see how the M-State looks in action.

   This analysis of cravings and addictions is in Chapter 4, The M-State in Action.
5. We'll look at the foods you crave and see how they act on your brain just as drugs do to create that imitation M-State. This is in Chapter 5, Food Cravings: Creating the Fake M-State.
6. To conclude the examination of cravings, we'll compare food cravings to other addictions and see how *all* addictions work to mimic the M-State. This is the subject of Chapter 6, Addictions: The Euphoria Principle.
7. We turn from an analysis of cravings in general to *your* cravings in particular. Do not skip to this chapter without reading about cravings first; I find that when my patients understand cravings, they do much better at Skinny School.

   Chapter 7, The Cravings Analysis Checklist gives you a genuine *cure* for cravings. When you're really cured of cravings, you won't even have to *resist* the foods that you usually crave. You won't even want them anymore.

The Cravings Analysis Checklist will help you discover exactly which foods are your "craving foods."

8. Next we present the Skinny School way to cure cravings and become naturally skinny. The complete program has three parts. First, you follow the Skinny School Anti-craving Diet that is right for you (based on the results of the Cravings Analysis Checklist). There are different diets to cure cravings for sweets and starches and for greasy, spicy, or salty foods.

   The Skinny School Sweet and Starch Cravers Diet and the Skinny School Greasy and Spicy Food Cravers Diet are based entirely on taste. There are *no* instructions like, "Boil one skinless chicken breast for six hours. Discard broth. Enjoy."

   Taste has been totally overlooked in diets, yet only by understanding taste can you ever control your weight. Your brain is designed to respond to taste, not only to calories or nutrients. By choosing food according to taste, you can use your body's own natural mechanisms for completely natural weight control. It's amazing and it really works.

   Because the concept of using taste to control your weight is so new, Chapter 8, All You Need Is Taste, and Chapter 9, How to Taste and Smell, explain how this works.

9. The Anti-craving Diets use a specific balance of tastes to cure each craving. Chapter 10, Tastes That Cure Cravings, explains the eight basic tastes, and shows you which tastes work for each craving.

10. Chapters 11 and 12 contain the two Skinny School Anti-craving Diets themselves, plus meal plans to help you begin *using* taste to cure your own cravings.

11. The second part of the Skinny School cravings cure is a targeted plan of specific nutritional supplementation to correct deficiencies, using supplements that are available at your local health food store.

   Research at Skinny School has shown that *everyone* who has cravings also has severe deficiencies of certain key vitamins, minerals, and other nutrients.

   Here you will find an extremely precise program of nutritional supplementation to cure *your* cravings. But this program *must* be used along with the Anti-craving Diets—for reasons that you'll see

clearly. If you follow the diet and take the recommended supplements, your cravings will be cured in four to eight weeks.

   You'll find the supplement program for your cravings in Chapter
13, Anti-craving Supplements.

12. The third part of the Skinny School cravings cure is the food-
    behavior modification exercises called "Lard" Lessons. The lessons
    work to retrain your eating habits. They are extremely effective, but
    cannot work until your cravings have come partially under control.
    At Skinny School we do not begin the lessons until patients have
    been on the program for four weeks.

    The "Lard" Lessons are found in Chapter 14.

13. Chapter 15 answers the most commonly asked questions about
    Skinny School.

14. Chapter 16 is a look into the future, for a life without cravings.
    You'll see what it is like to be naturally skinny—which is exactly
    what you learn at Skinny School.

15. Finally, the Appendix gives you recipes and food taste lists.

HOW TO END DIETING FOREVER

This is a diet book, and it does have all the traditional material that you
have a right to expect from a medically sound, health-oriented weight
control program. There are meal plans and recipes to go along with the
diets—all important, all helpful. But the real focus of this book is much
more on how to free yourself from compulsive cravings than on what
you should eat to lose weight.

   Curing your cravings is absolutely vital for permanent weight loss.
Certainly you can lose weight without getting rid of your cravings for
food. People do it all the time—temporarily. It takes tremendous amounts
of self-deprivation and willpower, but it can be done. You've undoubt-
edly lost weight yourself in this way, but since your cravings weren't
cured, you gained it back.

   Unless your cravings depart permanently, never to darken your oral
doorway again, you will inevitably gain back any weight you lose, and
often you will gain back much more than what you lost.

   When your cravings are cured, you will not only lose weight, you'll also find it easy to keep it off. If you actually don't *want* to eat anything that isn't good for you, keeping your best weight is literally no problem at all.

NATURALLY SKINNY PEOPLE

The craving cures in this book come from research done over the last twenty years in Skinny School, my weight control centers in the Los Angeles area. If you've read my previous books, you already know something about the Skinny School program. But even if you haven't read these books, you might still be aware of the program because there are many physicians across the country who are using with great success the Skinny School program we developed.

The name "Skinny School" was invented by my late colleague, a brilliant and innovative physician, Murry Buxbaum. We like it because it is light and cheerful; but I want to set your mind at rest about what we mean by "skinny." What we *don't* mean is that you should try to be super-thin. We believe getting you the right weight for you: to a slender, *comfortable* weight based on your own best look and energy level. We want you to look good and feel terrific.

NATURALLY SKINNY

What we *do* mean by "skinny" is being like those people who are just naturally skinny. Naturally skinny people absolutely don't have cravings. They aren't driven to eat any "bad" foods, so they just eat whatever they want. They never diet because they're not plagued by certain foods that they just can't resist or that they find themselves eating compulsively.

To naturally skinny people, food is just food. They like it but it doesn't drive them crazy. To us, that's what the word "skinny" means: not super-thin, not obsessed with dieting, not even worried about dieting. Just relaxed, comfortable with food, and permanently at your best weight without having to think about it at all.

This is the way I want you to be, and the way you will be when you've completed Skinny School. Once your cravings are totally cured, your dieting days will be over.

And after all, isn't that what you want from this book?

1

THE REALITY
OF
CRAVINGS

Let's begin by taking a look at what a craving actually is. A "craving" is what we call those almost-irresistible desires for any food that you shouldn't be eating. The relief of obtaining an illicit chocolate chip cookie at break time, the inevitable "Yes" when the squawky voice at the drive-thru asks, "Fries with that?" or the midnight dish of ice cream—these are all cravings.

CRAVING FOODS

Craving foods are the ones that tempt you away from your healthy meal plans, make you eat too much, and destroy your looks and even your health.

In this book, the word "cravings" is used mainly for food. When the same concept of an obsessive, irresistible desire is used about substances other than foods, I call it "addiction." But the fact is that while there are some differences in degree, food cravings are addictions and share all the important characteristics of the more classic addictions to drugs and alcohol. (I'll return to this point in Chapter 2.)

From the very beginning, we realized at Skinny School that cravings for specific foods are the real cause of overweight (and of a lot of illness as well). We also discovered early on that cravings are extremely specific. When it comes to overeating, no one overeats everything. At the buffet table of life we end up making very definite choices. What you "choose" to develop a craving for speaks volumes about your inner makeup.

THE MOST COMMON CRAVINGS: SWEETS AND STARCHES

Since no one overeats everything, the first step in curing cravings is to determine for each person just what he or she, in particular, craves. Every person with a weight problem has just a few "problem" foods, many times just a single one, and seldom more than three or four. You, too, have a few "problem" foods—though you may not be aware of what they are at this moment. If it weren't for these particular foods, you would have no trouble at all following any diet you might choose.

Many people, for example, have a problem with bread. These are people who eat very good, normal, balanced diets, except that they cannot resist bread and might eat two, or four, or five, or even more slices at a meal. We had a patient at Skinny School, Maria C., who had gained one hundred pounds, basically by overeating bread. It was literally her only problem food. Another man, Morris K., ate a *loaf* of bread with every meal, but since it took him six weeks to admit it, he had us puzzled for a time. He couldn't believe he was curable. He was.

SMALLER CRAVINGS, BUT THE SAME PROBLEM

In most people, of course, the cravings aren't as pronounced as Maria's or Morris's. I have had countless patients who might be ten, fifteen, or twenty pounds overweight, who have gained that weight just through eating a relatively small amount of bread every day. Just two slices of bread per day above what you actually need could account for a thirty-pound weight gain in just one year.

The craving for bread is an example of what we call the "starch craving." Other starch cravings are cravings for pasta, rolls, and tortillas.

SWEETS AND STARCHY SWEETS

The starch craving is extremely common, but almost as common is the sweets craving—the actual need that many people have to eat something sweet. If they didn't have a sweet dessert after every meal (and usually something else between meals), they would have absolutely no weight problem at all.

Corey L. was a good example. He'd often told me how healthful his diet was, and I couldn't help wondering why he was twenty-five pounds overweight. Then one day I ran into him in the grocery store. He was at the checkout register buying a cake. It must have been the shock of seeing me, because he admitted then that he ate an entire cake for dessert *every night*. Corey's craving was for *starchy sweets*—cake has both sugar and starch.

Again, most people won't do what Corey does. But a sweets craving can pile up pounds just as effectively as a starch craving. Just one 350 calorie chunk of brownie or cookie, or a little dish of ice cream, if they are more caloric than what you are actually burning up each day, can pile up twenty-five to thirty-five pounds in a year. This is the insidious quality of cravings.

GREASY, SPICY, AND SALTY FOOD CRAVINGS

While many people have a great problem resisting either starches or sweets, there is another great number of people who crave foods that are either spicy, salty, or rich in grease or oils. If you are one of these people, you have a tremendous desire for something fried, like fried chicken, or for a grilled steak, meat, or simply cannot resist eating the chicken skin.

Another example of this craving is mayonnaise. Some people have become fat exclusively because of their need to put mayonnaise on everything. To them, tuna is something to hold the mayonnaise together. If you have a greasy food craving, you will have no trouble resisting sweets or starches. You may feel superior to your friends who eat bread or dessert, but you won't be able to pass up the butter, or the creamy sauce, or the sour cream—foods which are terrible temptations for you.

RICH DESSERTS

There are also some people who think they crave sweets but who are actually greasy food cravers. A patient named Lucille W. was typical. She told me that she was a sweets craver, but it turned out that she craved only very *rich* sweets. She always fell off diets with foods like danishes and croissants, which are made with butter. Or she would eat the butter frosting off a cake and leave the cake.

After she completed the Cravings Analysis Checklist she turned out to be an intense greasy food craver. It was the butter she was craving, not the sugar.

Even a chocolate bar, which seems to be a classic sweet, derives two-thirds of its calories from cocoa fat. Chocolate mousse is another notorious greasy food which masquerades as a sweet. Just because it is a dessert doesn't mean it is a sweet.

You shouldn't assume at this point that you know for certain whether you are a sweet and starch craver or a greasy and spicy food craver— wait until you have completed the Cravings Analysis Checklist in Chapter 7. Some cravings are very misleading. Ice cream, for example, is a food that is craved equally by both sweets cravers and greasy food cravers, since it is both sweet and rich at the same time.

In our research at Skinny School, we have found that the following foods make up 98 percent of all food cravings:

1. CRAVING FOODS*

CATEGORY	EXAMPLES
Sweets	Candy Chocolate Soft drinks Cake Frosting
Starches	Bread Potatoes Spaghetti, Pasta Tortilla Pretzels
Starchy sweets	Pie Doughnuts Coffee cake
Fried foods	French fries Onion rings Fried zucchini
Rich foods	Cheese Cream Sour cream Dip Butter Fat meat
Salty food	Salted nuts Potato chips Pretzels (see also Starches) Corn chips
Spicy food	Mexican food Italian food Thai food Chinese food (Szechuan, Hunan)

*Foods people desire because of their effects on brain state.

CRAVINGS ARE NOT GLUTTONY

But whatever your specific problem food, cravings are the problem for all dieters—and they are the *only* problem. Having a craving does not mean you are a glutton, nor does it mean you lack willpower. You know that you have plenty of willpower in other areas of your life. You simply have one or two problem foods. These cravings need to be cured, not ignored.

Once we cure your craving for one or two foods, it will be very easy for you to diet, and weight loss will stop being an agonizing seesaw.

DIETS THAT FEED CRAVINGS

No other diet or diet book has dealt with the problem of cravings, simply because no one else has had the necessary tools. The strong implication of every other diet program is that your cravings would go away if only you were a good enough person.

Other programs, especially strict fasting programs, assume that even if you do have to tough it out with your cravings while you're dieting, once you've lost the weight, your cravings, too, will disappear somehow, perhaps by magic.

The implied premise is that since thin people seem not to have cravings, if *you're* thin *you* won't have cravings either. If you believe this, I have a bridge I would like to sell you.

First of all, there are thin people who have just finished diets but who are struggling with their cravings and who will regain the weight sooner or later (usually sooner). Then there are also people who do not have cravings, and they are indeed thin, but they are thin because they don't have cravings, not the other way around.

Ignoring cravings comes partly from denial (don't mention a problem and it doesn't exist), partly from a lack of real-life experience. Of course, it's a handy attitude to have if you have no solution to offer.

DENYING CRAVINGS WON'T CURE THEM

Where have you ever seen it written in a diet book that on the third day you are going to be ready to kill for a cookie, and here is what you should do. Nowhere. Day three is the same as day one: Eat your broiled fish and some spinach and be quiet about it. If you want something else, you have to struggle with that dirty little problem on your own.

Since diets have rarely if ever dealt realistically with cravings, many people with weight problems end up seeking out diets (or diet books or diet doctors) that let them eat the foods they crave.

If you are a greasy food craver, for instance, you will often choose a high-protein diet that lets you feed your cravings for fatty meats. "Eat all the steak you want and still lose weight." And/or die trying.

People who crave sweets or starches will usually choose a lower-protein high-carbohydrate diet that emphasizes fruit (which is very sweet), pasta, bread, or whatever. The magic words that draw them into the diet might be "complex carbohydrates," or "good for your heart," or "cardiovascular fitness," but the real reason they choose that diet is that it lets them eat what they crave.

DON'T WALLOW IN YOUR CRAVING

You can see that many people who diet go from their usual fattening, unhealthy diet to a weight-reducing but extremely unhealthy diet that gives relatively free rein to their craving foods. This is not the basis of a cure. It's giving yourself permission to wallow.

If you can't stay *with* a diet, it's because you crave foods that are not *on* the diet. It's that simple. So you choose a weight loss diet that consists almost solely of the foods you crave. Unfortunately, this has the effect of making your cravings even more severe (I'll explain *why* this happens in Chapter 5). Even if you do lose weight, at the end of the diet you will rebound far past your beginning weight.

HOW CRAVINGS UNDERMINE DIETING

Here are a few examples from my Skinny School files of how cravings undo a diet.

Kathy L. was a schoolteacher who was about twenty pounds over her best weight. Before coming to us she had been a year-round off-and-on-again dieter. Her pattern went like this: She would begin a diet, usually on a Monday, and do well through Wednesday afternoon. Wednesday night she had a faculty meeting and worked late. She would have a cup of coffee in the late afternoon, to keep herself going. No problem there—the diet she had chosen in the past let her drink coffee, ''as much as she wanted.''

By the time she got home she would be draggy, and would find herself wanting a taste of something sweet very badly.

''I would feel deprived,'' she told the Skinny School nurse. ''I thought, 'I worked so hard and I can't even have something to make me feel better.' '' She felt she just *had* to have just one Oreo. But once Kathy started, she couldn't stop. (After all, RJR/Nabisco doesn't want you eating just one Oreo; cravings and addictions are good for their business. And this doesn't apply just to RJR/Nabisco either, of course.)

Each Oreo actually made Kathy feel better, calmer, more cared for. She would decide that she didn't care about her diet. Her *feeling* was more important. Oddly enough, in its strange, limited way, the Oreo *worked*. (You'll see *why* in Chapter 4.) People only take drugs that actually work.

OREOS AT THE HELM

Even more oddly, Kathy also felt that the cookies would help her get control of her cravings. (''If I just have a few Oreos, I'll be able to control myself just fine at dinner.'') And to a limited extent this was also true. Kathy didn't overeat at dinner—because Oreos, her craving food, weren't on the menu. She didn't have cravings for everything, just for Oreos.

And so it would go. Kathy's craving, her desire for her problem food, would just become too strong, and the current diet of the month would be finished. But at Skinny School we finally focused on her sweets craving. Since we have the right tools, within a few weeks she was cured. She still had to diet to lose her weight, but with her craving for Oreos gone, she *could,* easily.

"SOMETHING WITH A LITTLE *BODY* TO IT"

Another patient, June A., talked about her craving for greasy food. She said it would hit her in fast food restaurants, when she'd be having salad bar. (Why did she go to a hamburger place for the salad bar? Unadmitted cravings, of course.)

"Especially if I was stressed, I would just feel so *cold* with only salad," June said. "Salad is great, I love lettuce and all that, but I used to feel like I needed something more *solid*. Something with a little body to it. Something that would *hold me*. When I was under pressure, what I needed wasn't more salad. It was a cheeseburger and fries."

June, too, was cured of her greasy food craving at Skinny School. We realized that if we didn't find out why people have cravings, we would never understand obesity, and never cure our patients. We'd just be giving them a lifetime pass to the revolving door, as so many diet programs clearly do.

THE STRANGE ILLUSION OF WILLPOWER

Getting rid of cravings actually does not require either willpower or a supreme effort of renunciation. It can't, because willpower is ultimately of no use in losing weight. Food cravings, if not cured, can overcome any willpower, and eventually will. And here is the difficult part: the longer you put off giving in to a craving, the stronger that craving actually becomes. When you *do* give in and eat what you crave, you are likely to eat much more of it than if you had given in immediately.

Willpower is not the answer. The craving must be uncovered and cured or you will never be free.

"WHAT IF I DON'T CRAVE *ANYTHING*?"

At Skinny School we always find a small but consistent percentage of patients who feel that they don't have any particular cravings. They say that they simply eat whatever is there. This type of patient usually says something like "I don't have cravings, I'm just *hungry* all the time."

Yet close analysis shows that this is never completely true. There are *always* cravings, though it may be a challenge to discover them immediately. If you are very ashamed of your cravings, your wall of denial will be very high.

The fact is that while the concept of cravings is fairly easy to entertain in the abstract, when it comes down to your very own cravings you may not find them so easy to recognize or to admit to them. Even people who are fifty to one hundred pounds overweight may say that they don't crave anything in particular. They are not lying—they just don't realize what a craving is or recognize its sneaky presence in their lives.

Cravings can be so pervasive that they seem almost built-in. You may be so used to eating what you crave (whether it is bread, chocolate, potatoes, ice cream, butter, or any other craving food) that you don't even think of it as a craving. It simply seems natural to eat that food. You may assume everyone eats it. You may not even be able to imagine life without it.

UNCOVERING THE CRAVING

When patients on their first visit to Skinny School deny having problems with any particular food, we ask them about foods that they snack on, that they eat late at night or in the car or in front of the TV.

Unless we specifically ask, these foods may never be mentioned. Even if we ask, we sometimes don't find out until much later.

Sometimes cravings are ignored or suppressed because of shame. Some patients pretend even to themselves that they don't eat these foods because of scoldings they received as children, or because people in their lives still make hurtful remarks. People fear anger and hate being scorned.

It is surprising how vulnerable most people feel—even confident people—about their eating habits. They are very self-protective about them, and will make schoolkid-type distinctions like "Oh, Doctor, I thought you were asking what I had for *lunch*. I just had a few Fritos *after* lunch." Patients tell me, and believe themselves, that even though they eat Fritos every day, those Fritos are a slip-up, a lapse, or a rarity.

CRAVING FOODS ARE *IMPORTANT*

Yet these foods—craving foods—are deeply ingrained into our food patterns, and *deep down* most of us feel that we could barely exist without them. Eating the foods we truly crave is like breathing—we hardly think about it. We hardly can.

Our ho-hum snack, eaten in the kitchen while washing up the dishes, is actually *far* more important to us than that piece of skinless chicken that was the official offering at dinner. In the kitchen is when the real eating takes place. Relaxed, alone, you can finally do something for *you*. But no one can see you, so perhaps it didn't *really* happen. . . .

If no one could see them, many people would skip dinner completely and just enlarge their before- or after-dinner snack. People who live alone or who eat alone from time to time sometimes do just that. With a guilty sense of transgression, they will snack throughout the evening and skip dinner completely. Regular proper food is the chore. The snack is the reward.

LITTLE ALICE

I was once right behind a young child, perhaps four years old, in a buffet line at a party. The little girl's mother had told her to help herself to what she wanted to eat, but then had started talking with friends and hadn't helped her daughter through the line.

Little Alice had simply filled her plate with cheese curls. The plate looked so funny that everyone who saw it laughed; but behind the laughter was the recognition that most everyone there would have liked to do the same thing; we just didn't dare.

Alice was being a "good girl" and just following orders. It wasn't her fault she was 100 percent in touch with her cravings and innocent enough to admit it.

In fact, it takes a great deal of insight and courage to own up to your cravings. You may have already seen yourself in the mirror of our examples. But don't worry if you still aren't sure about your craving foods. We sometimes have to work with our Skinny School patients for a week or two before they see their cravings clearly.

YOU'LL FIND YOUR CRAVINGS, DON'T WORRY

In Chapter 7, The Cravings Analysis Checklist, you'll be going through the steps that we take our patients through at Skinny School. When you've done the checklist you will know which foods are problems for you. Once you know that, you'll be ready to start the cures, which are much easier than you now can imagine.

2

WHAT CRAVINGS ARE FOR

Food cravings ruin diets, destroy willpower, and make you feel guilty, driven, and sometimes desperate. They're tough to deal with. They not only make you fat, they can make you sick.

All true. And yet cravings are not just something to be ashamed of. Cravings are also both natural and positive. They are almost *good*. We're supposed to crave—it's built in to what makes us human.

Unbelievable? Perhaps, but this is the paradox of cravings. Cravings are *for* things that are unhealthy, yet the act of craving is perfectly healthy. Or, to put it another way, you have cravings for things that are bad for you, yet what you are *actually craving* is something good.

Still not clear? Okay, what *is* it that you are actually craving when you have those urges to eat your own particular "craving foods"? What are you looking for when you "have to have" a candy bar or a bag of fries? Surely these foods alone, unhealthy and unromantic as they actually are, wouldn't have such power over you, would they?

No, they wouldn't—not all by themselves. It's *not* the food itself that you want. No matter who you are or what food you give in to, it is always something other than the food itself that you are craving. Whether your cravings seem to be for sweets (such as candy, soft drinks, or sugary frosting), for starches (such as bread, pasta, or rolls), for greasy foods (such as steak, hamburgers, or fried foods) or spicy foods (such as Italian or Thai), what you are actually in search of is a particular *feeling*.

Craving foods are not an end in themselves. They are a *means* to get a particular feeling.

A MAJOR DISCOVERY: YOUR FEELING BRAIN

This is the major discovery of Skinny School: Food cravings (and, in fact, all cravings, including cravings that are really addictions, such as cravings for drugs, alcohol, and cigarettes) are cravings not actually for the substance itself, but for a certain special state of your brain—and the special feeling that goes with it.

Now that I know this, I can understand why human beings do so many things that we know are bad for us. It's not because we are crazy, but simply because we are trying to feel better. Our research tells us that people are well-intentioned. This includes alcoholics and drug addicts as surely as it does people with food cravings.

Giving in to a craving is not so much a sign of weakness as an instinctive, unsuccessful attempt to improve your current feelings. That's why feeling ashamed or guilty about cravings is a big mistake.

The feeling we're craving comes out of a particular part of the brain, and is based on a special configuration of brain waves and brain chemistry. (We'll cover the brain chemistry in Chapter 3.) It's a feeling that, as human beings, we are strongly programmed by our genes to need.

THE SHADOW AND THE REALITY

In fact, we want this particular feeling so much, and are programmed so thoroughly by our genes to try to get it, we will develop tremendous attachments to, and cravings for, anything that even resembles or mimics this feeling.

The fact is that all craving foods have the ability to trigger our brains into *something resembling* this feeling. What makes you crave a particular food is its ability to act upon your brain—regularly and reliably—to create a false but still convincing substitute for the feeling you are searching for.

WHEN THE GOING GETS TOUGH, THE TOUGH GET BETTER

What is this feeling you're looking for, exactly? And why do you want it so badly? To answer this question for yourself, think back to those moments in your past when your diet has gone wrong.

Maybe it was at a moment of the kind I described in Chapter 1, when you were alone in the kitchen after a hard day, trying to deal with feelings of fatigue, depression, irritation, pressure, or any other feelings you didn't want to have. Or maybe the moment came while you were in your car, or at work, or out at a restaurant. Feelings are very personal, yet wherever you were, and whatever you were feeling *exactly,* the common thread is that you were under stress and you needed something to make you feel better.

When you meet stress, your brain automatically wants to find a way of dealing with that stress. It tries to get itself to work better so that you can deal with the stress and survive.

THE TWO PARTS OF THE FEELING

The feeling your brain seeks has two parts:

1. Complete inner calm and tranquillity
2. Intense alertness

There is a great deal of research to support this, as you'll see in the coming chapters. But it's more important for you to think about it for a moment in terms of the way you yourself feel when you have cravings, and your diet fails you.

Let's say your moment of diet breakdown most often comes in the kitchen, after a hard day at work and just before your family pours in with all its demands. At this moment you don't feel so great, but you definitely need to feel better, and quickly.

You definitely want to calm down. If you're tense, wound up, or irritable, you might yell at the kids when you don't really want to, or take it out on your husband. And you need to be wide awake; if you're tired or draggy you just won't be able to *do* everything you have to do. Deep inside, you *know* what the feeling you need is like. It's a feeling of settling down, becoming more centered, more aware of yourself. Some people describe it as simply coming back to themselves. You're a little "off," and you need to get back "on."

When you schlump down with a bag of corn chips, this is what you are trying to get back for yourself. You know from past experience that inside that bag is the calmness and alertness you so desperately need. It's not the chips you want, it's the feeling they give you.

THE TASTE CONNECTION

"Oh, no, Doctor," I remember a patient of mine, Sandy L., saying when I first explained this to her. She happened to be a starches craver who couldn't resist pretzels. "When I eat pretzels," Sandy said, "I don't care about the way I feel. I'm not even *thinking* about my family, or how I want to act around them, or about *anything*. I just want those *pretzels*. If I'm thinking about anything, it's about the way pretzels taste. Or about the way they feel in my mouth. That's all!"

As I told Sandy, this is exactly how cravings work in many people. When you're looking for a feeling, you often don't realize that's what's happening. You're caught up in the compulsion. The seeking occurs automatically, the way you might pull the covers around you while you're sleeping: you're trying to get warm, but without thinking about it.

With craving foods, you are automatically seeking out the reaction they trigger in your brain—but without thinking about it. The pleasure of the feeling gets attached to the taste of the food. When Sandy told me she mainly thought about the *taste* of her pretzels, I explained that the taste of a food is a shorthand way that your brain has of knowing what effect the food will have on your feelings.

TASTING THE FEELING

All foods have distinct chemical compositions, and these chemicals react in your body and in your brain. The taste "encodes" the chemicals in a food, in a way your brain can easily read. When your brain tells you it wants a certain taste, it's actually telling you that it wants a certain chemical reaction that will create a feeling. Taste is a code for the feelings that you will get from any food.

This is why taste is such a vital part of the Skinny School program. Taste is the way food communicates with your inner, feeling brain. But we'll come back to this in Chapters 8 and 9, which are entirely devoted to the subject of taste.

SURVIVAL VALUE

So when you seek out the particular taste you crave—which could be the taste of pretzels, or chocolate, or ice cream, or any of the craving foods—you're actually experiencing a *craving for a chemical reaction in your brain*. The chemical reaction will change your feelings to make them both calmer and more alert.

But why do you need this feeling so much that, as science tells us, it is actually programmed into your genes? The reason you need it is simple: *It has tremendous survival value.*

Think about this concept of "survival value." Suppose you are a Los Angeles cave person—someone living a simpler and more primitive life in the days when saber-toothed tigers and giant mammoths walked about the Los Angeles basin. (Of course, some people might say life is more primitive and dangerous *now* in L.A. In fact, maybe they're right.)

Now suppose that every night a saber-tooth comes stalking around your camp looking for a snack. You have to be alert at the right time, or that snack is going to be you, personally. Just a little bit of dullness at the wrong time could be fatal. You also have to be very calm; if you're tense or wound up you could make a mistake and jump right when you meant to jump left. Also fatal.

In short, your survival depends on your being rested, healthy, balanced, and on the qui vive—just as it does today. But you're one of the lucky ones. Whenever you see that tiger, your brain reacts just as it should. You become instantly calm, but alert. You don't get eaten, you have a large family of cave children, and your fine genetic makeup is passed along.

UNSURVIVAL VALUE

But suppose you have a friend who gets very upset whenever he sees the tiger. His tension makes him consistently wander away from the campsite at the wrong time, so that one day the tiger eats him. Since his brain didn't allow him to react well to stress, it didn't have the survival value yours did. So his genes didn't get passed along.

We are all the heirs of the people who *did* survive—the ones who could outwit saber-toothed tigers, marauding mammoths, and everything else. Our brains all have the potential to react to stress with the calmness and alertness we need. The ability is there—otherwise *we* wouldn't be here.

THE FOOD SUBSTITUTION

You can see the survival value of this feeling of calm alertness. You have to have it when you need it—in today's world as well as in the distant past. But what does it have to do with food cravings? What kind of survival value could there possibly be in pretzels or corn chips?

Well, suppose you're back in prehistoric Los Angeles. This time the saber-toothed tiger shows up on a night when you aren't feeling especially well. You're tense and inattentive instead of calm and alert.

But suppose you happen to pop into your mouth a few bites of roasted corn seasoned with a little sprinkling of that white stuff with the great taste you pick up around the salt lick, just as the tiger starts to growl.

And you find that it perks you up noticeably. It calms you down just enough, and gives you a little burst of energy, and you start to feel better. You don't feel totally better, but you feel okay for the time being—well enough to avoid the tiger for one more night. For now that's enough.

PRIMITIVE CRAVINGS

Repeat this over a period of time, and it gets to be ingrained. Whenever you feel tired or worried, you reach for those nice salty bits of corn, and every time they pep you up and contribute to your survival.

True, the effect of your prehistoric corn chips is short-lived. They help you for only a little while. You may feel worse afterward. You gain weight. People snicker and make fat cave paintings of you. You get a reputation around the campfire as someone who can't resist the corn. But for a little while they help.

Can you see where you might end up a cave person with a craving?

SURVIVAL VALUE—TODAY

Today survival has different parameters, but the way we use particular foods to manipulate our brains is the same. In other words, the stresses we have to deal with aren't saber-toothed tigers, but they are every bit as stressful and threatening—if not more so.

Getting yourself from the hunting grounds (i.e., the office) to the campsite (home) doesn't require negotiating your way through wild beasts. But it requires braving the freeways, where, let's face it, you could also be killed (50,000 people are killed there every year, after all).

Around the campfire (the dinner table), if you feel too depressed or too irritable, or too angry—if your brain isn't as calm and alert as you want it to be—the tiger won't eat you, but your family may chew you up in other ways. When you go off hunting (to work), if you're too tired or dull to bring down the mammoths (the competition), you may literally not have anything to eat.

We're used to these stresses. We don't even think about them—

they're just *life*. But they are there, and they affect us all constantly. So if we find that some particular food or drug helps us deal with them, even if the help is only temporary, we use them. This is survival value in the modern sense.

BOOSTING THE BRAIN: UP AND OVER . . .

Chapter 4 describes the precise mechanics by which the "craving foods" (see figure 1, page 5) work to bring temporary calmness and alertness to your brain. Foods like Fritos, Chee-tos, Screaming Yellow Zonkers (if they still exist), Häagen-Dazs, Whoppers, chocolate, and all the rest of them actually do have biochemical mechanisms to make you feel better.

. . . AND THEN DOWN

The "boost" they give the brain is temporary, and it carries a high cost. All craving foods have a seesaw effect. They stimulate your brain, yet they do not give the brain real nourishment, so there is a dangerous slump afterward. The slump, naturally, makes you feel even more in need of your craving food, so you reach for it, and the process begins again.

Craving foods do not actually give you what you *need* to meet stress. What you actually need is a state of *revitalizing* calm and alertness, one that comes from a part of the brain completely different from the part stimulated by craving foods.

Chapter 3 is all about how to give your brain what it really needs; you'll see that craving foods give you only an imitation of it. So if you have food cravings, it indicates that you habitually pick the wrong things to stimulate your brain because of a lack of alternatives. You are choosing a quick fix rather than a real cure. You don't get the true survival value you are looking for. You may injure your health or reduce your attractiveness.

Yet the act of craving is not to blame. What's wrong lies in the *object* of the craving, not the craving itself. Having cravings is part of being human. It's just that the choices we make to *satisfy* our cravings have to be changed. Guilt about having a craving is like guilt about being a person. A waste of time.

WANTING, LIKING, AND CRAVING

Many of my patients ask me whether having a craving for a food is the same as liking a food. Actually they are completely different. Liking any food is not a problem. If you like, say, fish for dinner, and you go out to a restaurant and order it, and it tastes good and is not too dry, everything is fine and you haven't hurt yourself in any way. This is not craving— it's eating, one of life's true pleasures.

But a craving is quite different. Cravings override the feelings of wanting or liking particular foods, and have little or nothing to do with feeling either hungry or full.

Suppose you have a craving for ice cream. The ice cream will be there in your mind with a special sort of feeling-glow around it. There is always a sense that the ice cream is going to deliver some sort of thrill or charge that you need, beyond the ice cream itself.

Suppose, then, you go ahead and order a healthy fish dinner, even though all you really can think about is ice cream. At the end of the meal you will still crave the ice cream, even though you are full. "There's always room for ice cream." Even if there isn't, you can always pack it in. There *has* to be room, because your craving *demands* it and you're not going to feel right until you satisfy it. Your feeling brain is giving irrational compelling orders that you *must* follow.

BRAIN STATES AND FEELINGS

Craving foods are foods that stimulate your brain in definite biochemical ways. Even though the various craving foods have different ways of achieving their brain effect (you'll find them explained in Chapter 4), they all achieve a result of increased *feelings* of calm and alertness.

Brain states are experienced as feelings. The brain consists of billions of nerve cells, surrounded by billions of nutrient cells called neuroglial cells. You don't experience all those billions of cells directly. You experience them together, as feelings.

The complexity of feelings is completely mirrored in the complexity of brain states. Brain states are extremely complicated biochemical events—which you would expect. When you can have a feeling as complicated as "anticipation mixed with a little dread, some doubtfulness, and a tiny thrill of excitement"—just for a relatively simple example—you can imagine how complex your brain state would have to be.

The way you experience the effect that a particular food has on your brain is through the feeling it creates in you. All craving foods are foods that have feelings of increased awareness, relaxation, and excitement associated with them.

PEOPLE TELL IT LIKE IT IS

My patients say things like this when talking about their craving foods (notice that they are all "feeling" statements):

"If I don't have bread with my meal, I just *don't feel right*."

"I just *can't relax* until I've had my dessert."

"Nothing makes me *unwind* at the end of the day like sitting down and eating some cheese and crackers."

"It just doesn't *feel like* coffee without the cream."

"If I don't eat something spicy, *I'm not happy*."

"If I don't have butter on my bread, *I feel like I haven't even eaten*."

This list could continue indefinitely, because feelings are completely individual. Yet I'm sure you can see the common thread. It's the sense that certain foods are important to us because of the feeling that comes with them.

FEELING FOODS

The interaction of food and feelings is a vital point in getting to understand cravings. All the foods that we crave are foods that give us a certain feeling. Feelings are important. No, make that stronger. Feelings are vital. If certain foods didn't have strong feelings attached to them, no one would get fat, because everyone would follow their computer-correct diet.

Craving foods become important to us only when there is a gap in our feelings for them to fill. When you are feeling sufficiently calm, alert, rested, happy, healthy, and in control of your life, you don't crave particular foods. (That is why the cure of food cravings requires a complete program to restore balance to your life. A quick-cure "diet" will never work, because the need for the feeling of calm alertness is too strong. If you don't have it, you'll always return to those foods that *seem*, though falsely, to give it to you.)

As long as you feel the need, at moments of stress, to stimulate your brain into a temporarily heightened state of calm and alertness, you will always reach for foods that do, in fact, have this effect on the brain. Only foods that have this effect are *ever* craved.

CHARD-EATERS ANONYMOUS DISBANDED

No one eats too many carrots. Hardly anyone craves cottage cheese. There is no such self-help group as Chard-Eaters Anonymous. These foods aren't on the list because they are literally craved by no one. As one patient remarked, "I know I ought to be eating cottage cheese for lunch, but it just doesn't thrill me." If a food doesn't give you the "thrill" (actually a temporary state of brain stimulation), you will certainly never develop a craving for it.

You might have a taste for these foods, but that's quite different. Many people have a well-developed taste for fresh fruit or vegetables, and say they "love salad," but they are also secretly relieved that crudités are no longer hip.

You don't notice anyone actually oohing and aahing when they bring around the vegetable cart, do you? In fact, there is no such *thing* as a vegetable cart. The honor of being wheeled up to your table after a great meal in a fine restaurant is reserved for the dessert trolley. You may stare blearily at it after a large meal, but the question is never "whether" but "how much" (as in, "Do we split the chocolate mousse cake, dear, or should we each have one?").

You might quite enjoy skim milk, but you don't rush into the house, tear open the container, and swallow the entire half-gallon when you come in from the market. Nor do you wolf down all the zucchini you bought for tonight's dinner in the car coming home. That's because these are foods that don't have a thrill to them—they don't have the brain effect you are looking for.

CHEMICAL FOODS

The craving foods come from different "food groups." Some are carbohydrates (sweets and starches). Some are dairy foods (butter, cheese, and cream) or animal foods (chicken, fish, or meat). All these foods are chemically different. The way they work to stimulate your brain is different (as you'll see in Chapter 4). But they all share another characteristic, which is that they are *partial,* as opposed to *whole,* foods.

A whole food is a food that is eaten in the same form in which nature produced it. Whole grains, for example, are seeds; when we eat a whole grain such as brown rice, we are eating the whole seed. White rice, by contrast, is a seed from which the outer hull has been removed. White flour is also from a grain, wheat, and again, it is from a grain from which part of the seed has been removed. All refined grains are partial foods—just a part of what nature put there.

WHOLE FOODS VS. PARTIAL FOODS

Vegetables are whole foods. So is fruit. Vegetable or fruit *juices,* on the other hand, are partial foods. Oils are partial foods. They are a part of a seed, nut, or fruit, or else are part of the milk or the fat part of an animal.

The meat we eat is a partial food. Meat is the muscle of an animal, separated from its tendons and blood vessels. When carnivorous animals eat meat, though, they eat everything. A coyote who eats a mouse eats the entire mouse—including the stomach and the vegetable matter that is in there. To them, meat is a whole food, but to human beings it is a partial food.

PARTIAL VS. WHOLE FOODS: THE BRAIN EFFECTS

This is a vital distinction because the effects that partial foods and whole foods have on our brains are completely different from one another. Whole foods contain a much wider variety of chemicals than do partial foods, and the variety of chemicals they contain act to *balance* one another. The balancing effect means that whole foods do not have a strong stimulating effect on the brain.

Partial foods, by contrast, do not have this natural balance. When part of a food is removed, the chemical effect is *simplified* and made *stronger*. Where a whole piece of fruit or a whole grain has many different chemicals in it that balance and offset one another in their effects, sugar and white flour have such a comparatively simple chemical structure that their effects are unbalanced and very pronounced.

We crave partial foods precisely *because* of their strong impact on us. In fact, the simpler and less complete a food is, the more it resembles a *drug* rather than a food. A very perceptive patient once remarked, "I know you always tell me that brown rice is better for me than white rice, Doctor, but brown rice is so much work to eat. With white rice, you eat it and it *hits* you. It's *quicker*." In short, more like a drug.

Most drugs, in fact, *are* partial foods. Many drugs are derived from herbs, but they are only part of the herb, what is called the "active ingredient." Alcohol is a drug that comes from grain or fruit or vegetables. Tobacco and marijuana are plants (though not foods), and smoking them brings a *part* of the plant, not the whole thing, into your body.

All the foods for which you can develop a craving are partial foods. In a sense they are actually drugs rather than true foods because we *use* them for their chemical effects on our brains rather than for nourishment.

Whole foods, as you will see when we come to the Skinny School Anti-craving Diets, are an important part of curing cravings. Whole foods are never craved because their effects are too balanced to stimulate the brain the way craving foods do.

Yet simply making a *major effort* to eat whole, rather than partial, foods will not cure your cravings. Willpower, as we've seen, is useless. Curing cravings requires the entire Skinny School program: the right diet, the right supplements, the "Lard" Lessons. Above all, it requires creation of a true state of inner calm, centeredness, and awareness—so that your brain can deal with stress without the need for craving foods.

SOMETHING BETTER IS THE ONLY CURE

Your cravings will never be cured unless the feelings that you get from craving foods can be replaced by even better, more satisfying feelings. If a craving food makes you feel better when you need to, no one has the right to take it away from you unless they can offer you something better.

You will never give up something that has survival value, except for something with *more* survival value. The life force within you would simply not let you do it.

If chocolate, potato chips, or any other craving food works for you, you're going to keep right on eating it—and so you should. If you have found something that helps you, I have no right to ask you to stop—unless I can replace it with something better. Fortunately, I can—as you'll see in the next chapter.

3

THE M-STATE: THE FEELING YOU'RE LOOKING FOR

Craving foods are foods that, because of their chemical structure, stimulate your brain to make it feel temporarily better. They all work to give you a sense of "readiness" to deal with stress, a feeling that mimics an important feeling of intense inner calm and alertness that you are genetically programmed to have.

To stop eating craving foods, then, you must find a way to get this feeling *without* your craving foods. What, precisely, is the feeling of calm alertness you're looking for? What does it feel like, and how do you know when you really have it? If you can be fooled by craving foods, how do you know when you have the real thing?

These are the questions that have to be answered in order to eliminate cravings from your life.

THE FEELING YOUR BRAIN NEEDS

I've said that the feeling we are looking for in craving foods is one of inner calm and alertness. Think for a moment about what this means. At those moments when you give in to cravings, it's invariably because you need to "fix" some other feeling that you don't like. You may feel stressed, nervous, upset, jittery, fatigued, down, or out of gas. Whatever the feeling, it's not the way you want to feel.

Notice that these feelings are quite different from feelings you have when you simply *want* a particular food. A patient named Shelley H. asked me whether she craved ice cream because she sometimes wanted to eat an ice cream cone on a hot day, just as a treat. I found that Shelley didn't have a craving for ice cream because she wasn't trying to deal with stress or to "fix" a bad feeling. She was simply hungry and wanted something nice to eat.

No, we're talking here about something different: those times when you don't even necessarily *want* something, yet you have a strong, virtually uncontrollable urge to eat it anyway. That is a true craving, because what you are looking for is a particular brain effect that will change your feelings. The food is a means, not an end.

THE TWO "PROBLEM" FEELINGS

The bad feelings, the ones we're trying to fix, fall into two categories: depression and anxiety. "Depression" is the general term for any feeling you might have of being "down." You have a touch of depression whenever you feel a lack of energy, when you feel fatigued, or at any time when you are dragging instead of zipping around.

"Anxiety," by contrast, is the general word for any feeling of being too "up." You are experiencing a touch of anxiety whenever you feel nervous. If you feel wound up, or "hyper," if you're irritable or jittery or just can't seem to settle down, you are suffering from too much anxiety.

FIXING THE FEELINGS

Notice that the two "bad" kinds of feelings aren't the opposite of each other. The opposite of anxiety isn't depression. The opposite of being *anxious* is being *calm,* not depressed. And the opposite of being *depressed* is being *happy and alert,* not being overexcited. You wouldn't reasonably try to cure your anxiety by becoming more depressed, or your depression by becoming more anxious.

You especially wouldn't want to be both depressed *and* anxious, yet often this is just what happens when you try to fix your feeling with craving foods.

Doreen K., a secretary at a community college, told me, "I usually get my craving for a candy bar in the middle of the morning. By that time my morning coffee has worn off, and I find myself feeling kind of down." She would go to the candy machine and buy a stimulating chocolate bar, simply to feel more cheerful.

I asked Doreen if it worked. "Sort of," she said. "I would feel a little better as I was eating the candy bar, but I would end up with a real buzz by the time I was finished—more than I wanted." Her response was typical. We do eat craving foods to cheer ourselves up, yet craving foods don't actually make us more alert, they simply make us more wound up.

When depression changes to hyperactivity, we miss the feeling we really want, which is precisely that sense of calm alertness that is the opposite of both anxiety *and* depression.

THE REAL FEELING

Craving foods do not deliver either true calmness or true alertness. What they do is to "offset" depression with a feeling of increased stimulation, which is actually hyperactivity; they also "offset" anxiety with a feeling of reduced alertness, which is actually dullness, not real calm. There is enough seeming value in these effects to make you think you are getting the true calmness and alertness that you need. "Better than nothing," you'd say.

Yet the truth of the matter is quite different. The truth is that the sense of inner calm and alertness you need is created *naturally* by your brain when the two main parts of your brain begin to work in a special way.

You get the brain state that you are looking for when you use your brain in that particular style that is traditionally known as "meditation." This meditative brain state gives the true feeling of calm/alertness that is actually the goal of all cravings.

This is extremely important, because it will help you see later where cravings fit into this picture, and why craving foods partially succeed but ultimately fail to give you the feeling you're looking for.

SCIENTIFIC SOURCES

Only the most recent scientific knowledge makes it possible to understand what true inner calm and alertness really is, and how craving foods work to mimic that state. The research I am drawing on here has come from three principal sources:

1. Recent research on the biochemistry of food. This research has focused on the ways food acts to create various emotional states within us, both by stimulating neurotransmitters in the brain and by affecting the balance of hormones and other chemicals in our bodies. (I'll describe these effects in Chapter 5.)
2. Important new research on the physiology of meditation practices such as Zen meditation, yoga, and Transcendental Meditation. This research shows exactly what "calm alertness" really is—within the brain, in the body, and in purely "feeling" terms.
3. My own research, conducted during two million patient visits to Skinny School, on food cravings and their cure. In my Skinny School research, I made use of what is now known, both about the biochemical effects of food and the effects of meditation, to create a complete program that *gives my patients the true calm and alertness they need*. When this need is satisfied, cravings disappear because the *object* of the craving has been achieved.

MEDITATION RESEARCH

These three areas of research have contributed tremendously to my understanding of food cravings, yet it is the meditation research that has done most to unlock the puzzle of why we do things we know are bad for us.

"Meditation" is not part of most of our life-styles, so it makes sense that the brain state it creates would be missing in most people. If meditation creates a brain state and a feeling that we all *need*, then it is perfectly logical that my patients would suffer from a strong sense of craving something very badly. And if certain foods (as well as drugs like alcohol and tobacco) give *something like* that feeling, it is logical that our craving for the meditation brain state would attach itself to these foods and/or drugs. This is exactly what happens.

The research on meditation has been done partly on very experienced practitioners of meditation ("yogis"). Bringing yogis into the laboratory has produced unexpected blasts of insight to long-standing medical and biochemical problems. But some of the research has been on ordinary people who have simply been taught an easy technique of meditation—which means that the results of the research are useful for all of us.

THE M-STATE

Research shows that when people are engaged in certain kinds of meditation, their brains actually become both deeply calm and tremendously alert. I call this state of inner calm and alertness the "M-State," which is my own term for a state that goes by many different names in the scientific literature and elsewhere.

"M-State" stands for "meditation state." But in fact, it is not only formal, structured "meditation" practices that give you M-State. Many people have told me that they get a similar state through various quiet activities, such as looking at the ocean, being out in the mountains, and listening to music.

You can, indeed, get your brain to go into the M-State in these ways. The *feeling* that you get is one of total relaxation, yet with a profound, heightened sense of inner awareness and alertness—a feeling that is often described as "being in touch with your real self," or as being "at one with and at peace with everything."

Unfortunately, the M-State you get when looking at the ocean and such is not easy to study. It is difficult to bring into the laboratory for research. For another thing, such moments of M-State tend to be unreliable. One day you may feel total calm alertness while watching the ocean, but the next day you might feel nothing.

Meditation, by contrast, does put your brain into the M-State each time, and can be done quite easily in the laboratory, where it can be studied.

So meditation gives the *clearest possible example* of the brain state that I mean. When people are doing meditation, we *know* that they are in a state of calm alertness, and so we can study it precisely. Besides, they stay put. Scientists have been able to look at their brain waves, breath, blood chemistry, and many other aspects of physiology. If it weren't for meditation, we wouldn't have such a clear concept of what the M-State actually is.

THE HOLISTIC MEDITATION STATE

Science has been looking for about the last twenty years at the particular brain state that is induced by the practice of meditation. Over these years scientists have gradually approached an understanding of it. Then a great explosion of research has occurred within just the last five years.

Research has been conducted on practitioners of Zen meditation, Transcendental Meditation, yoga, and a few other meditation practices. The vast majority of the research has been done on the Transcendental Meditation (TM) group. What has been found is that people who meditate reach a very special state of both restfulness, or tranquillity, and alertness.

During meditation the body becomes very quiet. Meditators show a depth of relaxation that usually comes to people only when they are sleeping deeply. Yet meditators aren't asleep. Their minds stay alert and awake rather than "switching off," as the mind does during sleep. The *combination* of relaxation and alertness is what is so unusual and significant.

This combination of relaxation and alertness occurs *holistically*. In other words, the two changes occur together, as a unified package, rather than being produced one by one by separate mechanisms. One process, meditation, does both. You don't do one thing to become calmer, and something else to become alert—hence, the process is holistic.

Figure 2, below, shows some of the indications of the calmness and alertness of the M-State.

2. PHYSICAL RESPONSES DURING THE M-STATE

Restfulness:

1. Reduction in oxygen consumption
2. Periodic suspension of breathing
3. Reduction in metabolic rate
4. Increase in galvanic skin response (signifies reduced stress)
5. Reduction in brain "noise" component (increased in stress and fatigue)
6. Not disrupted by outside events

Alertness:

1. EEG—general increase in alpha and theta activity (signifies wakefulness)
2. Hemispheric symmetry of brain waves—unified brain
3. Reaction time to stimuli quicker—more alert even at rest
4. Coherence of brain waves—thinking and acting parts of brain more unified
5. Better memory—long- and short-term
6. Fully aware of outside events

This is the M-State: a totally unique combination of deep restfulness (calm) and tremendous inner awareness and alertness. I find it extremely interesting that a completely natural state like this should exist yet be almost totally unknown to the vast majority of people in the world.

This does a great deal to explain why our levels of anxiety and depression are currently so high, and why there is such widespread use of craving foods as well as alcohol, tobacco, and drugs. It comes back to the fact that we are all looking for something vital that has dropped out, inexplicably, from our lives. If we can get it to drop back in, we won't have cravings and we won't gain weight.

THE NEUROGLIAL BRAIN: HOME OF THE M-STATE

The uniqueness of the M-State centers on another fascinating fact: The M-State is created in a part of the brain that until recently was considered relatively insignificant. This is the part of the brain known as the neuroglia, or neuroglial brain.

The brain we all know about is that grayish-white, convoluted structure that occupies the top part of our heads. This is, however, only part of the brain, the part known as the neural brain. It is made up of nerve cells, or neurons, all of which are in constant activity, firing off in response to countless events going on all around us.

THE NEURAL BRAIN: HOME OF THOUGHTS AND FEELINGS

The neural brain is responsible for all our thoughts, perceptions, feelings, memories, and movements, even the involuntary movements of our inner bodies. Up until recently, science thought this *was* the only significant part of the brain.

But there was something else all along: a completely different set of brain cells called neuroglial cells. These cells surround and support the nerve cells like a trellis, acting as nourishers and as protectors. The neural brain and the neuroglial brain are intertwined and rely on each other, yet work completely differently.

It was thought until recently that the neuroglial brain had no particular function except to nourish the "real" brain, made up of the neurons. It wasn't thought to make any contribution to consciousness.

Today, research is indicating that the neuroglial brain also provides the supporting framework for a different *kind of consciousness* from the kind supported by the neural brain—one that may be even *more* important to our total selves.

THE WHOLENESS OF LIFE—A NEUROGLIAL EVENT

It appears that the neuroglial brain may well be responsible for our inner sense of *connectedness* and *continuity*. Whereas the neurons react to the separate *parts* of life, the neuroglial brain reacts to the *underlying wholeness* that binds life together. It is the organ that makes sense out of life.

The neuroglial brain is what tells you when you wake up in the morning that you are the same person who went to bed the night before. It's what gives you a sense of continuity with your childhood self— despite the fact that you look different, are a different size, and may think and feel differently about everything.

The M-State is created in the neuroglial brain. When your brain goes into the M-State, what happens is that you *activate* your neuroglial cells. In the M-State, the entire set of neuroglial cells acts like *one single cell*, even though it is made up of billions of cells. The neuroglial brain literally becomes so profoundly coordinated that it is like a single cell—and this in turn brings that tremendous sense of calmness and serenity to your neural brain, and, through it, to your entire body.

When you experience moments of M-State in your daily life, what is happening is that your neuroglial cells have become activated somehow, in an unpredictable fashion. When you practice some kind of meditation, then you are using a specific technique (such as a mantra, or gazing at a candle) that is designed to activate neuroglial activity in a reliable fashion.

The neural brain is indeed supported and nourished by the neuroglia, but in a more profound sense than was previously thought. The neuroglia support the actual *consciousness* of the neural brain. Without this support your neurons would be like a computer, constantly processing information but unable to make sense out of it.

Computers are modeled on the neural brain. They have no neuroglia—no consciousness. And no amount of memory or processing power will give it to them. And of course computers do not experience the M-State. They have artificial intelligence but no consciousness.

THE REFRESHMENT OF THE M-STATE

Many of my patients who have experienced the M-State have described the feeling it gives them. They say, for example, "It's just a nice, refreshing feeling." "I get some inner peace." "It cools me out." Or, "I can't explain it, but it just makes me feel better." Or, "I felt total bliss."

The M-State *is* extremely refreshing and revitalizing. Yet it is rather quiet and unassuming. It doesn't give a "rush" of pleasure—the main feeling it has is just one of complete and wonderful relaxation. But it does refresh you so that you feel much better than you did before.

Studies that have been done on meditators have shown that regular experience of the M-State is very beneficial. It improves physical health and gives people more stable emotions. It also helps them be more effective in a job or at home and to have better coordination in sports.

What happens during the M-State is that the coordinated cells of the neuroglial brain produce a powerful, coordinated signal. Instead of the brain acting like many different cells, each one doing its own thing independently, the neuroglial influence integrates all the parts of the neural brain so that they perceive, think, and act with a unified purpose, without interference or static.

It's like what happens when a UHF station that has been drifting around and giving fuzzy sound and a bad picture is fine-tuned and comes into sharp focus. The whole picture gains meaning, texture, and coherence. The M-State tunes the entire brain to one station—the station of the inner self.

This powerful signal acts to "reset" all the body's systems to their genetically programmed setting. It's as if our bodies were looking back at their blueprints and becoming "like new" again.

Mental and physical health come from the deep sense of inter-connectedness and balance coded in our genes. All of the separate, individual facets of life, which our *neural* brains handle, tend to disrupt this interconnectedness. The neuroglial brain goes into the M-State in order to restore the connectedness. And this restoration is something we all deeply need.

A moment or two of the M-State allows your basic, healthy nature to reemerge from behind the static of the neural brain. It's like pushing the reset key on a computer. It puts everything back to normal.

In figure 3, below, you can see some of the ways that regular experiences of the M-State affect meditators' lives. Notice, especially, that people who experience the M-State have less need for cigarettes, alcohol, drugs, and craving foods. This is because the actual craving for the M-State is being satisfied, so it doesn't spill over onto substances that only *seem* to give them increased calm or alertness.

3. BENEFITS OF THE M-STATE

1. Improved physical health
   a. More efficient metabolism,
      reduced oxygen consumption,[1] heart rate,[2] and breath rate[3,4]
   b. Improved physical resistance to stress[5,6]
   c. Better brain integration[7,8,9]
   d. Better glandular balance[10]
   e. Improved nervous system function[11]
   f. Refinement of the senses—more acute hearing[12]
      more accurate posture in space[13]
      increased breadth of vision[14]

2. Better functioning
   a. Increased intelligence[15] and creativity[16]
   b. Improved coordination[17] and reactions[18]
   c. Improved productivity[19]
   d. Better learning[20] and academic performance[21]
   e. Improved athletic ability[22]
   f. Improvement of personality[23] and increased self-actualization[24,25,26]
   g. Tranquil alertness[27]

3. Reduced disease and disruption
   a. Reduced tendency to depression[26,28]
   b. Lower blood pressure[29] and cholesterol[30,31]
   c. Reduced asthma[32]
   d. Reduced tendency to drug abuse and improved ability to give up drugs, cigarettes, and alcohol[33]
   e. Reduced cravings and weight gain[34]
   f. Reduced insomnia[35]
   g. Reduction in biological age (rejuvenation)[36,37,38]

THE M-STATE IN YOUR LIFE

When so many benefits come from a single source, it makes tremendous sense that you would have a great desire to experience the M-State. People who do have this experience show a sense of being very satisfied with their lives, even when (to an outside observer) they don't seem to have lives that are very different from other people's.

On the whole, people who have the M-State (such as meditators) have lives just like other people's. They have families, jobs, challenges, things they love to do and things they can't stand. Yet they tend to feel more of a sense of happiness and enjoyment from their lives. It does not seem to be just a Pollyanna attitude either; if they just imagined they felt better, they wouldn't have the same range of physical health benefits that they do. This is integration, not self-delusion.

When you come to the Cravings Analysis Checklist, the very first section is designed to determine how much of the M-State *you* have in your life. My research at Skinny School has shown that if you have less M-State, you will have more food cravings, and if you have more M-State, you will have fewer, or less intense, food cravings.

Because food cravings are nothing more than your *need* for the M-State, gone painfully awry.

BUT IS THIS REALLY TRUE?

I remember a patient who once said to me after I'd explained about the drive for the M-State, "Doctor, you have to be kidding. I didn't even like the Beatles, let alone Ravi Shankar, and I think meditation's weird. I'm *positive* that's not why I crave salted cashews."

So let me bring this idea a little closer to home. In the next chapter I'll give you a case history of the way the M-State actually works. You'll see that far from being something exotic or strange, the M-State is something you know or have sensed in your own life. Making it a *regular* experience is really a vital part of curing your food cravings.

4

THE
M-STATE
IN ACTION

Even if you've never thought of meditating in your life, when I mention the M-State, you naturally recognize the feeling I'm talking about. All my patients do. Everyone knows the feeling: It's just the sense of starting to feel right again. The sense of coming back to yourself. It's what you feel when you take a deep breath and realize that everything is, against all odds perhaps, going to be okay.

Many patients have told me that they get a moment or two of this feeling when they walk quietly along the beach or through the woods, and come back refreshed and with a better perspective on their problems. You might have a taste of it when you listen to music, or when you unwind in a hot shower, or when you lie in bed quietly at the end of your day, or first thing in the morning before you get up.

Many people get a little taste of the M-State just before they drift off to sleep. Others get quick moments of inner peacefulness in the midst of their daily lives: that sudden feeling in the city when all the sounds blend together into harmony, or the nice sense you get when you look up from the newspaper and see someone you love puttering around in the kitchen.

ARE YOU SAYING I HAVE TO
MEDITATE TO BE SKINNY?

The difference between these *tastes* of the M-State, which so many people enjoy, and the M-State that comes with meditation, is that you can never be sure where your next *taste* is coming from. There's a catch-as-catch-can quality to these experiences. With meditation, research shows that when you sit down to get the M-State, you do get it—it's reliable.

Since meditation is so vital in curing cravings, I always recommend it to my patients. There are many kinds of meditation available today: Christian meditation, prayer, Zen, Transcendental Meditation, chanting, many others. I generally recommend Transcendental Meditation (TM) for the simple reason that most of the research has been done on TM.

I feel confident that other meditation techniques also work, and I have no reason to doubt people's experiences. My recommendation is based on scientific research, and that is important to me. But you should do what you feel comfortable with.

THE M-STATE IN ACTION

Here's an extended case history from my Skinny School files, to show you three aspects of the M-State:

1. The way the M-State works in action
2. The way a *lack* of the M-State leads to cravings
3. The way food is used as an M-State substitute, to create a fake or partial M-State

This case history is of a patient named Barbara K. Barbara came to me wanting to lose about fifteen pounds. Within a few weeks we had uncovered her starchy-sweet craving—in her case, cake. Barbara is a public relations executive whose husband, Mort, is an attorney. Mort and Barbara have been married for three years, and Mort has two teenaged sons from his previous marriage.

Barbara told me of a certain scenario in her life, one that repeated itself over and over. It occurred in three different versions. It seems that whenever Barbara has an especially difficult day at work, that's the day Mort's sons will always choose to do something she doesn't like—such as listening to the stereo at a deafening decibel level while they have seven friends over to play video games.

Here are her three versions of this scenario. See if there's anything here you can recognize in your own life.

THE FIRST VERSION: CHAOS

Barbara arrives home from the downtown pressure cooker exhausted and stressed out. She's too tired to deal with the blasting music and the gang of kids sympathetically, so she gets angry, yells, and causes a lot of resentment.

The boys respond that she can't tell them what to do because she isn't their "real mother," which considering everything she does for them is not exactly what she wants to hear. She explains to them that they are ungrateful brats. The whole thing goes rapidly downhill from there, with Barbara upset with Mort before he even gets home.

Mort comes home from work (himself suffering from end-of-the-day stress, and hoping for a "restorative" martini), only to find the house in chaos, teenage boys sulking noisily and slamming doors, and Barbara in their bedroom fuming, regretting the day she ever met him. He makes his martini a triple.

This is not ideal domestic life; and there's no M-State anywhere.

THE SECOND VERSION: A WONDERFUL LIFE

As Barbara told it to me, this was her best-case scenario. It happens sometimes—not often. Barbara has had an okay day at work. Traffic is flowing. In the car coming home she somehow manages to relax a bit and gets in touch with her inner self. Then, in the driveway, she switches off the car engine, closes her eyes for a moment, and switches off her own motor before going into the house.

In this quiet moment she sometimes gets a little taste of the M-State. Her neuroglial brain fulfills its function of restoring order and coherence to her neural brain and thus to her entire self. She draws, as it were, on an *inner*, built-in source of inner strength.

When this occurs, she always finds she can handle the boys with much greater finesse. In this mood, she empathizes with their high spirits and their independence rather than being aggravated by them. She feels her own strength and centeredness, and as a result she goes into the house feeling very relaxed and capable. She finds the kids' antics amusing rather than personally insulting.

Later on, when Barbara had begun to meditate as part of her cravings cure, this was the way she felt every day, since she had the moments of M-State she always needed. But at the time she was describing, this version of the scenario was quite rare. What would happen was that she would calmly ask the kids to turn down the stereo, negotiate a respite for herself by offering them a snack, and then get them to go downstairs and plug the video games into the big TV.

Mort would come home to domestic tranquillity, and unwind with a mineral water instead of a martini. Domestic bliss flowed like milk and honey.

THE THIRD VERSION: CAKE FOR M-STATE

This third version is the one that, before Skinny School, would actually happen most of the time. In this one, Barbara would find herself feeling exhausted as she drove home. She knew she was going to have to deal with the kids, and she couldn't quite face it. She certainly didn't want to lose her cool with them, as in version 1, but she suspected she probably would unless she felt better by the time she got home.

But experience had taught her that if she were to stop in the convenience store on the way home and have a quick snack—a sixteen-ounce coffee and a piece of packaged crumb cake—she would feel a whole lot better. Somehow those reserves of patience and energy that were used up at work would be replenished, and she'd be able to be a better step-mother and act the way she would prefer to at home.

Barbara told me many times that she didn't really want the cake or the coffee. She didn't feel really "hungry," she didn't want the calories, and the coffee would keep her awake at night. But she needed the feeling—the sense of coming back to herself that cake and coffee always delivered. And in a contest between health and feelings, feelings always win.

So she has the snack. Now, this is what happens:

The Physiology of a Snack

1. The *sugar* (in the cake and coffee) enters her body and, by a series of chemical reactions I'll describe in Chapter 5, tranquillizes her brain while increasing her alertness.
2. The *fats* in the cake and the cream she takes in her coffee enter her body and, by a separate series of chemical reactions (also described in Chapter 5), increase the sense of calm and alertness in her brain.
3. The *caffeine* in the coffee turns up the voltage in her brain even higher by increasing the rate and speed of firing of the cells in her neural brain.
4. The *taste* of both coffee and cake floods her entire system with a sense of temporary well-being linked to the brain events described above.

All these events come from the *neural part of the brain*. There is no neuroglial involvement. The *true* M-State can come only from the powerful neuroglial brain, which is the only part of the brain with the power to create a *global* sense of inner calm and alertness that can cascade throughout the whole body.

IMITATION OF THE M-STATE

Yet, even though the cake and coffee don't activate Barbara's neuroglial brain, they are able to create an imitation of the M-State—to the limited extent that it is possible to do so through the neural, not the neuroglial, brain.

Given this fact, it is not surprising that Barbara had become addicted to coffee and cake. It is, in a sense, a wonderful tribute to her ability to function as home-made chemist and self-taught druggist. Without any formal training in biochemistry, Barbara had put together a set of chemical reactions that would get her close to feeling the way she needed to feel. Unfortunately, she couldn't create the *real* M-State because she was working with the wrong part of her brain. Yet, within its limitations, her scheme did work.

Back in the cake-and-coffee days, Barbara would get home after eating her cake feeling energized and collected enough to take charge of kids and get them to go into the family room. It wouldn't be exactly peaceful with the music and their voices coming through the floor, but it would be tolerable, and at least they were out of the way.

Mort would come home to the throbbing of the bass from below and a wife about to go into post-cake-and-coffee letdown—but at least Barbara would be semifunctional. He would have one martini (just a single) and glaze out in front of the TV—the local news. In short, an average time would be enjoyed by all.

THE PRICE THEY PAID

But it could be worse, and it has been—often. So everyone was *reasonably* happy. Fake M-States were everywhere—Mort's from alcohol and TV, Barbara's from coffee and cake, and if truth be told, the kids' from the bizarre brain effects of U2 played very loudly. Barbara and Mort were both very unhappy about the weight they were putting on, and the boys were going deaf, but they were willing to pay the price for relative peace in the home.

Though Barbara and Mort were both worried about their expanding waistlines, they thought of that as a separate problem, not as a consequence of this one.

Even so, when Barbara struggled with her cravings for coffee and cake on her way home from work, she thought it was because she lacked willpower. Mort felt the same way about his martinis. Neither one realized how their cravings grew out of their unfulfilled drive for the genuine, complete M-State.

LEARNING TO CRAVE

Barbara and Mort have their own particular substitutes for the M-State, but this switch is something that *everyone* with food cravings makes.

How have Barbara, Mort, and you acquired your acute knowledge of biochemistry? How is it that you *know* that the substances you crave (whether cake, alcohol, cigarettes, mayonnaise, or any other craving substance) will give you the kind of boost you need? You know it, very simply, from experience.

Some of your cravings may have developed as far back as early childhood; others, you've acquired in later life, but the process is the same.

THE BIRTH OF A CRAVING

What happens is this: Cravings begin with stress. There are countless ways to stress your system; stress can come from literally anything that overloads your ability to cope, anything that is just "too much."

Not all stressful events are negative. Stress can come from very nice events. A child might become stressed from too much excitement, from too many birthday presents, for instance, or from something more difficult, like a failure at school. An adult can become stressed by a positive but demanding change, say, a new marriage, or by any of the negative events that bombard us these days.

Imagine yourself as an overloaded, stressed child. You're showing typical childlike stress reactions—you're crying, yelling, stamping your feet, sulking, or throwing things on the ground. Obviously you need something to help you get back in control.

If you were a lucky child, your mother was able to help you restore your inner tranquillity without using food to do it. Maybe she gently but firmly got you to go off by yourself for a minute, away from all the stress, to rest and be quiet until you felt better. If you were *really* lucky, she did this without screaming back at you and saying that you had to stay in your room because you were such a bad kid.

If you had that kind of mother, you had the chance to experience a little M-State in your lucky life. Your mom might have let you know that you would become calm again all by yourself, given the chance with a little quiet time.

HAVE A NICE COOKIE

More likely, though, your mother did what most mothers do. She stuck a cookie in your hand. Which you promptly ate, and within a few moments felt better. The cookie created in you a state that gave you something (though of course not all) of what you needed. And in this way learning occurred. You learned that next time you felt bad, a cookie would help.

I'm not trying to single out mothers for blame. They are trying to deal with their own stresses and their own cravings, and they don't have this information to help them. They themselves were given cookies in their own childhoods; besides, a crying child is a powerful inducement to do something, anything, to get him to stop. A new mother recently told me that when her three-month-old baby cries, she would fix him a hamburger and fries if she thought it would get him to shut up.

Just a few months later, I saw this baby with a cold Tater Tot in his little fist.

STRESS AND CRAVINGS

But even though it wasn't your mother's fault, over time, the way you could get yourself to feel better with a cookie (or some other craving food) was tested in many situations. Stressed feelings came in many forms, but what they have in common is that you want to "fix" them so that you feel better right away.

All of them call out for relief and resolution, if not through the actual M-State, then through whatever you have learned will help a little.

FIGHT OR FLIGHT VS. STAY AND PLAY

The drive for the M-State links up directly with the discomfort of stress. A number of studies on people who practice Transcendental Meditation have shown that in many ways the changes that occur during meditation are actually the opposite of the changes that occur in the body during stress.

"Stress" has been quite well defined in terms of increased adrenal activity (the "fight or flight" syndrome) by researchers such as Hans Selye (*The Stress of Life*). In "fight or flight," all the systems are revved up. Blood pressure increases, muscles become tense, blood flows out into the arms and legs so that you are ready for action. In TM, exactly the opposite effects occur. Muscles relax, blood pressure goes down, blood flows away from arms and legs and back toward your inner organs. The adrenal glands calm down. You feel calmer and more settled. The effect is so much the opposite of "fight or flight" that TM researcher Dr. David Orme-Johnson termed the meditation response "stay and play."

It certainly makes sense that in stressful situations you would seek out a state that will offset and balance the harmful results on the stress you're going through. Craving foods don't give you the real antidote to stress—they only trick you into thinking they do.

The real, the *actual* M-State is the antidote you need, and seek, in stressful situations. If a situation is challenging, you need to face it with true inner calm and a genuinely wide-awake mind—not a fake state that you've created for yourself out of sugar, grease, salt, or some combination of them.

NATURALLY SKINNY PEOPLE

People who are naturally skinny are people whose minds are very good at going into the M-State—either because they happen to have been born that way, or because they have taken up a technique of meditation and used it regularly.

Naturally skinny people don't use craving foods to get a fake M-State. Instead, they use the *right* foods to actually *support and increase their ability to have the real M-State*. When you've finished the Skinny School program, this is the way you, too, will be using food.

The Skinny School program is designed to support your natural ability to have the real M-State, not the fake. The M-State is a completely natural state, programmed into our genes. You will have it—but you do have to take some time for it. Any very positive, healthful action that you take actually helps you enjoy more M-State experiences, and have deeper feelings of inner calm and alertness.

M-STATE DEFICIENCY

If you are very stressed, on the other hand, you will have great difficulty in getting into the M-State. To experience the M-State deeply does require a well-balanced, fairly healthy mind and body. The M-State is natural, but it can be disrupted greatly by too much stress.

You know that if you are very tired, it is much harder to relax. Your mind keeps buzzing. You can't get even a moment of M-State relaxation. Very busy people often find it almost impossible to take a vacation—they are too wound up even to move toward the *possibility* of relaxation. When your life is so busy it offers not even an occasional quiet moment, then you find yourself with what I call "severe M-State deficiency."

Even though as a baby or a child you might have enjoyed the M-State, as a twentieth-century adult you may have lost it totally. Life's stresses— work, family, money worries, even environmental stresses such as pollution—can drive the M-State right out of you permanently.

I have also found in my research that another great source of M-State disruption is our present-day diet—which doesn't give your neuroglial brain the right kind of support. Food is not supposed to be *used*, like a drug, to create a fake M-State; but it *is* supposed to provide nourishment that supports the real M-State. The food you normally eat is too deficient in nutrients (because of overprocessing, hybridization of plants and animals, and soil depletion) to nourish your brain fully. It is also too deficient in *taste* to support the real M-State. You'll be hearing more about this in coming chapters, of course: I've designed the Skinny School diets and supplementation programs to correct these problems.

Even more than diet, substances like drugs and alcohol distort and even destroy your natural ability to have the M-State. This is a tremendous paradox, because the search for the M-State is behind all use of drugs and alcohol in the first place.

It is when you lose the natural M-State *totally* from your life that any craving—whether for food or something even more harmful—reaches its fullest intensity. In your quest for inner quietness, you'll take the fake if you can't get the real. But in accepting the fake M-State, you make the real much harder to achieve.

GETTING BACK THE M-STATE

The Skinny School cravings cure is based on restoring your natural ability to have the M-State. You need the real M-State in order to lose your taste for the fake one—and unless you have it, your cravings will never be totally cured. The best you can hope for is to transfer them from food to something else.

The Skinny School program will work for you whether your body has almost completely lost its ability to experience the M-State (in which case you will have extreme cravings), or whether you have the ability to experience the M-State but just aren't giving yourself a chance to enjoy it regularly (in which case your cravings will not be as intense).

Before you begin the program, I want you to know something about the way the various craving foods work to create the fake M-State, so we'll look at this in Chapter 5. This information will help you see more clearly the way you use food as a substitute for the M-State, and will help you understand and use the Skinny School program more effectively to cure your cravings.

5

FOOD CRAVINGS: CREATING THE FAKE M-STATE

No craved food or drug can ever create the real M-State because no craved food or drug has the power to activate the neuroglial brain. It's that simple. All you can ever do with any substance is to create an effect in your *neural* brain—the part of the brain that is affected by food, drugs, and indeed by actions of any kind. When you try to work through that part of the brain to create a chemical effect that will feel absolutely "right," the way the real M-State feels absolutely right, you're barking up the wrong tree. The M-State is just not up the neural tree.

You know the feeling you have when you go into the kitchen in quest of the *right* food—the one that will give you the feeling you want? You have an English muffin, and that doesn't quite do it. So you have a few olives, and they don't work, so you finish off the cake from last week . . . and that doesn't work either.

And so it goes: you graze and graze, but nothing feels quite like "it," so you don't stop until you're stuffed and furious at yourself. Now do you see why? You're trying to manipulate your neural brain to create a feeling of inner calm and alertness—a feeling that can come only from a completely different part of the brain.

Yet all your craving foods *do* affect the *neural* brain very strongly. This is why your need for the M-State is able to switch over and attach itself to these foods: because of their powerful effects on the neural brain. Each of the craving foods has its own specific chemical way of imitating the M-State. Each one, in other words, has its own pathway for creating a *fake* M-State in the neural brain.

I've been emphasizing throughout this book that you will develop cravings only for foods that affect your feelings. No other cravings are possible. Foods work their magic on your feelings precisely through their influence on the neural brain.

CRAVING FOODS AND BRAIN CHEMICALS

You already know that no one craves everything. Each person has just a few problem foods, sometimes just a single one but almost never more than three or four. My research at Skinny School has shown me that all these various foods fall into two major categories:

1. sweets and starches, and
2. greasy and spicy foods

Each of these two main categories has its own way of chemically stimulating your neural brain.

Sweets and starches belong to the group known chemically as "refined carbohydrates." Whether your craving foods are sweets (such as cake, candy, sugar, frosting, or soft drinks), starches (such as bread, pasta, rolls, or tortillas), or starchy sweets, which are a combination of sweets and starches (for example, cookies, doughnuts, or pie), the chemical effect on your brain is similar.

REFINING THOSE CRAVING FOODS

The only difference among craving foods is that sweets are more refined than starches. Starches are the least refined, and starchy sweets are in the middle. In the process of refining a grain, a portion of the grain is stripped away. The part that's lost contained proteins and fats that would have *balanced* the carbohydrates that remained, as well as vitamins and trace elements that would have moderated the impact of the pure carbohydrate on the brain. Starches such as flour have *some* of these moderating substances still with them, while sweets have none; they are pure carbohydrates.

White sugar itself is the most refined of all the carbohydrates. As a result, sugar has the *strongest* effect on your brain. White flour, white rice, and other refined starches have an effect that is similar to sugar's, but since these foods are not as drastically refined as sugar, the effect on your brain isn't quite as strong.

Greasy and spicy foods, by contrast, work on your neural brain in quite a different way from the way sweets and starches work. The feeling they create is also one of calmness and alertness, but it is a different sort of calm alertness than the other, one with its own "flavor" to it. The reason? It is created through a different set of brain chemicals.

Oils are "refined" by being extracted from the foods that bear them— nuts, seeds, grains. So their impact, again, is pure and takes place out of the context of a whole, natural food.

YOUR MAIN CRAVING

You will find, when you've completed the Cravings Analysis Checklist, that you are *mainly* either a sweet and starch craver or a greasy and spicy food craver. Your main craving tells you which set of brain chemicals you usually prefer to create in yourself when you are under stress.

It is quite possible to crave both sweets and starches *and* greasy or spicy foods. Many people do. Since the feeling that each class of food gives has its own "flavor," you may crave them under different circumstances.

As one patient told me, "I need sweets when I feel down; but when I'm jittery I always crave a really greasy hamburger—it makes me feel more centered and settled." Other people crave sweets in the morning and greasy foods at night. But you always have just one *main craving:* the one you will turn to when your need for the M-State is highest. This craving is based on your genetic tendency (see *Dr. Abravanel's Body Type Diet and Lifetime Nutrition Plan*).

Since the brain chemicals involved are different, the Skinny School Anti-craving Diets to cure these cravings are different. You will always follow the *diet for your main craving*. If you also have other cravings, we'll cure these through targeted nutritional supplementation (see Chapter 13).

SWEETS, STARCHES, AND THE BRAIN

To delve more deeply into the way sweets and starches work on your brain to give you a fake M-State, I will use white sugar as an example. Sugar is the most extreme example of the way sweets and starches work; the others work in the same way, but with a less drastic effect.

Sugar has, of course, a terrible reputation and very bad press coverage. It is deserved, I might add. In "under"-developed countries, where people eat less than seven pounds of sugar per year, cavities and heart disease are almost unknown. (Here, by comparison, we put away 130 pounds a year—every one of us.)

Most people think that sugar (and other refined carbohydrates) provides an energy "boost." Many of my patients have told me that they eat sweets to pick up their energy "when their blood sugar level is low." They believe it helps their mood. "I'm a terror when my sugar level drops," one patient told me.

Yet the truth is that sugar, while it may raise your blood sugar level briefly, does *not* change your mood in this way. Experiments conducted at MIT by researcher Dr. Richard Wurtman have shown that for most people, the amount of sugar you have in your blood is not a direct factor in your mood or your energy. Sugar does have an effect on your mood, but the effect comes from brain chemicals, not blood sugar level.

SUGAR AND SEROTONIN

Sugar's effect on your mood actually comes from brain chemicals (called neurotransmitters) that operate in your neural brain. When you eat a candy bar, your pancreas produces insulin to metabolize the sugar in the candy bar. The insulin then makes available to your brain an amino acid called tryptophan, which converts into serotonin, a major neurotransmitter.

Serotonin is a "well-being" brain chemical. When it travels between the cells of the neural brain across the synapses, it has the effect of making you feel less stressed, less anxious, more focused and relaxed, and less hungry. It is a natural calmant, or tranquilizer.

Serotonin's mood-raising effect is also indicated in a study done at the National Institute of Mental Health. This research indicates that if you become depressed during the winter months (a common form of depression called seasonal affective disorder, or SAD), you have depressed serotonin levels in your brain due to light deprivation. The researcher, Dr. Norman Rosenthal, suggests that many people eat refined carbohydrates like sugar during the winter "as a form of self-medication," to raise their levels of serotonin. Again, sugar is being *used* as a drug, for its brain effect.

BRAIN WAVE COHERENCE

The increased calmness that comes with eating sugar is reflected in greater *coherence of brain wave patterns* in the various parts of the neural brain. Coherence means that the activity of the neural brain is occurring in a more organized way. Parts of your brain are made to work together, which makes you *feel* more together.

Yet the brain wave coherence of the "sugar brain" is very superficial in comparison with the *total coherence of the brain in the M-State*. In the M-State, the neuroglial cells work together in the most coherent and connected way possible: they function as if they were a single cell. This produces much more total coherence, and coherence of a greater magnitude, than the neural brain coherence that comes from eating sugar or any other craving food.

Figures 4, 5, and 6 show the difference in coherence between your brain when you are in normal everyday consciousness (figure 4), in the M-State (figure 5), and in the state of *partial* coherence that is created when you eat sugar or other refined carbohydrates (figure 6). You can see that there is *just enough coherence* in the "sugar brain" to give you a convincing illusion of the M-State. But no more.

4. WAKING STATE BRAIN

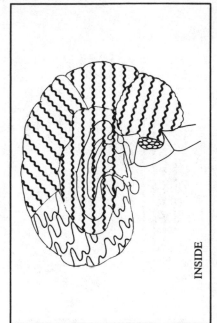

INSIDE

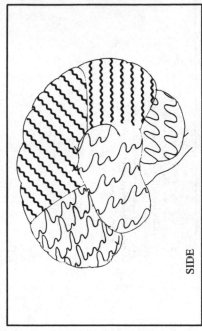

SIDE

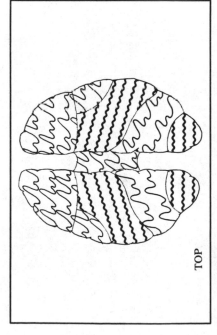

TOP

WAKING STATE BRAIN,
EYES CLOSED

DEEP BRAIN SLIGHTLY COHERENT.
BACK BRAIN—ALPHA.
REST OF BRAIN—NONCOHERENT RIGHT/LEFT,
UPPER/LOWER, AND FRONT/BACK.
IF YOU CLOSE YOUR EYES RIGHT *NOW*
THIS IS HOW YOUR BRAIN WAVES WILL LOOK.

5. M-STATE BRAIN

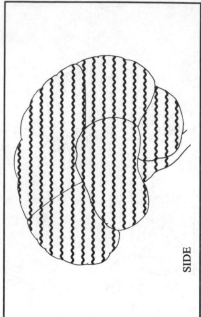

INSIDE

SIDE

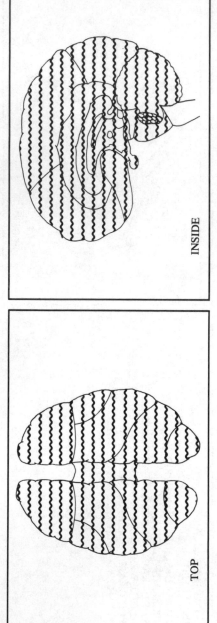

TOP

M-STATE BRAIN

TOTAL COHERENCE THROUGHOUT AND ACROSS BRAIN—UPPER AND LOWER, FRONT AND BACK, RIGHT AND LEFT. WAVE FORM FREQUENCY SAME ALL OVER BRAIN.
THIS IS NONSYNAPTIC, NONMOSAIC ORDERING.

6. SUGAR BRAIN

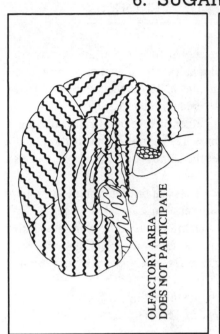

OLFACTORY AREA
DOES NOT PARTICIPATE

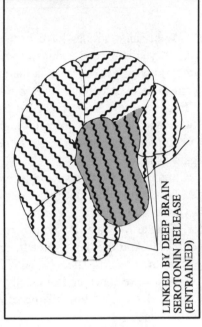

LINKED BY DEEP BRAIN
SEROTONIN RELEASE
(ENTRAINED)

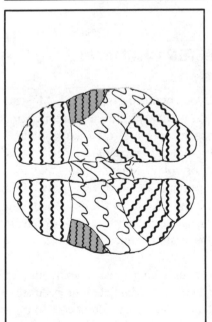

SUGAR

MOSAIC OF BRAIN COHERENCE.
SEROTONIN RELEASE DRIVES COHERENCE
OF FRONTAL CORTEX WITH LIMBIC SYSTEM—
CEREBELLUM.
REST OF BRAIN NOT COHERENT WITH
THESE BUT MAY BE COHERENT WITHIN
ITSELF, THEREFORE MOSAIC
SMALL, CHANCE OF MOMENTARY M-STATE.

HOW MUCH SUGAR IS ENOUGH?

Dr. Wurtman's studies have further shown that if you are at a normal weight, you will need about two and a half teaspoons of sugar to feel the way you want to feel. This is the amount of sugar necessary to get your brain to produce enough serotonin to create a fake M-State.

But if you are overweight by 20 percent (for example, if you weigh 150 pounds, but your normal weight is 125), you will need three and a half to four teaspoons of sugar to get the same fake M-State—about half again as much.

Unfair, isn't it? You should be eating less sugar, but you need more to get the same effect. But that's the way cravings are. And it gets worse. If you're more than 20 percent overweight, you require even *more* sugar for the fake M-State. As with heroin, the more sugar you eat, the more you need. And the more you eat, the harder it becomes for your brain to go into the real M-State.

If you have more and more difficulty in getting to the real M-State, your need for the tranquilizing effect of serotonin becomes even more acute.

OILS, FATS, AND BRAIN CHEMICALS

This is how carbohydrates stimulate your brain to give you an M-State-like condition. By a different pathway, and using different brain chemicals, fats and oils provide *their* particular version of the fake M-State.

Foods that are rich in fats or oils—butter, mayonnaise, fried foods, meat—are generally also either salty or spicy. Meat is salty, and fried foods like potato chips, fries, and peanuts are also very salty. Rich ethnic dishes (such as Italian, Thai, or some kinds of Chinese foods) are both rich and spicy. The addition of salt and spices to oily or greasy foods *reinforces* the stimulation of the brain chemicals involved in this version of the fake M-State.

What happens is that when you eat something greasy, your pituitary gland, which is located inside the brain, is stimulated to produce a chemical called vasopressin and another one called adrenocorticotropic hormone, or ACTH. The effect of vasopressin and ACTH is to give you a feeling of power and a sense that your mind is very well organized (a sense that most of us find very welcome).

Because greasy foods convey this feeling of power, greasy food cravers very often correspond to the traditional picture of the "meat-eater"—belligerent and overbearing. In fact, the "flavor" of the fake M-State that greasy food cravers feel is rather different from what sweets and starches cravers feel. After sweets or starches are eaten, the feeling of calmness and alertness comes from serotonin, which gives a calmer sense than the feeling of *powerful* calm and alertness that comes from vasopressin and ACTH. Yet each type of craving food does "deliver" a sense of the fake M-State.

THE GREASY FOOD CRAVERS' BRAIN WAVES

Vasopressin and ACTH also create a sense that the thinking parts of your brain are working together in harmony—an effect that actually *does* occur in the real M-State. The vasopressin acts as a neural brain activator, and the ACTH acts as an endorphin to increase the sense of "reward" and satisfaction that comes from your thoughts and actions. So you get a strong feeling that everything you do is just right.

Yet the harmony and coherence that you feel after eating greasy foods is much less profound than the sense of harmony that comes from the M-State.

Figures 4, 5, and 7 compare the effects of greasy and/or spicy foods on the brain (figure 7) with the brain in normal activity (figure 4), and the brain in the M-State (figure 5). Notice that there is increased coherence of brain wave patterns in the greasy food craver's brain; yet the brain wave coherence is created across only *part* of the brain. This is a *partial* M-State effect; figure 5 shows that the *real* M-State involves coherence across all parts of the brain and goes much deeper.

THE GLANDULAR CONNECTION: YOUR BODY TYPE

In these ways, the two main types of craving foods, sweets and starches and greasy and spicy foods, stimulate your brain chemicals to create

7. GREASY FOOD CRAVERS BRAIN

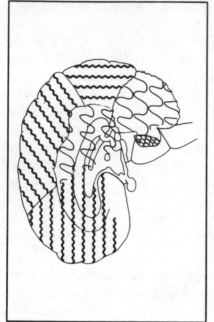

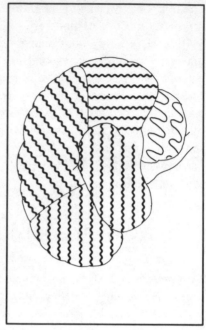

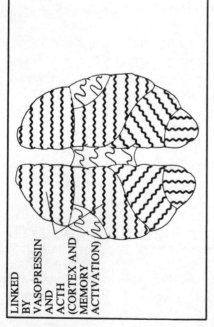

LINKED
BY
VASOPRESSIN
AND
ACTH
(CORTEX AND
MEMORY
ACTIVATION)

GREASY FOODS

RELEASE OF ACTH AND VASOPRESSIN FROM
PITUITARY RESULTS IN LINK OF
FRONTAL AND TEMPORAL CORTEX
DIFFERENT MOSAIC WITH GENERAL
INCREASE IN ACTIVATION OF BRAIN.

something resembling the M-State in your brain. The brain chemicals I've discussed do not exhaust the mechanisms that craving foods use to work their spell on you; science is involved today in unraveling many of the mysteries of the neural brain, and more pathways to the fake M-State are being discovered as this research continues.

But there is another *major* pathway that craving foods use to change your feelings: by *stimulating your body's glandular system.* Your glands produce their own chemicals, called "hormones," which also have powerful effects on the way you feel.

The glandular effects of craving foods reinforce the brain effects. The same foods that stimulate your brain to produce those chemicals that make you feel better—even if temporarily and at a high cost—also stimulate your glands to produce other chemicals that also contribute to your temporarily improved feelings.

I described these glandular effects of food in my earlier work on body types (*Dr. Abravanel's Body Type Diet and Lifetime Nutrition Plan* and *Dr. Abravanel's Body Type Program for Health, Fitness, and Nutrition*, published by Bantam Books).

In the introduction to *Dr. Abravanel's Body Type Program*, my second book, I wrote:

> What is it about your metabolism that makes you want one food over another? It's the fact that we use food not just for nourishment but for its mind-altering effects. What each of us is looking for in food is a *particular change in our state of mind*. We want the food that will make us feel both calmer and more awake. . . .
>
> What happens is that each and every food provides stimulation to some part of the glandular system. . . . Dairy products have a strong, stimulating effect on the pituitary gland. Sweets are thyroid stimulants. Meat and eggs stimulate the adrenals; greasy and spicy foods stimulate the gonads.
>
> *Each of us has a built-in tendency to eat foods that stimulate our dominant gland and get us to the state of mind we want in a particular way.*

The "change in state of mind" I was referring to was, in fact, the "M-State." Each of our glands works on our feelings *in its own way* to give us a fake M-State feeling.

BODY TYPES AND DIFFERENCES

The Body Type books focus only on the glandular pathway by which foods create the fake M-State rather than the entire picture of the way the *need* for the M-State causes *all* cravings. The Body Type books are about the *differences* from one Body Type to another. Skinny School is concerned more with the *similarities* of all cravings. Each craving is different—but each craving does have in common that it is really a craving for the M-State.

Your Body Type is a shorthand way of saying which of your body's four major glands (the pituitary gland, thyroid gland, adrenal glands, and the gonads, or sex glands) is *dominant* in your metabolism. Each person has one gland that is stronger than the other three, and it influences everything about you, from your body's shape to your personality, to which foods you crave.

(To find your Body Type, refer to the Personal Metabolic Inventory in *Dr. Abravanel's Body Type Diet and Lifetime Nutrition Plan*).

In each Body Type, hormones from your dominant gland are the ones that give you the best *feeling*. If you are a Thyroid Type, then your *feelings* are most affected by thyroid hormones. Adrenal Types respond to adrenal hormones, Pituitary Types to pituitary hormones, and Gonadal Types to the sex hormones.

Your own dominant gland's hormones are the ones that make you feel calmer and more alert—more like the M-State. And they cascade into your system right along with the brain chemicals that your brain produces from your same craving foods.

THE STIMULATING FOODS

Sweets and starches are very stimulating to the thyroid gland. For this reason, Thyroid Types have the strongest chance of being sweets and starches cravers. When you eat sweets or starches, your body becomes more responsive to thyroid hormone; this reinforces the feeling of calm alertness you get from the brain chemical serotonin.

Most Pituitary Types are also sweets and starches cravers because the pituitary gland responds to the sugar found in fruit as well as to the milk sugars found in light dairy products.

Greasy and spicy foods stimulate both the adrenal glands and the sex glands. As a result, Adrenal and Gonadal types are most likely to be greasy and spicy food cravers. These foods cause your glands to increase your body's supply of adrenal and sex hormones, which is a second source (along with vasopressin and ACTH, the brain chemicals) of the feeling of power that you get from eating these foods.

When you eat salt along with your greasy or spicy food, the effect is to raise your blood pressure, which creates a strong, very turned-on alert feeling. Salt, for greasy and spicy food cravers, works in the same way that caffeine works for sweets and starches cravers: It reinforces the fake M-State effect by increasing your inner feelings of calm alertness.

THE DOWN SIDE: CARBOHYDRATES AND CAFFEINE

Constantly stimulating your dominant gland through craving foods has a tremendously harmful effect in the long run. After all, as with every craving food, you are using the food like a drug, not a food. Its purpose isn't nutrition, it's a feeling, a change in brain state.

If you have a craving for sweets or starches, and constantly stimulate your thyroid gland by eating them, your thyroid will eventually become exhausted and stop functioning. Many, many sweets and starches cravers have weakened thyroid glands, and this is the reason.

If you are overweight and have a strong sweets craving, I recommend that you see your physician to have your thyroid checked. It is a possibility that you have worn your thyroid gland out with constant overstimulation.

Also, if you crave either sweets or starches the chances are good that you also crave caffeine—coffee, tea, cola, and diet cola. Caffeine is the most widely used psychotropic drug in the world. The effect of caffeine is to reinforce the action of the starches and sweets in stimulating your thyroid, which contributes still further to its exhaustion. Another reason to have your physician check it.

THE DOWN SIDE: GREASY AND SPICY FOODS

The results of overstimulating your adrenals or your sex glands with greasy, spicy, or salty foods are also debilitating, though in a different way from the sweets craving. Greasy food cravers overload their gall bladders, and gall bladder disease becomes common.

The cholesterol in greasy foods contributes to elevated cholesterol levels, and this is associated with risk of heart disease. Greasy foods also stimulate the ovaries in women, which can result in overproduction of estrogen. This in turn can be associated with increased risk of breast cancer. This is a known fact. For this reason alone, women who crave greasy foods should complete the Skinny School cure for this craving.

SUMMARY: THE FAKE M-STATE

Creating a fake M-State, as you can see, is a complex process that takes a lot of chemical input from various foods. In fact, the very *difficulty* of putting together anything *like* the M-State goes a long way toward explaining the phenomenon of overweight.

If you want to become calm yet alert, you might need some sweets to create serotonin, some oils to create vasopressin, ACTH, and endorphins, some coffee to perk up your thyroid, and something spicy to stimulate your gonads. A ''snack'' like this alone could amount to 3000 calories. How much easier and better to get the real M-State. And what a savings of calories and money!

Figure 8 summarizes for you the biochemical mechanics by which all the foods you crave work to give you that painfully created simulacrum of the M-State.

THE PARTS ARE MUCH LESS THAN THE WHOLE

At Skinny School, my nurses and I confront the reality of cravings every day. We know how difficult it is to give up a craving food—which at

8. BIOCHEMICAL EFFECTS OF CRAVING FOODS

FOOD	BRAIN EFFECTS	GLANDULAR EFFECTS	FEELING
Sweets	1. Serotonin release 2. Vasopressin release	Adrenal: stimulation Thyroid: "fake" stimulation	Calm, satiety, reduced sensitivity to shock Alertness (short-lived)
Starches	1. Serotonin release 2. Slow ACTH release	Thyroid: little stimulation Adrenal: stimulation Pituitary: suppression	Slight arousal, calm Calm, alertness Slight arousal
Dairy	1. Prolactin production 2. Beta-endorphin release	Pituitary: posterior and anterior stimulation Adrenal: cortisol release	Abstract thought, memory organization, arousal Tranquillity, insensitivity to pain, slight arousal Deemphasized sexuality, reduced socialization
Fruit	1. Vasopressin release 2. Serotonin release	Pituitary: posterior stimulation Adrenal: slight stimulation Thyroid: "fake" stimulation	General alertness, intellect Calm, decreased sensitivity to pain General arousal (short)
Cholesterol	1. General activation 2. Dopamine release 3. ACTH suppression	Adrenal: hormone production Adrenal: medulla activation (adrenaline) Pituitary: reduced activity	Global arousal Aggression, insensitivity to pain Decreased arousal (later)
Salt	1. Vasopressin stimulation	Pituitary: ACTH release Adrenal: cortisol release	Calm, clearmindedness General arousal, reduced depression, increased power
Spices	1. Endorphin release 2. Olfactory bulb activation 3. Limbic activation	Adrenals: cortisol release Pituitary and pineal: stimulation Ovaries: stimulation	Calm, hunger, arousal General brain activation (like M-State) Nesting instinct, mothering

least provides some help with the stresses of life—even when you *know* that the harm done far outweighs the benefits.

Only when you begin to experience the real M-State for yourself do you find your cravings starting to subside. This is because if you compare the fake M-State with the real, the artificially induced M-State has so much less reality than the real thing that there is no proper comparison.

If you compare the *feeling* of the fake M-State with the feeling of the real, you find yourself comparing a *collection of separate parts* with a process that you experience as a *unified whole*. Because the fake M-State has separate parts, you're constantly trying to tweak one part or the other to regain balance. You usually do this with extra snacks.

THE JUGGLING ACT

My patient Barbara, whose experiences I described to you in the last chapter, used to give herself a lift, and "fix" her anxious, worried, stressed feelings, with a snack of coffee and cake that gave her the fake M-State. At other times Barbara used to experience some minutes of quietness that gave her a taste of the real M-State.

She told me that she noticed several major differences between the two experiences.

First, Barbara said, the feeling she got from the fake M-State was *incomplete*. "I wouldn't feel really, totally better," she said. "The cake didn't *totally* fix the way I felt." Part of her tiredness or irritability would remain. "I might feel more energy from the cake, or maybe from the coffee, but I'd still have a feeling of tiredness underneath."

This is something you can always sense beneath your artificially induced "energy." If you eat a craving food when you feel "low," you may cheer up, but you will always be able to sense a nagging feeling of depression just beneath the surface. You feel that the waters of your spirit don't reach down deep, and that you lack reserves. Your depression invariably surfaces again as soon as the snack has worn off.

The real M-State, on the other hand, gives a *complete* feeling of restoration. When you actually take the time and allow your mind and body to experience the M-State, your tiredness, fatigue, depression, or anxiety will be genuinely relieved, not just covered up. "There's a big difference," Barbara said. "When I meditate instead of eating cake, I don't get that nagging sense that my depression is still pulling at me, or still needs to be dealt with."

OVERDRAWING THE ACCOUNT

Another difference you will notice for yourself is that where the fake M-State *depletes* you, the real M-State is *restorative*. When you use a craving food to fix a feeling, you're actually drawing down your energy reserves still farther. With the real M-State, you are allowing your total system to restore itself. You're not piling up further problems for yourself in the future.

Also, the fake M-State is *intense but short-lived,* and the real M-State is *more gentle, but lasts longer*. The real M-State feels less like an assault, more like a gentle and restorative suffusion of good feelings. After coffee and cake, Barbara told me, she would charge into the house like gangbusters, but would feel let down half an hour later. When she'd had her moments of real M-State, she'd come into the house in a mood of more genuine calm, which would last into the evening instead of wearing off.

Figure 9, on page 68, summarizes the difference between the real and the fake M-State.

9. REAL VS. FAKE M-STATE

REAL M-STATE	FAKE M-STATE
*Deep bodily rest[1,2]	*Speeds up body[39,40]
*Brain waves: coherence, diffuse[3,4]	*Brain waves: coherence local[18-20]
*Brain chemicals produced: decreased VMA, increased 5HIAA (quiet alertness)[5,6]	*Brain chemicals produced: sugar—serotonin[41] fats—vasopressin and ACTH[42] exercise—endorphins[43-45] spices—acetycholine and norepinephrine[46]
*Improves senses[74]	*Senses deteriorate[49]
*Endocrine stability[37,38]	*Endocrine disruption[71,72]
*Integration of mind with body[7-9]	*Disrupts integration[49-51]
*Increases ability to handle change because stable[10-13]	*Disrupts ability because brief[52,53]
*Type of brain activation— pineal/glial wave form[30]	*Receptor site activation— median raphe[47,48]
*Promotes evolution of receptors[31-34]	*Dulls and destroys receptors[54-56]
*Relieves anxiety, depression[14-16]	*Relieves anxiety, depression (briefly)[59,60]
*No calories	*Lots of calories[61]
*Feeling of power (long-lasting)[29]	*Feeling of power (short-lived)[62-65]
*The more you experience, the better for your health[21-24]	*The more you experience, worse for your health[25-28]
*Becomes more and more permanent[35,36]	*Doesn't last—effects deteriorate You need more and more[66,67]
*Body rejuvenates[35,36]	*Body ages[68]

6

ADDICTIONS: THE EUPHORIA PRINCIPLE

FOOD CRAVINGS AS ADDICTIONS

The mechanism of food cravings is extremely powerful. It is no small thing to be *driven* to eat certain foods because those foods create in you a fake version of a state you absolutely must have.

Yet it is only by understanding the origin of cravings that you can see how vital it is to cure them. Unless you have a cure that really deals with your underlying drives and needs, you will always struggle with cravings. You will never have the ease and comfort around food that naturally skinny people enjoy.

In this chapter, before we go on to the cures, we'll put food cravings into context with other, more classical addictions. As we noted at the beginning of the book, people crave many things besides food. Cravings can be for substances, such as drugs, alcohol, and cigarettes. There are also cravings for certain types of behavior, such as compulsive gambling and shopping, which also work to change your brain state and your feelings in the same way that certain foods and drugs do.

When the cravings are for drugs or for compulsive actions, they seem to be quite different from the simple cravings that you might have for chocolate or french fries. And certainly the effects can *appear* to be more serious.

But in fact these addictions are also nothing more than attempts to create the M-State. And although the actual method of curing these addictions might be different, the bottom line is the same: restore the real M-State, and the need for the fake one will gradually disappear.

The addictions we'll be comparing with food cravings are listed in figure 10, below:

10. THE MOST COMMON ADDICTIONS

1. Addictive substances
   a. Alcohol
   b. Tobacco
   c. Cocaine
   d. Opiates (heroin, morphine)
   e. Marijuana
   f. Amphetamines
   g. Barbiturates (phenobarbital, Seconal, others)
   h. Benzodiazepines (Valium, Ativan, others)

2. Addictive behaviors
   a. Gambling
   b. Shopping
   c. Compulsive sex
   d. Overexercising
   e. Working
   f. Lying

3. Addictive Foods
   a. Starches
   b. Sweets
   c. Salt
   d. Fried foods
   e. Spicy foods (slightly less than others)
   f. Protein (concentrated)

THE REWARD CIRCUITS

As you know, a true sense of calm and alertness comes from within you, and is created naturally by your brain. It can't be put together out of any addictive substances or any craving food. It comes from a very natural activity located in your neuroglial brain.

All the "pleasure" of whatever kind that you feel from addictions comes from some activity of your neural brain. Your neural brain is also designed to give you good feelings as rewards for healthy, life-supporting activities. In other words, your neural brain has built-in "reward circuits" that give positive feedback whenever you do something that's good for you.

When you eat a good, healthy, nourishing meal, you are supposed to feel good from it—this is a "reward circuit." When you exercise or rest, you are supposed to feel good. When you do good work or solve a creative problem, again, your neural brain will give you positive feedback from its reward circuits.

All addictive substances take over the reward circuits in the neural brain. This is called "usurping the reward circuits." It is another way of saying that people use craving foods, or drugs, or addictive behaviors, to mimic the M-State through the neural brain. And again, you will feel the *need* to do this only when you are deficient in the real M-State.

When your drive for the M-State is satisfied by the real thing, you will allow your neural brain reward circuits to reward you for good, healthy actions, and not *use* them to create a fake M-State.

THE TWO SIDES OF PLEASURE

Usurping the reward circuits of your brain—using them to create the fake M-State—is what all addictions are about. An addiction can get its hold on you only when it gives you something like the feelings you get from the real M-State.

When researchers have tried to understand the way addictions get their intense hold on people, they have looked at them in terms of the *euphoria*, or pleasure, they provide. They have come up with a "Euphoria Scale''—a scale that shows how much euphoria (pleasure) actually comes from the various things you might become addicted to. Euphoria, according to research, is made up of two main parts, which they call arousal and relaxation.

The two parts of pleasure correspond precisely to the two sides of the real M-State: calmness and inner alertness. "Arousal" refers to what we know as the "alertness" factor: it measures how much a food or drug makes you feel more "up," how much it relieves depression and mimics the true alertness you get from the M-State. "Relaxation" is the calmness or tranquillity factor: it measures how much a food or drug will calm you down and relieve your anxiety—how much it mimics the true inner calm the M-State gives you.

The more something calms you and wakes you up, the more pleasure, or euphoria, you will get from it. Of course, to be really pleasurable, relaxation should be a very rich, oceanic feeling of total calm—not a sense of dullness or sleepiness. And the alertness you derive, if it is to be really euphoric, should be a sense of heightened total alertness, like the feeling you get when you're in the presence of great art or with someone you truly love. It should have no trace of feeling "wired" and no sense of anxiety associated with it.

THE EUPHORIA SCALE

When euphoria is found to have two parts to it, it's only natural for researchers to want to create a graph, or Euphoria Scale (creating graphs is one of the more enjoyable parts of the job of being a researcher).

GOOD PLEASURE AND BAD PLEASURE

On the Euphoria Scale, you'll see that there are both *natural,* healthy states and various *unnatural,* unhealthy, and addictive substances on it. Both the *good* and *bad* things are located on the scale according to how much arousal and how much relaxation they give you.

You'll notice that familiar substances give different combinations of arousal and relaxation. The reason you choose one substance over the

11. EUPHORIA SCALE I

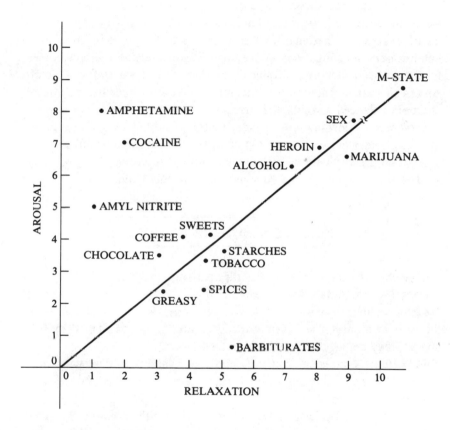

On this scale you can see many of the things that people crave and where they stand in a graph of their effects on arousal and relaxation.

Everything that people crave contributes to the balance and increase in arousal and relaxation. This is the reason they are craved in the first place. Different people will choose activities or substances which increase either the arousal, the relaxation, or both—usually both but in different amounts. Note that the things that are most universally used are closest to the diagonal line of balance on the chart.

Note also how far out on both scales sex and the M-State are.

other depends on what gives *you* the right feelings of arousal and/or relaxation—which differs very much from person to person.

The vertical markings on the Euphoria Scale show "arousal," and the horizontal scale shows "relaxation." The higher something is on the arousal side, the more it works to wake you up. The farther out on the relaxation side something is, the more it works to calm you down.

Look for instance at cocaine. Cocaine is a stimulant. So it is very high up on the "arousal" (vertical) line, but not very far out on the "relaxation" scale (the horizontal line). This shows that cocaine is stimulating but not very relaxing. Part of the intensity of cocaine's effect comes from the fact that it is a "refined" product. The coca leaf that South American Indians chew is the "natural" version of cocaine; its effects are more balanced and less addictive.

By contrast, sleeping pills are very relaxing and not very arousing. So they are farther out on the horizontal scale (showing relaxation) and not as high on the vertical scale (showing arousal). Anything that gives any kind of pleasure can be located somewhere on this scale.

DIFFERENT KINDS OF PLEASURE

The Euphoria Scale oversimplifies the real situation quite a bit, because "arousal" and "relaxation" are terms that cover a variety of different *kinds* of feelings. The arousal that you get from cocaine is different from the type of arousal you have from sugar, sex, or the M-State—and, of course, they are all different from one another.

Fear, too, is arousing—but it is hardly pleasurable, unless you know it's not for real, like the kind of fear you get in a fun house or a not-too-scary horror movie.

By the same token, the relaxation of sleeping pills is hardly the same as the relaxation you feel with, again, sex or the M-State. Things that are equally relaxing, or equally arousing, may deliver their feelings by quite different pathways. Feelings are highly complex. This is the limitation of the Euphoria Scale. Yet even so, it gives us a useful basis for comparison.

PLEASURE AND YOU

The Euphoria Scale, then, gives us a good idea of exactly how various substances provide us with pleasure. Some will make us happy mainly by cheering us up, others mainly by calming us down. Yet the Euphoria Scale can't tell us which substance any particular person will choose for their *own* pleasure, because this depends entirely on what the individual needs.

True pleasure comes from the *right balance of arousal and relaxation*. You know from your own experience that different things will strike you as pleasurable, according to your mood. Sometimes, when you're full of energy, you might want to spend the evening dancing, or in energetic conversation. Other times, you want to go to a movie, or listen to music, or even just watch TV. It all depends on how you feel.

The bottom line is, you're trying for the perfect balance between arousal and relaxation, and the same thing is true when you are "choosing" something to crave. Whether you'll choose something that is more on the arousal side or more on the relaxation side will depend upon what kind of needs you have at any moment. Your cravings will vary according to what you need most of the time.

If you generally have more of a need for arousal (to offset tiredness, fatigue, or depression), you will choose something that is more energizing, such as coffee or proteins with fats. On the other hand, if you're more anxious and uptight than depressed, it will be relaxation that seems more appealing to you, and you'll tend to crave starches or alcohol.

BALANCED EUPHORIA

Most of the time, for most people, our stresses are made up of some depression *and* some anxiety. So we are looking for pleasure that gives us a little bit of both arousal *and* relaxation. If something is well balanced between the two components of pleasure, it will be located on the scale along a diagonal line midway between the arousal and relaxation lines.

If you look at the scale, you'll see that there are two excellent,

healthy, natural choices on that line, ones that give a perfect balance
between arousal and relaxation: the real M-State and good sex. The
M-State has a perfect balance between arousal and relaxation: naturally
enough, because it works in a completely integrated way to give you a
state of inner calm and alertness. Sex, too, has been given us by nature
to cheer us up and calm us down. Good sex gets your brain very close to
the M-State. And it's the opposite of fattening.

But on that same line you will also find many other substances for
which we often have cravings. Tobacco is there, because smoking
relaxes and stimulates in about equal proportion. Alcohol is close to it,
just a little bit on the stimulation side.

Chocolate is right in there too (perhaps the most common single
craving/addiction). In fact, all the craving foods cluster around this line
as well. Sweets and spices are just a bit more on the arousal side, and
starches, and greasy and spicy foods are more on the relaxing side. But
all the craving foods mimic the M-State by providing a fairly balanced
proportion of arousal and relaxation.

THE MOSAIC EFFECT

The most important difference between the naturally balanced euphoriants
(M-State, sex) and the partial pleasures delivered by craving foods,
tobacco, and alcohol is that all the effects created by food or drugs are
mosaiclike in character. A mosaic is a picture made up of tiny bits of
glass, or tile, or stone—of various bits and pieces that are put together to
form the total picture.

The various substances we crave work by creating some little bit or
piece of the M-State: a bit of relaxation here, a trace of arousal there.
What we are doing with these substances is trying to put together a total
M-State experience out of these bits and pieces.

There are actually researchers who have spent their entire professional
lives trying to figure out, from what you ate last, what you'll eat *next* in
order to piece that fake M-State together. These scientists study the
effect on your brain of your last meal, and then try to predict what you
will crave at the next meal to balance the neurotransmitters you created
with the previous meal. They offer Fritos to the research subjects, then

weigh how many are left behind. And while they don't give specific attention to the M-State, a concept of the "ideal brain state" is *implied* in this research.

THE MOSAIC DOESN'T WORK

But the M-State cannot be created by this approach. There is no food and no combination of foods that will give the actual, true, and complete M-State. It is true that sugar, starch, grease, alcohol, and the other substances do give us some arousal and some relaxation. It's part of what we're searching for. But it is just a mosaic: a bit of this and a piece of that. The total effect can never become the complete whole, the true M-State.

As with a mosaic, when you look closely at the fake M-State, you can easily see the mortar, which holds the individual pieces together but which also keeps them apart. The real M-State, by contrast, is *seamless*. It creates a total effect that cascades throughout the system. The whole picture is there at once.

The mosaiclike characteristic of the fake M-State is why addictions or cravings, by their very nature, can *never truly satisfy us*. Convincing though it may seem at times, it isn't *really* even close to the real M-State. A mosaic looks like a complete picture only when you stand away from it. Come up close, and you can see the individual pieces only too well.

The mosaic of the fake M-State created by all addictions and all cravings looks convincing only when you are far from the real M-State. The closer you get to the reality, the more you can see how incomplete the fake really is.

This is why I emphasize constantly that cravings must be cured, not just masked or covered up. The parts can never make the whole. Where the whole—the real M-State—is restorative, the parts—the fake M-State— merely deplete the system further. Rather than helping, the fake M-State does tremendous harm.

Figure 12, on page 78, shows the tremendous harm done by each addiction. Contrast this to the across-the-board healthfulness of the real M-State that you saw in figure 3, page 37, and you'll see why cravings must be cured.

12. BIOCHEMICAL PATHWAYS TO THE FAKE M-STATE

Each substance/activity takes its own incomplete, convincing route to the fake M-State while doing the body tremendous harm.

SUBSTANCE/ACTIVITY	PATHWAY	FEELING	HARM
Alcohol	1. Suppression of inhibitory neurons[1] 2. Cortisol release from adrenals[4]	Euphoria/reduced anxiety[2] Energy/invincibility[5]	Postintoxication letdown (hangover), addiction, cirrhosis, poisoned tissues[3]
Cigarettes	1. Endorphin release[6] 2. Nicotine-ACH receptors[8]	Reduced anxiety/pain[7] Pleasure/stimulation[9]	Cardiac and lung disease, cancer, addiction[10]
Cocaine	1. Increased brain activity[11] 2. Overstimulation of pleasure centers[14]	Omnipotence[12] Orgasmic[15]	Dependency and depression from depletion of neurotransmitters[13] Permanent burnout of pleasure centers[16]
Amphetamines	Depletion of neurotransmitter chemicals from brain and nerves (dopamine and noradrenaline)[17]	Jittery euphoria[18] Appetite suppression[19]	Mania, dependency, rebound weight gain, lethargy, exhaustion, psychosis[20]
Compulsive behaviors (gambling, etc.)	Complex interaction of cerebral cortex and limbic system[21]	Arousal/relaxation ("fun")[22]	Distorts reality, addictive, profound disruption of social relations[23]
Exercise	Endorphin, vasopressin release[24]	Physical bliss, insensitivity to pain, reduced stress[25]	Addictive, depletion of body energy, negative impact on socialization[26]
Craving foods	Production of various brain chemicals and hormones[27]	Mosaic of restfulness/alertness[28]	Seesaw of obesity and stimulation/depression, blocks emergence of real M-State[29]
Opiates	Endorphin receptors[30]	Relaxation, "visceral bliss," detachment[31]	Severe addiction, poor social relations, increased susceptibility to disease[32]
Barbiturates	General depression of nerves and muscles, especially in brain[33]	Sedation and muscular relaxation[34]	Rebound hyperexcitability, addiction, overdose, coma[35]

7

THE CRAVINGS ANALYSIS CHECKLIST

This Cravings Analysis Checklist is a compilation of the methods my nurses and I use at Skinny School to determine your cravings. Since you aren't sitting in a room with us, I made the checklist *as close as possible to an actual conversation* as I could. It's just like being there.

You'll see that the checklist is not only a technique for finding out what you crave, but also a new way of thinking about your cravings. It focuses not just on the particular foods that you can't resist, but on the kinds of *situations* where you tend to get your cravings. The checklist will help you see which foods you have problems with, and also when your problems are most likely to occur. These are both important parts of your cure.

"I'M NOT READY FOR THIS, DOCTOR!"

A patient named Stephanie S. once told me, "Doctor, I don't want to find out for sure what my cravings are. Maybe I do crave chocolate, maybe I don't, but I'm not ready to stop eating it."

Stephanie's resistance to knowing her cravings was typical of a significant percentage of my patients. The stronger your cravings are, the more likely you are to resist focusing in on them—because you are wary of having to give up what is very possibly the only thing in your life that is giving you real pleasure. Basically, Stephanie was saying—change how I look if you can, but don't change the way I feel.

If you sense this kind of resistance in yourself, remember that you don't have to give up the foods you crave until you are ready. We always tell our Skinny School patients to simply begin the program. Begin your Anti-craving Diet and start the Nutritional Supplement Program for your particular craving. Don't promise that you'll never look at a chocolate bar or a french fry again. Until your cravings are cured, that promise is worthless anyway.

We know that the program works and will cure our patients' cravings within four to eight weeks. It will work for you in the same way. In the week that you start Skinny School, giving up your craving food will seem, and be, very difficult. By the second or third week, it seems much easier, and by the fourth week you will be wondering why you had so much trouble with chocolate in the first place.

THE FOUR SECTIONS

The Cravings Analysis Checklist has four sections:

> Section I: Your M-State Quotient
> Section II: Your M-State Substitution Quotient
> Section III: Your Craving Foods
> Section IV: Your Body Shape

Each section covers an important aspect of your cravings. In Sections I and II, you'll find out how much M-State you have in your life today, and how much you are substituting other things for the M-State. These two sections together will give an indication of the strength of your cravings.

The more M-State you are experiencing, the less strong your cravings will be, and the less likely you are to be making substitutions for the

M-State. By contrast, the less M-State you have, the stronger your cravings will be, and the higher will be your M-State Substitution Quotient.

The information you'll get from Sections I and II will tell you how strong your cravings are, and approximately how long your cravings will take to be cured.

Section III is where you find out *your* craving foods. In this section, I have you take a look at the foods you habitually use to change your feelings. The foods that you use in this way are the foods you are substituting for the M-State.

In Section III, I describe certain situations that are stressful for most people, and ask about what foods you reach for at those times. I do this because, whatever you crave, the craving will tend to come up in specific situations that happen to be stressful or difficult for you.

People are different. We are all stressed in our own ways. For you, a business meeting might be the ultimate in stress; for someone else, it might be a doctor's appointment, a long drive home in traffic, or a day alone with four children. Stressors (that is, things that cause stress) can be anything; for some people even success and celebrations are stressful, especially if they feel they don't deserve their successes.

It's important that when you go through Section III, you use your common sense to apply the situations *to your own life*. If I describe a situation where someone is celebrating because they've finished a big job, don't say to yourself, "This doesn't apply to me because I don't have a job."

Instead, think something like "I don't have an outside job, but I feel the same way when I finish a gardening project or successfully organize a fund-raiser. What foods do I reach for then?" In other words, *apply* the questions appropriately to *your* life. Don't try to wiggle out and play around. These questions are for *you*.

Section IV, the final section of the checklist, is about your body's shape. What does this have to do with cravings? It turns out that certain features of your body's shape are quite definite indicators of the foods you are *likely* to crave. If you know my work on body types, you'll see that the questions in Section IV are about your body type.

Your body's shape—whether you have long or short legs and arms, whether you are rangy or stocky, the shape of your hands, the shape of your head, and other such factors—is largely determined by which of your body's glands is dominant in your metabolism. If your thyroid is your strongest gland, your body will have a characteristic shape; if your adrenals are strongest, your basic shape will be different.

Each of the four major glands (thyroid, adrenal, pituitary, and gonads, or sex glands) gives you a particular and very distinctive body shape.

In Chapter 4, I described the way different craving foods stimulate each of the four glands to give you a fake M-State feeling. According to your Body Type, you will be likely to crave foods that stimulate *your* dominant gland, in order to get the feeling you want.

So when I ask about your body's shape, I am discovering which foods you will be most likely to crave, based on your Body Type. If you already know your Body Type, you know that Pituitary and Thyroid types are more likely to be sweet and starch cravers, and Adrenal and Gonadal types are more likely to be greasy and spicy food cravers. The questions in Section IV will help you focus on this factor in determining your cravings.

(If you want to know more about Body Types and cravings, or about the way Body Types help you choose a complete health program for yourself, refer to *Dr. Abravanel's Body Type Program for Health, Fitness, and Nutrition*, published by Bantam Books.)

SECTION I: YOUR M-STATE QUOTIENT
1. How stressful is your life?

    a. I'm ready to throw it all in today.
    b. Pretty crazy.
    c. Normal.
    d. Pretty nice!
    e. I feel like I live on a beach in Bali.

2. Do you have both a job outside the home and housework/childcare responsibility?

    a. Yes.
    c. Part-time job and/or part-time housework/childcare.
    d. I only have to do *one* of them.
    e. I don't have to do either one.

3. How old are your children?

   a. Oldest between ten and eighteen.
   b. Oldest under ten.
   c. Youngest over eighteen.
   d. No kids.
   e. All grown and out of my hair.

4. Do you consider yourself at or near the point of "burnout" in your life?

   a. Yes.
   b. Getting there.
   c. Sometimes I think so.
   e. No.

5. Do you have trouble asking others to help you with your responsibilities and burdens?

   b. Yes.
   c. I ask only on major things.
   e. No.

6. Do you have paid household help?

   c. No.
   e. Yes.

7. How many real vacations (one full week or more) have you had in the last year?

   a. None.
   b. One.
   c. Two.
   e. Three or more.

8. How many mini-vacations (3 to 4-day weekends, anything less than a week) have you had in the last year?

   a. None.
   b. One.
   c. Two.
   e. Three or more.

9. How do you feel about your vacations?

    a. I hate them—I can't relax.
    b. I don't like them.
    c. They're the same as ordinary life.
    d. It's nice to get away.
    e. I love every second.

10. Do you return from the weekend more tired than when you left?

    a. Yes.
    c. I feel about the same.
    e. No, I feel much better.

11. Is your workplace (or your home office) a refuge from your family life?

    a. Yes.
    c. They're about equal in stressfulness.
    e. No.

12. How many built-in nonfood "break periods" are in your day (e.g., midmorning read-the-paper break, hot bath before bed, etc.)?

    a. None—what's a break without food?
    b. One.
    c. Two or more.
    e. Three or more.

13. How much time do you spend actually alone in your day? (Time in the car counts only if you're not in a traffic jam.)

    a. Less than half an hour.
    c. One half hour to an hour.
    e. More than an hour.

14. Do you practice any kind of meditation, yoga, etc.?

    a. No.
    e. Yes.

15. Do you go to any religious service regularly?

   a. No.
   c. Yes, but I don't get much out of it.
   e. Yes.

16. How often do you work out physically (20 to 30 minutes)?

   a. Never.
   c. Once or twice a week.
   e. Three to five times a week.

Add your score for Section I here:

   a. _____ Multiply each "a" answer times 4. Total = _____
   b. _____ Multiply each "b" answer times 3. Total = _____
   c. _____ Multiply each "c" answer times 2. Total = _____
   d. _____ Each "d" answer is worth 1 point. Total = _____
   e. _____ No points for "e" answers.

SECTION II: YOUR M-STATE SUBSTITUTION QUOTIENT

17. How much alcohol do you drink? (Note: "one drink" is 12 ounces of beer, 6 ounces of wine, or one ounce of hard liquor.)

   a. I drink some alcohol every day.
   b. 5 drinks or more per week.
   c. 3 to 4 drinks per week.
   d. 1 to 2 drinks per week.
   e. I drink no alcohol at all.

18. Do you exercise more than five times per week, or more than an hour each workout?

   b. Yes.
   c. No.

19. How much do you smoke?

   a. More than a pack per day.
   b. Between a half pack and a pack per day.
   c. Less than half a pack per day.
   e. I don't smoke.

20. Do you use any illegal drugs?

   a. Yes.

   e. No.

21. Do you take diet pills?

   c. Yes.

   e. No.

22. Do you gamble?

   a. Yes, compulsively.

   c. Yes, once in a while, for fun.

   e. No.

23. Do you do any very dangerous actions, such as race-car driving, skydiving, rock climbing, hang gliding, motorcycle jumping?

   a. I do every one of these I can, and more.

   b. I do one dangerous thing.

   e. I wouldn't think of it.

24. Do you overspend for your income level?

   a. Yes, it's my cure for everything.

   b. Yes, a little, just at the holidays.

   e. No.

25. How many extra pounds do you have?

   a. 50 or more.

   b. 26 to 49.

   c. 10 to 25.

   d. Less than 10.

   e. None.

Add your total number of points from Section II here:

   a. _____ Multiply each "a" answer times 4. Total = _____

   b. _____ Multiply each "b" answer times 3. Total = _____

   c. _____ Multiply each "c" answer times 2. Total = _____

   d. _____ Each "d" answer is worth 1 point. Total = _____

   e. _____ No points for "e" answers.

SECTION III: YOUR CRAVING FOODS
(Note: This section is to help you determine which foods you crave under stress. Remember that you must *adapt* the "stressful situations" described below to *your own life*.)

26. Stressful Situation 1: The five o'clock slump.

You walk into the house after a hard day, the children start dragging on your skirt, there are eleven messages on your answering machine requiring your immediate attention, and the dog makes a run in your panty hose. You know you'll be able to handle this better after you get yourself:

    a. A candy bar.
    b. Some pretzels.
    c. Some cookies.
    d. Some chips with dip.
    e. A bag of spicy peanuts.

27. Stressful Situation 2: Midmorning freakout.

Your boss wants you to redo the entire project. The bank says you are overdrawn and have to show up in five minutes with money or they'll bounce the mortgage check. Your child calls up and you hear a sound of rushing water in the background, and when you ask what she's doing she says, "Nothing." You cheer up when you realize that once you're in the car you can stop and get:

    a. A Snickers.
    b. A bagel.
    c. A doughnut.
    d. A burger.
    e. A taco with salsa.

28. Stressful Situation 3: Sudden joy.

You just heard Jane Pauley say on TV that science has absolutely proved that there is no such thing as overweight, and the more you weigh the longer you will live, and in good health, yet. She personally has gone over to coffee and doughnuts for breakfast. She says that Willard Scott has been right all along. She then interviews Tom Cruise, who says in front of everyone that he has always preferred overweight women. You decide you will go out immediately and have:

a. A banana split with extra chocolate sauce.
b. A super-sized order of onion rings.
c. An entire cake.
d. An enormous chicken-fried steak.
e. An endless Thai (Mexican, Italian) meal (10 from column A, 10 from column B, etc.)

29. Stressful Situation 4: "Kid let out of school" syndrome.

You and your spouse have just come back from two weeks at one of those cardiovascular fitness camps where the diet is restricted to hay, oats, and nonfat yogurt. You can set your watch by your bowels. Now that you're home and there's no one to see how you're killing yourself, you head straight for the kitchen and stuff your face with:

a. Mallomars.
b. White bread.
c. Twinkies.
d. Cheese.
e. Sausages.

30. Stressful Situation 5: The big celebration.

This is the first time you've ever been to a Bar Mitzvah. There on this huge buffet table crammed with all kinds of semimysterious ethnic foods is a bust of the Bar Mitzvah boy, done in chopped liver with hard-boiled eggs for eyes. At the end of the buffet you look at your plate with everything on it and realize that you have absolutely no intention of eating the:

a. Chopped liver.
   (Why have protein when there are so many different desserts?)
b. Lox.
   (You'll just have the bagels.)
c. Bread.
   (Let them eat cake. Let *you* eat cake too.)

d. Celery.
   (You'll take the dip without the celery, thanks.)
e. Dessert.
   (You'll be far too full by that time on the pigs in a blanket.)

31. Stressful Situation 6: Sexual excitement.

You are incredibly excited about running into an old flame. You're
lunching together in a place with hushed tones, flowers on the table, and
a string quartet. He/she wants to meet again. You *know* that your most
significant other won't find out. You feel elated, guilty, and sexy. While
you're considering whether it would be wise to meet again or not, your
old flame asks what you want to finish off your lunch. You decide the
perfect thing would be:

a. Anything chocolate.
b. The rest of the bread sticks.
c. The entire dessert trolley.
d. Some Roquefort cheese.
e. A second shrimp cocktail.

32. Stressful Situation 7: Family vacation in the car.

You've been driving for almost four hours. Everyone says they have to go
to the bathroom, the interstate is all corduroyed because they're adding a
lane, and the little one has just thrown up tidily into the Styrofoam
cooler. You spy a "home-cooking" franchise at the off ramp. You're not
exactly hungry, but could choke something down to "settle your stomach." The best thing would be:

a. M&M's.
b. The bread of a sandwich.
c. One of those huge chocolate chip cookies.
d. A milk shake.
e. A microwaved burrito.

33. Stressful Situation 8: The big day.

This day is really important. You are being interviewed for a job that,
if you get it, will solve all your financial problems plus be interesting.

Afterward you have a date with a really nice man who gets along with all your children and wants to marry you, but only if you get the job. You usually have a really healthy breakfast of whole-grain cereal and decaf, etc., but today because it's so important you decide to "fortify" yourself but good with:

    a. A Coke.
    b. An English muffin.
    c. Pancakes with syrup.
    d. Steak and eggs.
    e. Huevos rancheros.

34. Stressful Situation 9: Success.

Everything went right for once. Everything. You got the job and he kept his word. And you're the one that made it all happen. It's a total fluke, you secretly think, yet you do truly deserve a fabulous reward. It's going to be:

    a. Fudge.
    b. A pasta salad with bread on the side.
    c. A gorgeous piece of cake.
    d. Steak.
    e. Kung Pao Three Flavors.*

35. Stressful Situation 10: Being in the house all day with the refrigerator.

Think back to your childhood. You knew that when you finally became a grown-up, you would always, no matter what Mom said, have as much as you ever wanted of:

    a. Marshmallows.
    b. Macaroni, hold the cheese.
    c. Oreos.
    d. Hot dogs.
    e. Chili peppers.

Give yourself a check for every answer in Section III:

    a. _____
    b. _____
    c. _____
    d. _____
    e. _____

SECTION IV: YOUR BODY SHAPE
(Note: This section should be taken if possible with a friend who can look at you from all angles and give you honest feedback about your shape. Next best is to take it in front of a mirror in which you can see yourself from front and back.)

36 A: WOMEN.
Consider your body's basic, ideal shape—that is, the way you would look if you were at your best weight. Choose the one that best characterizes how you would look:

   a. Slim but curvy—breasts medium to large for your size, small waist, rounded hips and rear end, rounded upper thighs, tapering calves, and slim ankles. Long, narrow face.
   b. Rather childlike in general shape—small breasts, fairly straight through the waist down to small hips, slightly rounded rear end. Cherubic, innocent face.
   d. Straight torso, broad-shouldered, large breasts, very small rear end, slender thighs, rounded calves. Square or round face.
   c. Small above the waist, narrow shoulders and small, well-shaped breasts, small waist, flat stomach, and prominent rear end that goes out straight back behind you. Fairly slender thighs and rounded calves. Small face and downward-sloping eyes.

36 B: MEN.
Consider your body's basic, ideal shape—that is, the way you would look if you were at your best weight. Choose the one that best characterizes how you would look:

   a. Fine-boned, slim for your height, broad shoulders, a very flat rear, long legs (again, for your height), and a long, narrow hand with long, flexible fingers. Long, narrow face.

b. Boyish-looking, narrow shoulders, small chest, slightly rounded rear, and delicate hands. Cherubic, innocent face.
d. Squarely built, sturdy-looking, a strong chest and rounded rear end, rather short legs for your height, and a square hand with short, sturdy fingers. Square or round face.

37 A: WOMEN

Turn sideways and look at the line of your back in the mirror, or ask your friend to look. If you are overweight, ignore the extra pounds and try to uncover the way you would look at your best weight.

a. Neck comes forward from shoulders, back is quite straight, and the line of the rear is rounded but not extremely prominent.
b. Shoulders are rounded, back is also rounded, and rear end is small and childish-looking.
d. Head is directly above the back, rear end appears to be flat and "tucked-under."
e. Back appears swayed and rear end sticks out behind you.

37 B: MEN.

Turn sideways and look at the line of your back in the mirror, or ask your friend to look. If you are overweight, ignore the extra pounds and try to uncover the way you would look at your best weight.

a. Back is straight and there is practically no rear end.
b. Back is curved, head comes forward from neck, and rear end is rounded.
d. Back is straight and rear end is rounded.

38 A: WOMEN.

Look carefully at the location of your extra fat. Where is it mainly located?

a. Around your middle. "Roll" around midriff, tummy, upper thighs.
b. All over, no single particular location.
d. Stomach ("potbelly" rather than midriff roll) and upper back.
e. Rear end.

38 B: MEN.
Look carefully at the location of your extra fat. Where is it mainly located?

   a. Around the middle in a spare tire.
   b. All over, no single location.
   d. In the front in a potbelly.

Add up your scores from Section IV:

WOMEN:

   a. _____
   b. _____
   d. _____
   e. _____

MEN:
   a. _____
   b. _____
   d. _____

Scoring the Cravings Analysis Checklist:

1. Add your total scores from Sections I and II.

This portion of the checklist indicates how strong your cravings are.

75 to 84: You have intense cravings.
Skinny School cure projection: 8 weeks.

50 to 74: You have fairly strong cravings.
Skinny School cure projection: 4 to 7 weeks.

25 to 49: You have moderate cravings.
Skinny School cure projection: 3 to 4 weeks.

0 to 24: Your cravings are fairly well controlled.
Skinny School cure projection: 1 to 2 weeks.

2. Add your total number of checks from Section III and Section IV.

Highest number of checks = a, b, or c:
You are a sweet and starch craver. You will follow the Sweet and Starch Cravers Diet (found in Chapter 9).

Highest number of checks for "a": You mainly crave sweets.
Highest number of checks for "b": You mainly crave starches.
Highest number of checks for "c": You mainly crave starchy sweets.

You will use the supplement program to cure this craving.

Highest number of checks = d or e:
You are a greasy and spicy food craver. You will follow the Greasy and Spicy Food Cravers Diet (found in Chapter 10).

Highest number of checks for "d": You mainly crave greasy foods.
Highest number of checks for "e": You mainly crave spicy foods.

You will use the supplement program to cure this craving.

ADDITIONAL CHECKING QUESTIONS

The questions below are to *confirm* or *check* your results for Sections III and IV. Take these questions to check whether you are a sweet and starch craver or a greasy and spicy food craver.

39. Which is your favorite taste?

   a. Sweet, sour, or spicy-sweet.
   b. Salty, bitter, or spicy-hot.

40. What do you usually add to your food:

   a. Sugar.
   b. Salt.

41. How often do you eat dessert:

   a. Quite often.
   b. Quite rarely.

42. The expression "America's breadbasket":

   a. Is strangely exciting.
   b. Leaves you cold.

43. Picture yourself pushing away from the table after a perfect dinner. You ate just the right amount for once, you aren't sleepy, and you feel like going salsa dancing. The thing you like best about this feeling is that you are:

   a. Livelier and more energetic than before dinner.
   b. Sexier and more powerful than before dinner.

44. You prefer to handle the difficult people in your life with:

   a. Charm or avoidance.
   b. Displays of strength.

45. You've been working like a galley slave all week, and Saturday has finally arrived. You can't wait, because you're finally going to get a chance to:

   a. Sleep until noon and then eat pancakes with syrup for brunch.
   b. Play 36 holes of golf, then drink some beer.

46. You've been off and on diets your whole life, and in a way there are certain diets you actually, secretly look forward to going on. If they only worked, they'd be perfect. The diet you secretly love is:

   a. *Fit for Life* or the *Beverly Hills Diet,* because you can eat fruit all day and have dates for breakfast.
   b. Scarsdale, Stillman, or Atkins, because you can eat steak at every meal and drink cream in your coffee.

47. All the time you're on any diet, you think constantly about:

   a. Cookies.
   b. Crispy chicken skin.

Add up your Checking Questions.

More "a" answers: confirms you are a sweet and starch craver.
More "b" answers: confirms you are a greasy and spicy food craver.

INTRODUCTION: THE SKINNY SCHOOL CRAVING CURES

Now that you know about your cravings, you are ready to begin the Skinny School craving cure. I want you to be really free of food cravings, to eat whatever you want and keep your best weight easily, the way naturally skinny people do. But for this to happen, you *must* do the complete cure and *not* just pick the parts you think will be easiest or will get you by.

Cravings are highly complex, as you've seen. They don't just mean you have a "lack of willpower." A craving has *nothing* to do with simply "wanting too much chocolate" or any such oversimplification. Sayings like "You just need to push yourself away from the table" are patronizing as well as totally inaccurate—they completely fail to do justice to the reality of the problem.

To cure your food cravings, you must:

1. Restore your body's natural ability to feel true calmness and alertness, based on natural neuroglial brain activity.
2. Learn to choose your food according to your body's innate chemical food-evaluation methods, that is, through using your senses of taste and smell.

3. Correct the massive nutritional deficiencies that come with *all* cravings.
4. Retrain your eating habits so that they are in harmony with the changes in your body's neurophysiology created by steps 1, 2, and 3.

All of these steps are necessary for a complete and lasting cure. If you omit even one of them, you will not be fully cured, and you will never maintain your best weight in an easy, effortless way. Losing weight at Skinny School means getting really cured and becoming, yourself, a naturally skinny person.

THE TECHNOLOGY OF THE M-STATE

The first step, restoring your natural ability to feel true inner calmness and alertness, means that you must make room in your life for experiencing the real M-State.

The M-State gives your body the ability to neutralize stress. It gives you contact with your sense of inner selfhood, and it "resets" your total physiology to its original healthy setting. It also creates in you a feeling that, *if you don't have it,* you will do literally *anything* to get.

All cravings are based on your attempt to put together, using chemical stimuli, something resembling the feeling of inner calm and alertness that comes naturally with the M-State.

For *all* these reasons, getting the real M-State is an absolute part of the cure for cravings.

How, exactly, you decide to do this is your own decision. Experiencing the M-State is not something that can be taught in a book. You need to learn a reliable technique of meditation from a trained teacher.

I recommend Transcendental Meditation to my patients, because it has been scientifically researched and shown to be very effective in giving you the M-State. Also, it is available everywhere (simply look in the white pages of your phone book).

Other similar techniques may well be effective. *Simply be sure that what you are learning does, in fact, give you a sense of inner calm, tranquillity, heightened awareness, and relief from stress.* Your own experience is always the best guide. If you begin a technique and it doesn't give you a real sense of the M-State right away, don't waste time thinking it will change. Move on to something that works.

DIET, SUPPLEMENTS, AND "LARD" LESSONS

Steps 2, 3, and 4 are accomplished by following the right Skinny School Anti-craving Diet, by taking the nutritional supplements that cure your craving(s), and by doing the "Lard" Lessons, a series of food-behavior modification exercises.

These now follow in the next seven chapters. Simply remember that the entire program works together as a whole. The supplement program is designed to work *with* the diets. Do not imagine that you can just take the vitamins and minerals and your cravings will be gone. Supplementation cures the part of your cravings associated with physiological deficiencies, but that is not the whole story of cravings.

It's true that the Skinny School supplements, which are targeted to specific cravings, seem to work like magic but alone are not sufficient for a complete, permanent cure. Unless you take them along with the right foods, your body will not be able to use them and you will not get the results you want. You need the "instructions" that come with the right tastes, in order to use the supplements.

The "Lard" Lessons are designed to work *after* your food cravings have been already partially controlled with the diet and supplements. You should not begin the "Lard" Lessons until you have been on your diet and taken your supplements for at least four weeks. They work to restructure the neural reward circuits that have developed around your cravings.

If you do follow the complete Skinny School program in this way, you will find, as have my patients, that within four to eight weeks, your food cravings will be finally cured.

8

ALL YOU NEED IS TASTE

The Skinny School Anti-craving Diets are the most natural diets in the world. There are no calories to count; you don't have to know the nutritional content of the food, and you don't think about fiber or anything else. All you have to know about food is its *taste*.

"Taste?" a patient named Jane B. said incredulously. "What could taste possibly have to do with a *diet*? Vitamins, sure. Vitamins I can understand. Also protein, carbohydrates, and fats. Fiber, even. *Calories,* certainly. But a diet based on *taste?"*

Yes, taste. Or, more accurately, taste and smell—these are your two *chemical* senses, and are closely linked both in their action and in the brain. These are what you must consider in choosing your food. Until you understand how to *use* taste and smell in the right way—to eat the right combination of the eight tastes, and to choose the tastes you need to satisfy your body and brain—you will never be in complete control of your food destiny.

This may seem incredible to you, as it did to Jane B. and countless other Skinny School patients, if you have been accustomed to counting calories or analyzing your food's nutritional content for many years. But it is true. Taste and smell together make up an extremely precise, totally accurate, and incredibly sensitive mechanism, given to you by nature to choose the foods that are exactly right for you at any time.

SUBJECTIVITY IS THE KEY

Using taste and smell is a *subjective,* personal way of evaluating food—as opposed to the *objective,* scientific way that nutritional analysis uses.

When science tells you about food's heat-producing ability (that is, its calories), or its biochemical components (its proteins, carbohydrates, or fat content), or its quotient of trace elements and catalysts for the digestive processes (its vitamins and minerals), then you know something about that food. But you *don't* necessarily know whether that food is right for *you* at any particular moment, or not.

The scientific way of analyzing food is very valuable, of course. It has helped us greatly to understand the biochemistry of food and to develop a scientifically grounded approach to our nutritional needs. But it really needs to be *complemented* and *supplemented* by a more personal approach to food.

Knowing the science of food doesn't help you make the right choices from within yourself. Science may know food, but it doesn't know *you,* your DNA, or your brain-chemistry profile. And it is of no help at all at those moments of diet failure, when cravings overwhelm you and all your knowledge becomes useless.

KNOWLEDGE ISN'T POWER

Another patient, Lucinda P., told me about an insight she had one day at lunch. Lucinda had about 35 pounds she wanted to lose, and before Skinny School had been an expert dieter who had lost weight on every diet in the world (and then, unfortunately, gained it back).

She told me she was lunching with a friend and had just finished the kind of lunch she used to hate herself for eating—basically starch topped by grease, and capped with a dessert of mousse cake. At the end of the meal, she said, she burst into tears and told her friend, ''I just ate 3260 calories in under fifteen minutes.'' She was crying because she knew the exact calorie count of everything she'd eaten, but it hadn't stopped her from taking a single bite.

It's always like that. My most overweight patients are the most knowledgeable: they know everything there is to know about food, most particularly how many calories there are in everything they put into their mouths. They could write those little books you find by the checkout counter. It simply doesn't help.

Skinny people, on the other hand, almost never know the calories of food. They don't think that way. If you ask one of them which has more calories, a brownie or a baked potato, they usually haven't the slightest idea—and couldn't care less. That's not the way they choose their foods. They use taste and smell.

NATURE'S GUIDELINES

Taste and smell are not "extra" features of food. They are its very essence. Nature gave you these senses so that you would be able to make precise, accurate evaluations of everything you put into your mouth (or even near your nose). Taste and smell work on your brain. When you taste and smell a food, it tells your brain:

1. Exactly what you are eating.
2. Whether that food is good or bad for you.
3. How your body should *digest and use* that food. The taste and smell actually contain *instructions* to your body about digestion and utilization; without the right tastes and smells your body cannot fully utilize a food.
4. When you have had enough. Your appetite is regulated by taste and smell. If food doesn't taste or smell right, your brain never reaches the conclusion that you are full, and you never feel satisfied enough to stop eating. But when you are full, food stops tasting and smelling appetizing, and you automatically want to stop.

Tasteless food can't give you any of these messages. That's why it makes you fat.

THE CHEMICAL SENSES

When I say taste and smell are chemical senses, it means that these senses have evolved in your body over billions of years as ways to evaluate the chemical content of food and check it against your needs.

When you taste or smell a food, you are taking a chemical sample of that food actually into your brain. In the brain, you then compare how that food will "fit" with what your body needs. In foods that you don't crave—your nonproblem foods—the comparison is very simple. Foods that will "fit" your needs smell and taste good; foods that don't fit your needs smell or taste bad.

When you taste or smell a food that you crave, then your brain uses its chemical analysis of the food to check and see whether it will give you the *M-State substitute* that you are searching for.

Since taste and smell are methods for *checking* a food's value to you, the smell or taste will depend on what is going on inside you at that moment, both physically and mentally. Studies tell us that food tastes vary according to the condition your body is in. For instance, the taste of bitter orange is very appealing if you are very hungry. It tastes and smells just wonderful—but as soon as you have eaten something and aren't quite as hungry, it starts to taste too bitter.

Just as some foods are nearly always good for you, some foods will nearly always taste and smell appealing. Liking for certain tastes and smells is genetic. Your body type is a good indicator of what tastes and smells you will like. Thyroid or pituitary types always enjoy sweet foods, and adrenal and gonadal types always like spicy and salty tastes. Besides this preference, nearly everybody has some enjoyment of sweetness—it is a characteristic of all primates.

WHAT TASTE IS FOR

A Spanish poet, Antonio Machado, wrote, "It's good knowing that glasses are to drink from; / the bad thing is not to know what thirst is for." I agree. It's good to know how many calories there are in everything; the bad thing is not to know what taste and smell are for. They are there to give us satisfaction, and to protect us as well.

Today, we are "microsmatic"—which means we don't use our sense of smell very much, or very well. If you tried to track someone with your nose, you wouldn't get two feet. But if you lived in the wilds, where life is more obviously treacherous, you'd need to use these senses constantly, just to survive. Soldiers in Vietnam reported that they grew adept at smelling the presence of enemy camps in the jungle. The senses themselves are still there, as capabilities—it's just that we don't utilize them very much.

If you were less civilized, you'd have to smell and taste your food *very carefully* before eating it just to see if it was edible. In strange countries, or in strange new restaurants, we all do smell and taste new foods more carefully than we do at home. We're testing it out to see if the food will "agree with us"—one of the important functions of taste.

Babies are very much in touch with their natural taste-testing ability. Nobody will spit something out faster than a baby—who certainly isn't counting calories. The whole world is strange and new, and babies are definitely on the qui vive.

SMELL: THE MINI-LABORATORY OF THE BRAIN

Of the two chemical senses, smell is the one you use first in evaluating a food, because smell works at a distance from the food—before you put it into your mouth.

What you smell is actually nothing more than vaporized molecules of the food itself, which float off the food and into your nose. That's actually why you sniff: to make a little breeze to draw in a mini-sample of the food.

Inside your nose, the food comes into contact with a nerve ending whose other end is actually *in* your brain; there is no synapse or gap intervening between the brain and the nerves in the nose. So when you smell a food you are bringing it into actual, direct contact with your brain.

If you have a sensitive sense of smell, you are like a cat; cats have extremely sensitive noses and reject many foods on the basis of their smell, which is why we think of cats as finicky. Owls are even more finicky. Ernest Hemingway had an owl that he used as a taster—or, rather, as a smeller. The owl would sniff Hemingway's food, and if the owl wouldn't eat it, Hemingway wouldn't either, because he knew it wasn't fresh enough.

When your sense of smell brings food into contact with your brain, it does more than just tell your brain what the food smells like. Smell has four vital functions:

1. Smell lets your brain evaluate the chemical composition of the food. If the food is rancid or poisonous, it will smell bad, and you can reject the food before putting it in your mouth. If the food is good, it will smell good, and you will proceed to eat it.
2. Smell sends a message to your mouth, telling it to produce saliva and begin the digestive process.
3. Smell sends a message to your stomach, telling it not just that food is coming, but what kind of food it will be, so that the right juices can start flowing.
4. Smell creates a sense of pleasure and satisfaction in your brain. And this, in turn, is part of a natural appetite-control mechanism. Good, natural smells from food are part of what satisfies your hunger, so that you stop eating at the right time.

TASTE: THE MINI-DIGESTION OF THE MOUTH

When you have smelled a food and decided that it "smells good," you have made a judgment based on the molecules of food that were volatile enough to float into your nose. If you sensed no danger in the food, and if you found the smell to be good, you would be ready to take the next step and actually take a bite.

If you were using your senses properly, you would be very cautious about your first taste of a food, because danger from the food might be deep inside it, not on the surface where it could be smelled.

The first taste of a food comes when you place it on your tongue. This is closely followed by chewing, in which you crush the food and release chemicals from *within* the food into your mouth. These chemicals pass up the back of your throat to your nose and again give you a chance to let it pass or fail the smell test.

When you first smelled the food, some outer molecules of it came into direct contact with your brain. Now the inner portion of the food touches your brain as well.

Taste is a mini-digestive process. The taste buds are in little "pits" in the tongue, which the food goes into just like it goes into the stomach. Your taste buds report what the food tastes like: whether it is sweet, sour, bitter, astringent, pungent, or "umami" (the term for richness of taste). The illustration of the tongue on the next page is a close-up of the tongue, showing the taste buds at the bottom of tiny mini-stomachs.

TASTE IS A COMPARISON TEST

Whether a food tastes good or bad to you at this moment depends partly on the composition of the food and partly on the current state of your body and mind. The moment of taste is another moment of comparison between the chemical composition of the food and what your body knows will be good for it.

Smell carries information both upward, to your brain, and downward, to your stomach. Taste does the same thing. While nerves from your tongue transmit information directly to your brain, a nerve called the trigeminal nerve gives your stomach more complete information about the food it will soon get.

Because of taste, your gastric juices start flowing, your blood moves into digestive position—all the reflexes get ready, not just for food in general, but for the precise foods that the tongue has just informed the body are on the way. Taste, along with smell, literally carries *instructions* to the body about how, exactly, to make use of your food.

DRINKING ORDERLINESS

Whenever you eat or drink, you are "drinking orderliness from the environment," in the Nobel laureate Prigogine's famous phrase. Energy from outside your body is brought to the inside, to serve your processes

13. THE "MINI-DIGESTION" OF THE TONGUE

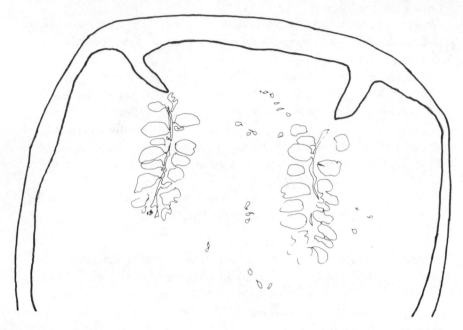

This is a diagram of the surface of the tongue which highlights the pits in the taste buds. The little sacs are actually below the tongue's surface. They receive the chemicals of the tasted food and relay their chemical composition to the brain and digestive tract. This allows the body to check its composition against that of the food and decide if it's right to eat. This is accomplished by a "Mini-Digestion" in the little sacs.

of growth and evolution. To be sure that what you are taking in is really orderliness, and not disorder (poison), you need the information you get from your chemical senses.

Taste and smell tell your body and brain what is coming in. They are designed to carry a clear message to the brain of exactly what you're eating and what the effect will be.

Our faculties of taste and smell have evolved in us over millions of years, in an environment filled with natural foods undisturbed by industrial processing. Natural food has its own very distinctive and characteristic tastes and smells. Our senses haven't changed. But the food we eat has. Today, the tastes and smells of all foods have changed drastically. And this change has had profoundly disturbing consequences for all of us.

STOPPING TO SMELL THE APPLES

My patient Jane B., who was so incredulous when she first heard that the Skinny School diets are based on taste, saw the point very quickly when I explained the way taste and smell are supposed to work. But she told me she was puzzled about one thing. "How does it work on apples that don't smell?" she asked me.

"I love apples," she went on. "They've always been my favorite fruit. I especially like the way they smell, and I would always choose the ones that smelled best in the market. I try not to let anybody see me, but I smell every apple I buy. But now I don't know if it's just me or what; I can barely smell them anymore."

It isn't just Jane. Apples grown naturally have a very strong smell. If you walk down the aisle of a supermarket stocked with naturally grown "organic" apples, the smell of the apples should be almost overwhelming. Today, I'd be willing to bet I could walk you blindfolded through the entire produce section, and you wouldn't be able to tell whether you were walking past the apples, the pears, or the peaches.

The apples in the market today are hybrid varieties that are equally lacking in both taste *and* smell. They have been bred for commercial qualities: to get ripe at the most convenient time, or to be easy to pick or ship or store. They have also been bred for microsmatic consumers who make food-buying decisions by sight, not smell. Red, mushy, tasteless apples are what we *buy*—otherwise they wouldn't be there. Ripeness today is a look, not a taste.

Apples haven't been purposely bred to be tasteless, but food producers know that consumers buy with their eyes, not their noses. We buy apples that are red. Because we don't seem to care about taste or smell, these qualities have gotten lost in the industrial process. The old apple taste—strong, tangy, bracing—has all but disappeared. Yet that's the taste your brain is looking for in an apple. Your brain hasn't changed, but apples have.

Another patient, who was raised in Europe, told a story of not being able to eat canteloupes as a child because the smell was too strong. It disturbed her. Today, she said, canteloupes barely have a smell. She can eat them, but it isn't worth the trouble.

A study of today's peaches shows that peaches, today, have only a fifth as many "flavants" as old-fashioned, organically grown peaches (see the peach flavants chart below). Flavants are the volatile chemicals that create taste and smell. This study merely confirms what you have probably suspected for a long time: Food today just doesn't taste as good, or as much, as it should.

14. PEACH FLAVANTS

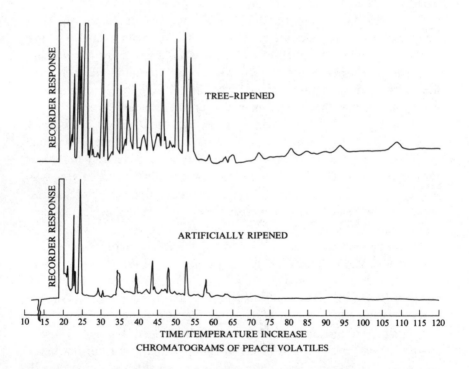

TREE-RIPENED

ARTIFICIALLY RIPENED

TIME/TEMPERATURE INCREASE

CHROMATOGRAMS OF PEACH VOLATILES

This chart shows the difference in amounts of flavor chemicals in tree-ripened and artificially ripened peaches. The artificially ripened peaches have about one fourth the flavants (hence flavor) of the natural ones. This is for modern hybrid fruit. Natural varieties have about three times as many flavants as the tree-ripened ones, a difference of twelve times (3 × 4). This is why so much supermarket fruit looks good and tastes so empty. They're sweet, and they look good, but they have no flavor and don't give you an M-State.

DID I EAT?

The implications of this loss of taste and smell are serious. Taste and smell are the messengers from the food to your body. They contain vital instructions about the food. So if food doesn't taste or smell right—and "right" means the way it has always smelled and tasted, through the millions of years of human evolution—then it throws your entire process of evaluating, eating, digesting, and using food into chaos.

Or, to put it another way: if you eat a peach with one fifth the taste of a *real* peach, your brain will not know what it is. Without the right taste and smell, the peach is unrecognizable. It is not, properly speaking, even food. Your brain won't know if you want this substance, or not. It won't be sure how to digest it, and it won't have all the "instructions" of how to use it.

Finally, after you have eaten this thing, your brain will feel that you have eaten, possibly, a fifth of a peach. If you were hungry for a peach, this peachlike thing won't satisfy you. You'll be only one fifth satisfied. Your confused brain won't want you to stop eating until you've eaten five peaches. But even five denatured peaches can't give you the taste of one whole, natural peach—because the real, concentrated taste is not there to give.

Is it any wonder you start eating and can't stop? If you can't taste anything, your brain won't even believe you've had anything much to eat—and it certainly won't want you to stop until it feels satisfied. Which it may never feel.

Satisfaction is the key step in natural appetite control; and only food that *tastes right* supplies it. Deliciousness is the key to weight control.

DELICIOUSNESS

What is good taste? Where does deliciousness in a food come from? It comes from the genetics of the food—that is, a peach tastes good because it has the genes to taste that way. But the genetic potential of a food can be expressed only if the food is grown properly.

Good taste develops as nutrients are absorbed from the soil. The

freshness and goodness of the water contribute to the food's deliciousness; so does the energy of the sunlight and the freshness of the air.

In animal food, deliciousness is part of the genetics of the animal; it
develops as the animal grows, supported by the animal's food, which
should come from the animal's free foraging for nonchemicalized, un-
sprayed, natural food.

Have you ever eaten a wild strawberry? If you have, you know that
they are tiny—barely a half an inch across—but that tiny berry is an
explosion of taste in your mouth. Compare it with a supermarket strawberry. They are huge, but taste like sawdust.

Steak? The story is the same. A patient told me he visited Brazil,
where cattle are raised nonindustrially. His heart sank when he saw the
tiny, thin piece of meat on his plate at his first Brazilian restaurant, but
when he ate his first bite, he realized the taste of a huge slab of marbled
American meat was concentrated in the small Brazilian slice. It was a
hundred times more satisfying.

You've heard about wine experts and the extreme subtlety that they
use when tasting wine. It's almost a joke to be that discerning ("It's a
demure little Burgundy without any real breeding, but I think you'll be
amused by its presumption"), yet the fact remains that a really good
wine taster actually can detect where a wine was grown (sometimes not
just the region but the field), when it was grown, and who made it.

All this information and more is encoded in the taste. The deliciousness of the wine accurately reflects the quality of the grapes and of the
soil, the weather, and the care that went into it.

That's wine—but the fact is that taste always reflects the quality of the
food and the way it was grown. If you were motivated enough, you could
become a skilled zucchini taster, and talk about "demure little zucchinis"
(not that you probably would). The point is, taste is not an arbitrary quality
that is floating around in a food. Taste, and smell, too, are what the food *is*.

THE TASTE OF CRAVING FOODS

The taste of craving foods is actually the *opposite* of the satisfying
deliciousness of natural foods. Jane B. tried telling me that *her* craving
food (which was chocolate chip cookies) was actually very delicious.

But she admitted that if she had the choice, she would *rather* eat wild strawberries. "I used to love fruit," she said ruefully. "It's just that fruit doesn't seem to taste that good anymore. With a chocolate chip cookie, I at least know I'm going to get something I can at least *taste*."

Craving foods are not delicious in the complex, satisfying way of natural foods. But they are *intense tasting*. Their taste has a druglike intensity, which results in intense changes in your brain chemistry—that is what attracts you to them. Foods that you crave have simple tastes: they are either very sweet, very salty, or very rich-tasting. These tastes are not natural—they come from commercial manipulation of your taste buds by industrial food processors.

In my research on taste, I have been struck by the fact that virtually all the research has been funded by the enormous industrial food producers worldwide—Nestlé, Beatrice Foods, Kraft. These huge food companies know everything there is to know about how to get you "hooked" on craving foods.

Highly industrialized craving foods—things like potato chips and cookies—are the subject of intensive research, which has given them just the right sweet, salty, or oily taste to make you keep on eating, but never enough actual taste satisfaction to make you feel you've had enough. If you were really satisfied, you'd stop eating. And ask yourself: would the manufacturer want you to stop, or not?

Ask yourself also, the next time you eat a potato chip: do you taste any *potato* in there? It's a long, long way through many industrial steps from a potato to a potato chip.

Since natural good taste has disappeared from most of your food, the food industry replaces it with artificial tastes. The real taste and smell of natural food are what tells your brain and body about the food's value. But an artificial taste (as in "artificial flavor added") or a "flavor enhancer," such as MSG, can't convey any useful information to your brain because the taste has nothing to do with the food itself. It's like making a decision about engine overhaul based on a paint job.

PEOPLE WHO DON'T SMELL ENOUGH

In 1986 *National Geographic* magazine (along with Avery N. Gilbert and Charles J. Wysocki, biopsychologists with the Monell Chemical Senses Center) conducted a smell survey of 1.5 million people. The results showed we Americans have actually *lost* much of our ability to smell.

In the survey, *National Geographic* asked its readers to "scratch and sniff" six smells:

1. Sweat (androstenone)
2. Banana (isoamyl acetate)
3. Musk (galaxiolide)
4. Cloves (eugenol)
5. Gas (mercaptans)
6. Rose

Only 70 percent of the women and 63 percent of the men were even *able* to smell the aroma of sweat. And only 26 percent of the women and 24 percent of the men could say what it was. The percentages are very similar for musk. Most people have actually lost their ability to smell these aromas.

National Geographic, interested by this finding, looked to see if the same thing would be true on other continents. It wasn't. People in Africa and Asia could almost all smell these smells, and people in Europe and Latin America couldn't smell them as well as Africans or Asians but still did better than Americans.

Even the smell of banana, which you would think everyone could identify easily, was identified correctly by only 53 percent of the American women and 49 percent of the men. Nearly half the people got it wrong!

What does this mean? It means that something is wrong with the way we are using our chemical senses. Anything that you don't use, you lose. We have obliterated natural tastes and smells from our food (and, for that matter, from *ourselves*), and substituted intense, unnatural tastes and smells that carry no real information about the food. As a result, we have lost our ability to use these senses for information; and the result shows up in our inability to choose the right foods—the ones that would make us skinny and healthy.

TASTING AND SMELLING RIGHT

Taste and smell are senses without many words attached to them. When you see a table, you automatically identify it. "That's a table." When you hear a sound, you know it's a voice or a car horn or a piece of music. But when you taste something, and even more, when you smell it, the experience is nonverbal, and floods your entire being with feelings and associations.

Marcel Proust's masterpiece, *Remembrance of Things Past,* is a huge three-volume book of memories that all flooded out of a single taste of a *madeleine*—a kind of French cookie—and some linden flower tea. But that's just the most famous example: the same thing happens to all of you when you smell a faint smell of cinnamon or of bread baking, or have a taste of a food out of your childhood, or hug your grandma.

Taste and smell are powerful, evocative senses. Their intensity and their lack of specific vocabulary give them an almost mystical quality in your brain. And in fact, this influence on the brain is part of the function of taste and smell. When you use your taste and smell, you create in your *neural* brain an experience that is very close to the way the *neuroglial brain* works when you have the M-State.

Natural tastes and smells, just because they are both powerful and nonspecific, create a calm, integrated feeling in your brain. They don't create the M-State, nor do they stimulate different *parts* of the brain to create a mosaiclike fake M-State. What they do is to *encourage the neural brain to work in a more orderly way.* In other words, they create the right preconditions for the M-State, and help your neural brain *retain* more of the calmness and alertness of the M-State, even while you are busy and active. When you do have the M-State, the effects last much longer.

When you learn to use your senses of taste and smell, your whole relationship with food will change completely. You will be able to select exactly the right foods for yourself simply by their taste and smell, and you will get from your food both a sense of satisfaction and a powerful feeling of well-being that comes out of a well-nourished brain.

The next chapter begins your true education in taste and smell. It's about how to taste and smell, and about which tastes you should choose to cure your cravings, balance your diet, and become the naturally skinny person you were meant to be.

9

HOW TO TASTE
AND SMELL

Choosing your foods because you like the way they taste and smell—the way naturally skinny people always do—will give you an infallible sense of what foods are right for you at any time.

Those irritating skinny people of this world choose their foods that way by instinct, but you are going to have to *study* taste and smell for a little while until you get the knack of it. It's not difficult, because it is natural. You'll soon be doing it yourself, and irritating *your* friends by your natural skinniness. (Only *you* need to know that you weren't naturally skinny—you learned how to be skinny at Skinny School.)

THE PRECISION OF TASTE

The most basic fact about taste is that every food has its own taste. No two foods taste quite the same, because every food has its own unique chemical composition.

Taste and smell give you a more precise technique for analyzing food than scientific analysis of its content. *Science* says, for example, that the carbohydrate in corn is chemically the same as the carbohydrate in rice.

Taste tells you that while they are similar, they are not identical. If they were identical, they would taste exactly the same—and, of course, they don't. Science can't distinguish them, but your mouth and nose easily can.

"Sniffer dogs" are much more sensitive at detecting smells than any instrument. Your own sniffer and taster are no less sensitive, if you learn to use them.

Using the precision of your chemical senses, you can choose a more precisely balanced diet than if you follow the scientific recommendations of choosing foods from the various "food groups."

Nutritional science tells you to choose foods from among these groups:

1. Meat
2. Dairy products
3. Grains
4. Vegetables and fruit

Each of these groups covers a lot of ground. "Grain" can be anything from wild rice to a tortilla chip. Vegetables and fruit range from artichokes to zucchini—are they all the same? What about meat: is there any difference between eating halibut and eating water buffalo? Are all meats the same, and are they all equally good for *everybody*?

Taste as a tool makes much finer distinctions among foods. If you choose from the four food groups, you will come up with a roughly balanced diet, but if you balance your food among the *eight tastes*, you will come up with a *precisely* balanced diet that is exactly right for *you*.

THE EIGHT TASTES

If you are going to use taste to determine what foods you eat, you first have to become very aware of the eight tastes and which foods they come from.

Different scientists recognize different numbers of tastes (as with so many things, various experts have various opinions). Some scientists say that there are more than thirty tastes; others say that there are an infinite number of tastes, since every food has its own distinctive taste. But my own research finds, and the majority of scientists agree, that there are eight basic tastes. These are:

1. Sweetness—is the most familiar and common taste, and even the youngest child recognizes and likes it immediately.
2. Sourness—the bracing taste of vinegar or lemon juice.
3. Salt—also instantly recognizable.
4. Bitterness—the dark taste of coffee or parsley.
5. Astringency—the "puckery" taste of fresh lettuce and tomato.
6 and 7. Pungency—the sharp taste of spices. There are two kinds of spiciness: a sweet kind of spiciness, like cinnamon, and a hot kind of spiciness, like pepper and cayenne. These two kinds are called (6) pungent/sweet and (7) pungent/peppery.
8. Umami—the commonly used term for the taste of richness. "Umami" is a Japanese word and is used because this taste was first recognized as a separate taste by Japanese taste researchers who then cloned it by inventing MSG. Occasionally you will see the term "unguency" used for this taste. "Unguent" has the same meaning as "umami"; but the Japanese term is more commonly used, and I prefer it.

WHERE THE EIGHT TASTES RESIDE

The two Skinny School Anti-craving Diets—for sweet and starch cravers and for greasy and spicy food cravers—are based on different combinations and balances of these eight tastes.

The Sweet and Starch Cravers Diet, as you'll see in Chapter 11, has breakfast based on astringent tastes, lunch based on astringent, pungent/peppery, and umami tastes, and dinner based on sweet, sour, and bitter tastes.

The Greasy and Spicy Food Cravers Diet, in Chapter 12, has breakfast based on sweet tastes, lunch based on sweet, sour, and pungent/sweet tastes, and dinner based on astringent, umami, and pungent/peppery tastes.

The diets contain complete guidelines on what foods to choose for each of the tastes—but by the time you have completed Skinny School, you will be an expert taster yourself. So you will be able to choose your own diet, based on taste, with great exactness and precision.

The diets contain complete guidelines on which foods to eat to get the right balance of tastes. As you follow your diet, your tasting ability will gradually improve until you don't need the guidelines anymore. *The ultimate decision-making power comes from your own taste buds.*

WHICH FOODS HAVE WHICH TASTE

To begin your education about taste, here are the *sources* for each of the eight tastes:

1. *Sweetness* comes from grains, fruits, and vegetables. Sweet fruits (such as peaches, melons, and bananas) are the strongest source of sweetness. Some vegetables (beets, sweet potatoes, and carrots) are very sweet, especially when they are cooked. All grains are basically sweet.

    Refined sugar, which has a totally sweet taste, comes from sugar cane, which is a vegetable. Honey and molasses also give the pure taste of sweetness.
2. *Sourness* comes from vinegar, some fruits, some vegetables, and some dairy foods. Citrus fruits and tomatoes are sour. Yogurt, buttermilk, and some cheeses are sour. Fermentation produces sourness; beer is sour, and wine is, too, at times, though it isn't supposed to be. Fermentation with yeast adds sourness to the basically sweet taste of bread.
3. The taste of *saltiness* comes from salt itself.
4. *Bitterness* comes from some vegetables (e.g., greens like mustard greens), some herbs (such as parsley), from coffee and quinine (the flavor of tonic water), and from some spices, including fenugreek, turmeric, and sesame seeds. Artificial sweeteners also have some bitterness along with their sweetness (and to some people they taste only bitter, not sweet at all).
5. *Astringency* comes in meat, eggs, beans and lentils, and some dairy foods, including butter, fresh cheeses, and goat's milk. Some fruits also have astringency: figs, purple grapes, and plums, and any other fruits that have a little "bite" to them along with their sweetness are astringent as well as sweet.

Astringency is also found in some vegetables: cauliflower, celery, lettuce, spinach, and sprouts, for example, are all sources for this taste. A big green salad is wonderfully astringent.

6 and 7. *Pungency* comes from herbs and spices, and from onions, garlic, and radishes. There are two kinds of pungency: *pungent/sweet* and *pungent/peppery*. Sweet pungency comes from spices like cinnamon, clove, nutmeg, ginger, and saffron. Peppery pungency is from black and cayenne pepper.

Of the pungent vegetables, onions and garlic are more pungent/sweet, and radishes are more pungent/peppery. Herbs such as dill and savory are pungent/sweet; thyme, oregano, and chives are more pungent/peppery.

8. *Umami,* the taste of richness, comes from oils and fats, including both animal fats (such as the fat in meats, the skin of the chicken, fish skin, and butterfat) and vegetable oils (oil that comes from olives, corn, sunflower seeds, peanuts, coconut, sesame, etc.).

Baked potatoes have umami as well as sweetness. Sugar and salt can also add umami to foods: sugar makes the taste of tomato sauce umami as well as astringent. Salt, added to nuts and other astringent foods, increases their umami taste. MSG (monosodium glutamate), a variant of salt used very commonly in the Orient as a flavor enhancer, adds umami to foods.

Every food has one of these tastes. Some foods have a combination of two of them, and a few foods have a combination of three of the basic tastes.

The Food Lists, which appear in the appendix, list the taste of all foods. Until your taste buds are fully trained, use the Food Lists to determine a food's taste.

When you begin to think about a food's taste, begin by asking yourself what food group that food belongs to: this will give you its basic taste. When you have an idea of its basic taste, you then ask yourself whether it is more or less sweet, astringent, sour, salty, bitter, pungent, or umami than other foods of the same kind.

The examples below show the steps of analyzing a food's taste, using the Food Lists as a guide.

1. Suppose you want to decide what is the taste of oats. Maybe you are thinking of having oatmeal for breakfast, and need to decide if it fits

into your diet guidelines. So first you think of the food group oats belongs to. You know that it is a grain, and grains are a source of *sweetness*. So oats is basically sweet.

But is it a sweet grain? You look on your grain list and you see that oats is sweeter than brown rice, barley, or rye, but not as sweet as white rice, whole wheat, or corn. You conclude that oats is a medium-sweet, medium astringent grain.

2. You are trying to decide what to have for dinner. You know that you need something with the taste of *astringency* at that point in your diet. Meat is basically astringent, so you decide you will have some meat as your main course. But what meat should you have? You look at the meat list and see that beef and lamb are the sweetest meat, and fish or chicken are the more astringent choices. So you make your choice based on whether you need a more astringent or a more sweet meat.

While you are using the Food Lists to determine taste, you should be simultaneously *checking the taste and smell of every food you put in your mouth*. This is how your tasting ability will grow. Don't rely on the Food Lists to tell you how a food tastes: *taste the food*. See if you agree with the list. Check the list against yourself.

Begin tasting your food immediately, even though you still have cravings and still eat foods that you will lose your taste for after a few weeks of Skinny School. When you really start tasting and smelling, you will find that a large percentage of the foods you now eat—especially the industrialized, highly processed part—will not taste good to you. If so, all the better. It's only because you *haven't* been tasting and smelling your food consciously that you have allowed these foods to become part of your diet in the first place.

HOW TO SMELL AND TASTE:

THE SKINNY GOURMET

A warning: Don't skip over the next few pages, thinking, "I of all people know how to taste and smell my food." Many people with cravings think they have gained weight because they like the taste of food, but the truth is that if you need to lose weight, you do *not* know how to taste.

True gourmets—people who really know and appreciate food—are almost never overweight. A patient named Randy L. told me that his sister was the best cook he knew, and he couldn't figure out why she never dieted but never gained a pound. I explained to him it was because she was too discriminating about tastes to gain weight.

If you eat only food that tastes really good, and is totally natural, your body and brain will feel entirely satisfied with just the amount of food that you actually need. Good food makes you feel full much sooner.

But if your food isn't really tasty, or has only artificial tastes, you will become a victim of your confused brain, acquire tremendous cravings, and overeat constantly, looking for satisfaction where it doesn't exist.

HOW TO SMELL

You are about to become like Randy's sister—too good at tasting and smelling *ever* to overeat. We'll start with smell. To begin using this sense, you have to first of all give yourself *a chance* to smell your food. If you smoke, you really should stop—it destroys your ability to use this sense. Do anything you have to do, but stop smoking.

If you do still smoke, or have spent the day outside in the smog, when you wash your hands before dinner be sure to snuff a little water into your nose as well. Clean off those nerve endings that go straight to your brain, so your brain will be able to get the smell message. Rinse out your mouth and brush your tongue too.

Then you need to take the time to smell. Smelling a food means holding it to your nose and sniffing it. Take little breaths that create turbulence around the food. This draws molecules that are detachable from the food into your nose.

When the smell registers, focus on how it makes you feel. Ask yourself whether the food smells good to you. Try not to be tricked by a dominant smell into ignoring the deeper ones. Spoiled food can be masked by strong seasonings. Compare the smells of the different foods on your plate. Which one smells best? Which ones smell like they would be good for you? Do you detect artificial, chemical-type smells? Try to classify the different smells. Does a food smell sweet, astringent, sour, salty, bitter, pungent, or umami?

THE SECOND SMELL

Smell different foods both raw and cooked, and note the difference. Smell foods when they are hot and then again after they cool off. You will find that the smell changes a great deal when the temperature changes. Often a food that smelled quite appetizing when hot loses its appeal when it cools down.

Continue exercising your sense of smell even after you have started eating. The *second smell* of a food comes when you chew up the food. If you are alert for it, you will see that again the smell that is released by chewing may be quite different from the first smell. Your brain is now coming into contact with the deeper levels of the food, which previously were buried inside.

When you smell a food, molecules from the food go into your nose, are absorbed there, give you the experience of the smell, and then are released again by your nasal membranes. The molecules you smelled actually leave your nose and come back out as you breathe out.

You can do an experiment yourself to verify this rather strange fact. Take a smell of something pungent (fresh ginger would be good, or garlic), but don't touch it with your hands. Then a minute later go into another room and have a friend see whether she can detect the smell of garlic or ginger on your breath. Breathe out through your nose, and get your nose close to your friend's. You haven't eaten the garlic or ginger, only smelled it—yet your friend should be able to detect the smell on your breath a few moments after you breathed it in.

NATURAL SMELLS

What's important, though, isn't so much the way smell works as what you are gaining by using this sense. If you reawaken your body's ability to smell, you will be able to evaluate any food and discover its effect on your brain and body. This ability exists; but it is largely unused and will remain dormant unless you take conscious steps to get it back.

Smell is there not just to evaluate your food, but to help you get the brain state you should have from food. While you eat to sustain your body, your *brain* is what tells you how successful you are being. Your brain state tells you that you have eaten enough and that it is time to stop. If you don't smell your food, or if your food has no smell, or very little smell, you will eat and eat that food and never feel the satisfaction you need.

It's not easy today to experience true, natural smells; the chemists of taste and smell have manipulated the responses that come from our brain and have separated smells from reality. What does "fresh scent" cleanser have to do with any reality? What is "fresh" about the smell chemicals they put into a detergent? Well might you ask. The goal of this manipulation of smell is simply to influence your buying decisions.

If you vacation in a natural environment (say, Alaska, or the Amazon, which I recommend) you will experience the natural relationship that should exist between the way things smell and the way they really are. You learn to trust your sense of smell again. But when you come back to big-city life in America, you see again how confusing and incoherent the smells are. There's not much help in them.

Nevertheless, it's vital to get back to using your sense of smell. When your food has a smell, and the smell tells your brain what the food really is, you're taking a major step toward getting over your cravings and getting true satisfaction from food. You need to do it to become naturally skinny.

HOW TO TASTE

Taste, the most important of all senses to naturally skinny people, must be done *with your inner being*. Tasting a food means experiencing it completely—as opposed to swallowing it hurriedly, heedlessly, or unconsciously.

Ask yourself as you taste: Does this food taste like something artificial (the way extremely sweet things like candy or extremely salty things do) or does it taste like something real? Taste a really fresh, organically grown piece of fruit and you'll see the difference.

Does it taste *good* or *bad*? If a food tastes bad, you should actually spit it out. If it tastes right, chew it and swallow. (Try not to run your first taste experiment at a dinner party.)

THE SECOND TASTE

"Second taste" is an extremely important concept. It means using your sense of taste to find the food's effect on the body. Some foods that taste sweet actually *sweeten* the body; other foods, which might *taste* just as sweet, have an aftereffect that is pungent, sour, astringent, or bitter. This second taste is detectable in your mouth about twenty minutes after eating a food.

At this point you may not be able to detect the "second taste" of foods. The Food Lists contain the second tastes of the foods; but in time, if you pay attention to taste, you will be able to detect it for yourself.

The second taste is actually a function of your stomach. When your stomach digests the food, the tasting nerves in your mouth get the taste of the digested food from your stomach, and pass it on to your brain. So what you are actually tasting is your *reaction* to the food.

Experiencing this taste requires more subtlety than tasting food that is actually in your mouth. What you do is to notice very carefully how you feel within your mouth about twenty to thirty minutes after eating. Check to see if the second taste is good or bad. It's much less important to decide whether you're getting a sweet, astringent, sour, salty, bitter, pungent, or umami second taste than to check if you feel good from the second taste.

HOW DOES THE FOOD MAKE YOU FEEL?

If you feel more relaxed, steadier, calmer, and more alert, then your reaction is good. If you feel heavy, bloated, gassy, uncomfortable, sleepy, or drowsy, or if you feel hyperactive, keyed up, or wired, these are bad signs.

Often you may find that you like the first taste of a *class* of food, but the second taste, your *reaction* to the food, is bad. For instance, you might enjoy the taste of frozen food, but have a bad reaction to it. Half an hour after eating, you may find a bad taste in your mouth, or feel very unenergetic. Others may find that freezing does *not* give them a bad reaction.

Check yourself for each of the four modern food groups: fast, frozen, canned, and snack. All may taste fine but have very bad second tastes for you. And if you eat them anyway, you may eat something else afterward to try to get rid of the bad second taste.

A Skinny School patient, Josie B., told me that she used to eat a certain brand of "gourmet" diet food. She thought it would be perfect for her—convenient, fairly tasty, and so on. But she eventually noticed that a half hour or so after eating one of these things, she would get a nervous feeling in her stomach, which she would interpret as being "hungry again." So she'd start nibbling. It took some time, but Josie finally realized that she was actually experiencing a bad second taste.

When she stopped eating the frozen meals, it became easy for her not to eat after dinner.

If you do feel nervous after eating, eating something else will *not* solve the problem. A six-ounce cup of plain hot water, however, will usually do it; it will relax your stomach and help it process the food and get through the bad second taste. Remember what you did wrong and file it away.

THIRD TASTE ("WHAT? THERE'S MORE?")

There is even a *third level of taste*, and if you can become aware of it, it will help you evaluate food even more accurately. But don't even try to notice the third taste until you've been on your Anti-craving Diet for at least a month. Your body won't be ready to show it to you until that point.

You get the third taste of a food several hours after eating. It comes from the reaction of your skin, muscles, and mucous membranes to the food. Some food may make your nose feel stuffy, for instance; some may weaken your muscles hours later; some makes you sweat or makes your skin become tight or oily. There is actually a taste in your mouth at this point, but it is very subtle and hard to notice until you become a very good and experienced taster.

A good example of third taste is my reactions as a child to bacon. I liked bacon. I liked the way it smelled and tasted, and I liked the satisfaction I felt soon afterward (the second taste). My stomach felt good (as far as I can remember) after eating it. But later that day and the next day I would have a stiff neck and feel some pains in my body—not much, as I was just a child and children don't get very stiff, but only a little. This was the bacon's third taste—and it was a bad third taste.

I did not understand this at the time, but I stopped eating bacon for a long time. But then I got my first microwave, and I heard that bacon comes out very nicely in the microwave, so I had some. By then I'd been working on Skinny School and the Anti-craving Diets for years, and knew about first, second, and third tastes. I was able to clearly see how bad bacon's third taste was. I was quite a bit stiffer the next day than I had been as a child, but my childhood reaction came back to me, and sure enough, I realized that if I'd known how to check for third taste, I would not have eaten bacon even as a child.

THE TOTAL BRAIN: TASTE AND SMELL
FOR MIND/BODY INTEGRATION

When I think back on my desire for bacon as a child, I realize I actually had a craving for it. I was eating bacon because it had a particular effect on my brain, and gave me a little taste of the fake M-State. When I ate bacon in spite of its bad effects, I was making a choice that is made by everyone with cravings: I was choosing my brain over my body.

I was eating the bacon for its brain effects; but the effect on my body was not good. I was harming my body for the sake of my brain. Whenever you eat craving foods, this is what you are doing.

Taste and smell, if you really use them, will prevent you from ever doing this again. The chemical senses are natural ways your body has for establishing communication between the brain and the body, and between the neural brain and the neuroglial brain. When you eat craving food, you ignore the messages of taste and smell. But when you use these senses, you will be able to select foods that are right for your body *and* your brain—foods that are completely in your best interests.

In the next chapter you'll learn exactly *which* tastes and smells you should be choosing to cure your cravings and become naturally skinny.

10

TASTES THAT CURE CRAVINGS

Although the Skinny School Anti-craving Diets are perfectly balanced among the food groups, and supply about 1200 calories per day, and are full of the vitamins, minerals, and other nutrients you need for health, they go far beyond these basic scientific considerations. These are the *beginning,* not the *end,* of craving-free nutrition.

The Skinny School diets achieve their balance through the right proportions and combinations of the eight tastes. Your diet will cure your cravings *and* help you create and maintain your own personal, true M-State. Using taste and smell is the unique quality that makes choosing food so absolutely natural you won't even feel that you are dieting. When you are eating the right tastes, it just feels like you are simply eating the right foods for yourself!

SATISFYING AND BALANCING TASTES

The two Skinny School Anti-craving Diets use *different* taste combinations, because the two classes of cravings are cured by different tastes.

For each of the diets, foods are divided into those with *satisfying tastes* and those with *balancing tastes*. For sweet cravers, a satisfying taste is the taste of sweetness; for spicy food cravers, it is spiciness, and so on. *Satisfying* tastes are the ones that satisfy you—you like them the most and reach for them most often.

Balancing tastes are ones that *contrast* with your satisfying tastes. People pick foods with balancing tastes to give variety to their diet, and because they have a bracing and invigorating quality. For example, sweets cravers pick astringent, "puckery" foods when they feel they have had enough sweetness and want something with a different, refreshing quality.

Naturally skinny people enjoy their balancing tastes *almost* as much as their satisfying tastes, because of their invigorating and tonic effect.

Naturally skinny people always eat a combination of satisfying tastes and balancing tastes, without having to think about it. This gives them a natural balance in both the neural and the neuroglial brain, and helps them maintain the M-State.

For *sweet and starch cravers,* the two kinds of tastes are as follows. Note that the taste that appears on the top of the satisfying list is the most satisfying, and the taste that appears on the top of the balancing list is the most balancing.

Satisfying Tastes	*Balancing Tastes*
Sweet	Astringent
Bitter	Umami
Sour	Salty
Pungent/sweet	Pungent/peppery

The foods you will naturally find most satisfying are the ones that are sources for your balancing tastes: grains, fruits, the sweet, sour, and bitter vegetables, and the sweeter spices and herbs. Foods that are sources for your *balancing* tastes are the ones that you will naturally eat for variety and to give a sense of balance to your diet.

Sweet and starch cravers *crave* foods with their satisfying tastes— mainly, the sweet taste. When you learn to use balancing tastes in your diet in the right way, you will be able to overcome this craving. As you will see in Chapter 11, your balancing tastes are used at key moments throughout the day; this strategy is extremely effective in curing your cravings.

For *greasy and spicy food cravers,* the two kinds of tastes are as follows. Note that the most satisfying taste is at the top of the satisfying list, and the most balancing taste is at the top of the balancing list.

Satisfying Tastes	*Balancing Tastes*
Umami	Sweet
Salty	Sour
Astringent	Bitter
Pungent/peppery	Pungent/sweet

The foods you will naturally find most satisfying are the ones that are sources for your satisfying tastes: proteins, including fish, meat, and eggs; salty foods; astringent fruits and vegetables; and the hotter, more peppery herbs and spices.

Foods that are sources for your *balancing* tastes are the ones that you will naturally eat for variety and to give a sense of balance to your diet.

Greasy and spicy food cravers *crave* foods with their satisfying tastes. When you learn to use balancing tastes in your diet, you will be able to overcome your cravings. As you will see in Chapter 12, your balancing tastes are used at key moments throughout the day; this strategy is extremely effective in curing your cravings.

CRAVING VS. SATISFACTION

When I explain this to my patients, they always ask something like "Do you mean the foods I *crave* are the ones that have my satisfying taste? What am I supposed to do, never eat a food again that satisfies me?"

I can understand the question, and it is an important one. Yes, you do crave foods that have your satisfying taste. But you crave foods that have that taste very *intensely.* There are many foods that have your satisfying taste which are *not* craving foods.

If you are a sweets craver, you *crave* the *intense* sweetness of sugar, but you are *satisfied* with the natural, balanced taste of sweet grains, fruits, and vegetables. If you are a greasy food craver, you *crave* the very *intense* umami taste of butter or mayonnaise, but are *satisfied* with the natural umami taste of baked potato or a small amount of a light vegetable oil.

The difference is vital. Getting rid of a *craving* for sweets or greasy food will free you to *enjoy* your satisfying tastes much more than you did before.

THE PRINCIPLES OF TASTE BALANCING

The Skinny School Anti-craving Diets are built around using satisfying and balancing tastes at the right times and in the right proportions.

A list of the principles of the taste balancing for the Anti-craving Diets follows. Then I explain each principle in detail. In Chapters 11 and 12, you will see how the principles are applied, specifically, in your own Anti-craving Diet.

Along with the diets there are Food Lists, meal plans, and recipes. Follow the guidelines in the diets carefully until the principles become second nature—which will happen sooner than you think. As you follow the diets you will pick up the principles automatically. By doing, you'll "get it."

Even if you are completely unused to tasting and smelling your food, within six to eight weeks you will have the taste skills to make your own food selections automatically, like a naturally skinny person. By that time, also, your cravings will be cured.

SUMMARY OF TASTE PRINCIPLES:
TASTES THAT CURE CRAVINGS

Sweet and Starch Cravers
Satisfying tastes:
sweet, sour, bitter, and
pungent/sweet

Greasy Food Cravers
Satisfying tastes:
astringent, umami, salt, and
pungent/peppery

Balancing tastes:
astringent, umami, salt, and
pungent/peppery

Balancing tastes:
sweet, sour, bitter, and
pungent/sweet

1. Breakfast: eat balancing tastes.
2. Lunch and dinner: protein from balancing tastes, grains and vegetables from satisfying tastes.

3. Lunch and dinner: grains and vegetables with a satisfying second taste.
4. Snack and dessert: fruits with balancing tastes.
5. Cooking and processing add sweetness, while raw, unprocessed food has more astringency. Choose the one that increases your satisfying taste. Sweet and starch cravers eat more cooked food, greasy food cravers eat more raw unprocessed food.
6. Eat only fresh, natural food.
7. Eat only delicious food.
8. To find the right *quantity* of food, use your fist (see below).
9. Sweet and starch cravers eat more protein than grain; greasy food cravers eat more grain than protein.
10. Lunch and dinner: eat something with *each and every taste*.

THE PRINCIPLES EXPLAINED

PRINCIPLE 1: BREAKFAST WITH BALANCING TASTES.
The most important meal of the day for taste balancing is breakfast. At breakfast, you must start your day with a balancing taste—this will actually help *prevent* craving attacks throughout the day.

For sweet and starch cravers, the right breakfast is nutritionally important to prevent cravings. For greasy and spicy food cravers, breakfast acts more to "steer" your physiology from the beginning of the day. It provides a rudder, rather than fuel, for your engine.

TO APPLY PRINCIPLE 1:
Sweet and starch cravers start the day with astringency. For breakfast, choose between an egg cooked in a small amount of oil (for umami, which is also a balancing taste), or a glass of warm *whole* milk with a pat of either butter or ghee (clarified butter), which gives astringency plus umami. Butter in milk may sound strange, but it works.

You are allowed a cup of partially decaffeinated coffee, despite the fact that the bitterness of coffee is a satisfying taste. The small amount of satisfaction will help you; but you must definitely *not* have sugar in it.

Greasy and spicy food cravers start the day with sweet and/or sour tastes. Orange juice is good. Eat whole-grain cereal or toast along with fruit from the sweet end of the fruit list. You can also have coffee—for you, bitterness is a balancing taste. You can have nonfat milk on your cereal or in your coffee if you wish, but no cream. You don't want umami at this point in your day.

PRINCIPLE 2: AT LUNCH AND DINNER, PROTEINS SHOULD HAVE SATISFYING TASTES AND VEGETABLES AND GRAINS SHOULD HAVE BALANCING TASTES.

The reason for this principle is to provide a sense of balance *during* the meal, and a sense of satisfaction *following* the meal.

When you choose foods from your satisfying tastes, that take longer to digest (that is, protein foods), you will have a sense of longer-lasting satisfaction from your lunch and dinner. Having a satisfying taste in your system that "trickles in" for hours prevents cravings. You can add to this effect by using your Anti-craving Spice Mix on your protein foods— this gives even more zing to this principle.

When you choose foods that take a shorter time to digest (that is, vegetables and grains) from your balancing tastes, you feel braced and invigorated after the meal, which adds to the anti-craving effect.

The pressure and stresses of daytime activity, combined with food habits that come from cravings, make all cravings increase throughout the day. Whenever a "slump" or a stress period comes, you have acquired the habit of using a craving food. Cravings become harder to resist as the day wears on, which is why most weight loss plans fail either at the end of the afternoon, or in the evening after dinner. At these times cravings are at their peak.

The taste plan in Principle 2 actually works to keep you both satisfied and balanced *as you move through your day*. You will be amazed how easy it is to resist craving foods if you follow this principle.

TO APPLY PRINCIPLE 2:

Sweet and starch cravers choose proteins from the sweet end of the protein lists, and vegetables and grains from the more astringent end of the vegetable and grain lists.

Greasy and spicy food cravers choose proteins from the astringent end of the protein lists, and vegetables and grains from the sweet end of the vegetable and grain lists. Note that your protein should be astringent rather than salty or umami. Salt and umami are satisfying tastes for you, but if you choose them you will be adding too much salt and/or oils to your diet. Choosing astringency will give you the same *satisfaction*, but without the health drawbacks and calories of salt and oil.

PRINCIPLE 3: AT LUNCH AND DINNER CHOOSE VEGETABLES AND GRAINS WHOSE "SECOND TASTE" IS SATISFYING.

To find the "second taste," look at the Food Lists in the Appendix. This will help you refine your grain and vegetable choices.

The reason for this principle is to increase your long-range feelings of satisfaction from lunch and dinner. You will be enjoying a feeling of satisfaction based on the taste of your protein foods; choosing vegetables and grains with a satisfying second taste will add to this feeling.

The more satisfaction you feel from your food, the less likely you are to experience the nagging desire for the M-State which is behind *all cravings*. The daily accumulation of stress and fatigue that usually causes cravings in the evening will be greatly reduced, and you won't be driven to secret after-dinner "I think I'll clean up the kitchen now" eating.

TO APPLY PRINCIPLE 3:

Sweet and starch cravers choose vegetables and grains with a sweet second taste.

Greasy and spicy food cravers choose vegetables and grains with an astringent second taste.

PRINCIPLE 4: FOR DESSERTS AND SNACKS, CHOOSE FRUITS WITH A BALANCING TASTE.

For both sweet and starch cravers and greasy and spicy food cravers, the best desserts as well as the best snacks are fresh fruit. Fruit is fresh, natural, and loaded with flavor "instructions" that help your body digest not just the fruit itself but all foods.

But fruit is light and digests very quickly. If you choose fruit with a satisfying taste, you run a risk of overstimulating your brain and invoking a fake M-State. This is especially a danger for sweet and starch cravers, who even can develop *cravings* for sweet fruit.

By choosing fruit with balancing tastes, you will avoid this danger, but still get the benefits of fresh fruit in your diet. Sweet and starch cravers should choose fruit from the astringent end of the fruit list, and greasy and spicy food cravers should choose from the sweet end of the fruit list. Greasy and spicy food cravers can have dried fruit, but sweet and starch cravers should never eat dried fruit, as it is much too sweet.

TO APPLY PRINCIPLE 4:
Sweet and starch cravers choose fruits from the astringent end of the fruit list.

Greasy and spicy food cravers choose fruits from the sweet end of the fruit list.

PRINCIPLE 5: COOKING ADDS SWEETNESS TO FOOD. RAW FOOD IS NATURALLY MORE ASTRINGENT. CHOOSE THE ONE THAT GIVES YOUR FOOD MORE OF YOUR SATISFYING TASTE.
Cooking makes all foods sweeter. The same thing also applies to processing. Various kinds of processing—including the process of fermentation, which turns milk into cheese, and the processing of vegetables by canning or freezing—add sweetness (as well as some sourness); these are satisfying tastes for sweet and starch cravers.

TO APPLY PRINCIPLE 5:
Sweet and starch cravers eat more cooked food than raw food.

Greasy and spicy food cravers stick faithfully to fresh, unprocessed foods, and eat more raw than cooked food.

PRINCIPLE 6: EAT THE FRESHEST AND MOST NATURAL FOODS YOU CAN FIND.
This principle applies equally to sweet and starch cravers and greasy and spicy food cravers. In following the Skinny School Anti-craving Diets, you must choose the freshest and most natural foods.

"Fresh" means that your fruits and vegetables should be fresh picked, locally grown, and in season. The best is homegrown. Next best is organically grown produce from your immediate geographic area.

"Natural" means that you should choose foods that haven't been through major industrial processing. Don't eat foods in which any of the ingredients have numbers. If you need to eat a frozen dinner, something made locally picked out of your supermarket deli case is better than something made in a huge factory who knows where. The less a meal looks like it could be served on an airplane, the better. If you must eat airplane food, try to get something that looks more like first class than coach.

Behind this principle is the fact that the taste and smell of your food should tell your brain what these foods actually are. It only confuses your body and brain when you eat foods whose smells and tastes don't correspond to what it really is. If your brain is confused, it can't tell your body how to use that food.

PRINCIPLE 7: NEVER EAT ANYTHING THAT ISN'T DELICIOUS. BORING FOOD IS ABSOLUTELY PROHIBITED.

This principle is extremely important, and I mean it very seriously. Anything you eat that isn't really good you should basically think of as a waste of precious nutrition. You're getting stuff to accumulate in your body, but you're not getting satisfaction, and if you're unsatisfied, you will just eat more food until you *are* satisfied.

You should forget about the boring food, the cottage cheese, the celery, and anything that doesn't thrill you. It's actually better to eat only chocolate mousse cake than to eat chocolate mousse cake *plus* cottage cheese.

The meaning of the phrase "less is more" finally becomes clear. Food that is less delicious, you eat more of. Food that is more delicious, you eat less. People who are less overweight eat more good food, and less boring food. And naturally skinny people are more healthy and more beautiful.

PRINCIPLE 8: TO FIND THE RIGHT *QUANTITY* OF FOOD, USE YOUR FIST.

Yes, your fist. This is the secret of choosing the right quantity of food for you. Overweight people always use *outside* measurements of their food: they use numbers of ounces or portion size (so many ounces of this, so many cups of that), or else they use the method of eating the whole thing, whatever it is—the whole fish, the whole chicken, the whole cake.

Naturally skinny people never think about it at all—they just eat until they feel like stopping. But you, now that you are learning to be naturally skinny, should use a unit of measure that is *connected with your own body size:* your fist.

Your fist, as it happens, is the same size as your unstuffed stomach; it's nature's gift to give us a visible measure of this invisible organ. By using your fist, you'll make your portions automatically the right size for your stomach and your body.

Here's the way it works. At lunch and dinner, the total quantity of cooked protein and grain that you eat should be equal in volume to your fist. Simple, portable, and personal—the perfect method. Nothing to buy.

To find the volume of your fist, put a small saucepan inside a larger one and fill the smaller saucepan to the *very top* with water. Then put your fist into the small saucepan, up to the *first* crease in your wrist. Pour the water that runs out of the smaller saucepan into a measuring cup and see how much it is. Say "eureka" while you do this, to remind yourself that this principle comes from Archimedes in the bathtub.

The amount of water that ran into the bigger saucepan is equal in volume to your fist. In most people it is between a cup and a cup and a half.

Of this total, the amount of grain that you will eat is the amount of uncooked grain that you can hold *in* your fist. It's not how much you can hold in your cupped palm. It's the amount you can pick up in your closed hand if you reach into a bag of rice.

Do the experiment now with rice or whole wheat. See how much you can actually grasp in your hand, then measure it. (In most people it is about a quarter of a cup of uncooked grain.) This amount is now known as "one grain exchange" for you.

When you cook your "grain exchange," naturally, it turns into a bigger amount, because it takes up water in cooking. So your quarter cup of raw rice, say, becomes about half a cup of cooked rice. So on your plate at lunch or dinner you should have a half cup or so of grains, and the rest of your fist-volume in protein (chicken, fish, or meat).

Vegetables, whether raw or cooked, and fruits are not included in your fist-volume. You can have whatever quantity of vegetables you wish because if you measure out your grains and protein correctly for your body, you will automatically want just the right amount of vegetables to go with them. Vegetables contain the "instructions" to help your body digest your grains and proteins, so your body will automatically *want* just the right amounts.

By the way, this is only complicated to explain, not to do. But I have included conventional weights and measures in the Anti-craving Diets to help you at the beginning. Compare your own fist measurements with the amounts of food given in the diets, and adjust them accordingly.

In time you will not even need your fist. You will learn to eat just the right amount of food by listening only to your body, just the way naturally skinny people do.

PRINCIPLE 9: SWEET AND STARCH CRAVERS SHOULD EAT MORE *PROTEIN* THAN GRAIN, AND GREASY FOOD CRAVERS SHOULD EAT MORE *GRAINS* THAN PROTEIN.

The reason for this principle is that protein foods have balancing tastes for sweet and starch cravers, and grains have balancing tastes for greasy and spicy food cravers. To cure cravings, you need to include *more balancing tastes* than satisfying tastes in your diet.

PRINCIPLE 10: EAT *SOMETHING* WITH EACH AND EVERY TASTE AT BOTH LUNCH AND DINNER.

It is important to eat *all* the tastes. The tastes carry the instructions for using all foods. For complete digestion and complete healthy food utilization, you need all the instructions contained in all the tastes.

You are a complete human being, and your diet should reflect that. Your brain needs everything that nature has provided for it, the complete range of experience. There is a spiritual dimension to this as well: Complete evolution of your spirit requires that you eat every taste.

USING THE PRINCIPLES AND THE FOOD LISTS

These are the principles of the Skinny School Anti-craving Diets. And while they have their own interest, it is much more important for you to *use* them than to understand them intellectually. If you think the principles are complicated, remember that first of all we are going for a *cure* of the very complex problem of cravings, and second, that they do become quite automatic after using them for a short time.

To begin using the principles, look at the Food Lists that appear in the Appendix. Then turn to your own Anti-craving Diet, either the Sweet and Starch Cravers Diet (Chapter 11) or the Greasy and Spicy Food Cravers Diet (Chapter 12), depending on your results from the Cravings Analysis Checklist.

The principles can be summarized very simply: they are ways of enjoying your food. If you use your senses of taste and smell, and become aware of the many ways that taste and smell affect you, the principles will fall into place as your experience in tasting grows.

As you become a naturally skinny person, you will find yourself becoming far more aware of taste, and enjoying your food far more, than ever before. Skinny people always enjoy their food, and never feel guilty. They know that for food to be delicious is not a drawback—it is a positive, intrinsically valuable quality that you can use for your benefit at any time. Delicious taste is far more important than calories, nutrients, or food group. It is the very essence of the Skinny School cure for cravings.

11

THE SWEET AND STARCH CRAVERS DIET

YOUR TASTE PRINCIPLES

Satisfying tastes for sweet and starch cravers are sweet, sour, bitter, and pungent/sweet.

Balancing tastes are astringent, umami, salt, and pungent/peppery.

1. *Breakfast:* eat astringent and umami tastes; salt and hot spices for seasoning.
2. *Lunch and dinner:* choose proteins from sweet end of protein list, grains, and vegetables from astringent end of grain and vegetable lists.
3. Grains and vegetables should have a sweet second taste.
4. For snacks and dessert, eat fresh fruit with astringent and/or sour tastes.
5. Eat more cooked than raw food, to increase sweetness.
6. Eat only fresh, natural food.
7. Eat only delicious food.
8. Determine quantities with your fist.
9. Eat more protein than grains.
10. Eat all of the eight tastes every day.

SWEET AND STARCH CRAVERS
SUPPLEMENT PROGRAM

Chapter 13 explains the Skinny School nutritional supplement program I have developed to eliminate deficiencies in sweet and starch cravers. *You should begin the supplements at the same time as the diet.* The supplements are designed to make it possible—and easy—to follow the diets. They work to eliminate the massive chemical imbalances that drive the craving for sweets and starches. For this reason, instructions on when to take your supplements are included along with the diet.

Without the support of the supplements, you will find that your cravings will continue to make it very difficult to stay with your diet, especially at the beginning. I don't want you to have a repeat of the experience you've been through so many times in the past, when you are left alone with your cravings at times of stress. Take your supplements and make this experience different.

If you do have cravings at the beginning of the program, remember not to worry. This is natural—you've had them for so long, and the cure takes four to eight weeks. And above all don't feel guilty about them. What you should do is *notice* each craving, and refer to Chapter 13 for supplements that will cure it. Within four to eight weeks all your cravings will be at least 90 percent cured.

THE M-STATE IS ALSO A
NUTRITIONAL SUPPLEMENT

Don't forget, also, that you should begin using a technique of your choice to experience the M-State. Start this at the same time as the Skinny School diet and the supplement program. If you want to be naturally skinny, don't neglect this part of your education.

Note: As with this or any other diet or supplement program, do not begin without consulting your physician.

The only part of Skinny School you *shouldn't* begin at this time is the "Lard" Lessons. They should wait until your cravings are at least 50 percent under control—in about the third or fourth week of the program.

THE SWEET AND STARCH CRAVERS DIET

FIRST THING IN THE MORNING: The first thing you should do is check your tongue in the mirror and scrape off any coating. Use a teaspoon and try not to gag yourself. The coating comes from toxic overload of digestion and cravings; getting rid of it will make following the diet easier. Next, if you are taking any of the amino acid supplements (Magic Pills, Brain Food, or Tri-Skinny), take them now, before eating. If you are taking the Graded Appetite Controllers, take your morning tablet now.

Breakfast:
CHOICE OF:

One 8-ounce glass of warm whole milk with a pat of butter or a teaspoon or clarified butter (ghee) (for a combination of astringent and umami tastes).

OR one egg fried in one teaspoon of vegetable oil (astringent plus umami). Season with finely ground white pepper.

One grain exchange from the astringent end of the grain list.

One cup half-decaffeinated coffee. NO SUGAR.

Supplements: Basic vitamin/mineral tablet (Skinny-All®); Anti-craving Mineral (magnesium, manganese, or Vitomag, depending on your craving).

WAIT 3 HOURS—LONGER IF YOU AREN'T YET HUNGRY.

Snack: Half piece of fruit from the astringent end of the fruit list.

WAIT 2 MORE HOURS.

Supplements: If you are taking the Graded Appetite Controllers, take your afternoon tablet one half hour before lunch.

Lunch:
CHOICE OF:

4 ounces cooked meat, fish, poultry, tofu, or legume from the sweet end of the protein or legume list. Season with Sweet and Starch Cravers Spice Mix if desired.

Large serving of fresh vegetables in season. Choose from the astringent end of the vegetable list. Cook with one teaspoon of butter or vegetable oil, for umami. Seasoning: Tamari or soy sauce (salt taste), spices from pungent/peppery end of spice list.

One grain exchange from astringent end of the grain list.

Tea or coffee (half with caffeine and half-decaffeinated)

Supplements: Anti-craving Mineral as above.

WAIT 3 HOURS.

Snack: Half piece of fruit from astringent end of fruit list.

WAIT 2 MORE HOURS.

Supplements: If you are taking the Graded Appetite Controllers, take your evening tablet one half hour before dinner.

Dinner:
CHOICE OF:
Sweet and Starch Cravers Vegetable Soup, or soup made from other vegetables from astringent vegetable list.

3 ounces of meat, poultry, fish from the sweet end of the protein list or tofu. Season with sweet spices or use Sweet and Starch Cravers Spice Mix.

Cooked vegetables with astringent tastes, sour and/or bitter tastes. Dress with a little oil and lemon juice (umami and sour tastes).

One grain or legume exchange.

Cooked fruit or fruit sherbet.

Supplements: Anti-craving Mineral as above.

BEFORE BEDTIME: 4-ounce glass of warm milk (optional).

Supplements: 1500 mg. tryptophan.

MEALTIME NOTES

THE LARGER AND SMALLER MEALS

In the Skinny School plan, lunch is the larger meal and dinner is the smaller meal. If you study naturally skinny people, you'll see that they almost never eat a big meal at night. Skinny people know instinctively that the body doesn't digest a large meal as well at night as it does in the middle of the day. Much of the food you eat at night turns automatically into fat, and the toxic overload on your digestion shows up on your tongue in the morning.

When you are free of cravings, it's easy to eat a smaller meal at night. It also gives you more energy in the evening. A big meal turns into an evening of falling asleep in front of the TV.

Today, since the majority of people are working outside of the home, it's convenient as well as healthier to eat your larger meal at lunch. "Larger" doesn't mean *large*. You still should never exceed your fist size; the old theory that you have to eat a lot to keep going is nonsense. You have to eat the right tastes to keep going. But you can have a more substantial meal at lunchtime and still digest it well.

If you eat out at lunch, find a restaurant that serves a selection of fresh, natural food. You can then make a smaller, simpler meal at home at night (saving time as well). If you are at home during the day, you can still make your bigger meal, and have more control over the freshness and deliciousness of the ingredients.

SUBSTITUTIONS

Since your Skinny School Anti-craving Diet is based on taste, all your *substitutions* should be based on keeping the same balance of tastes at each meal.

At breakfast you can substitute other astringent protein sources for the eggs if you wish. Two ounces of light-meat chicken or fish is a fine substitution. Not eating chicken at breakfast is a cultural prejudice. We eat fish (lox, kippers), pork (sausage, bacon), and meat (breakfast steak). Why not chicken?

At lunch or dinner you have great freedom to substitute within the taste categories given. As your ability to use your sense of taste grows, you will be able to make your own substitutions with confidence.

If you have read *Dr. Abravanel's Body Type Diet and Lifetime Nutrition Plan,* or are familiar with your body type diet, you can see that the principles of taste can be applied to make these diets more flexible. Some foods become possible which weren't possible in the body type format. For example, thyroid types were not supposed to eat fruit in the body type plan because the sugar in the fruit was too stimulating for their thyroid gland. But using taste principles, thyroid types can choose astringent or sour fruit, and avoid the overstimulation.

SKINNY VEGETARIANS

Being a vegetarian on the Skinny School program is easy, too, using taste principles. Vegetarians who don't use taste balancing usually have too much sweet taste and not enough astringent and umami tastes in their diets. This is a problem for sweet and starch cravers, because too much of the sweet taste doesn't give you the balance you need.

Using the taste principles, you can substitute other sources of astringency and umami, and maintain balance in this way. You can also balance your tastes using pungent/peppery spices. You'll notice that Indian food (the Hindu variety), which is traditionally vegetarian, is very spicy—because pungent/peppery tastes are balancing for a very sweet-intensive vegetarian diet.

THE MEAL PLANS AND THE SIMPLE MEAL

At the end of this chapter you'll find a week of suggested meal plans for sweet and starch cravers. I want you to look at these as suggestions, not as laws. Feel free to make up your own menus using the taste principles.

The meals I've suggested are not extremely elaborate, but they all involve some cooking and some time spent assembling ingredients. I want you to have some real *taste* in your meals, because taste is the key to satisfaction. Without satisfaction, you'll never be cured of your cravings.

But tasty meals do take time to prepare. And time is in chronically short supply. So you should have in your repertoire a simple meal that is tasty, that contains all the tastes, and that works for you as a sweet and starch craver.

You can always fall back on this meal; if you want, you can have it every day, with minor variations. It will work, it will satisfy you, and it will cure your cravings. Here it is:

SWEET AND STARCH CRAVERS SIMPLE MEAL

One small piece of chicken (breast or thigh), skin *not* removed. Crack bones before broiling to improve taste. Sprinkle with fresh herbs or Sweet and Starch Cravers Spice Mix. Broil.

When you eat the chicken, chew on the cracked bones for additional flavor, and take a bite of the skin. Both of these are to make the chicken a more complete food. Primitive hunters did this automatically. If you don't, a piece of chicken is *almost* a processed food.

Or, have one piece of fresh fish, sprinkled with herbs or Spice Mix and broiled.

Or, for vegetarians, have four ounces of tofu sauteed in one teaspoon of olive oil and sprinkled with your Spice Mix.

One-half cup of brown rice.

One large serving of vegetables from the astringent end of the vegetable list, lightly steamed.

DESSERT

Sweet and starch cravers cannot live by astringent vegetables alone. I know that and so do you. You need something sweet or you'll never be able to stay with the program.

Everything in the Skinny School program is designed to help both *cure* your craving for sweets and *satisfy* your natural desire for the sweet taste.

As your cravings come under control, you will truly lose your desire for sugary desserts (and also for refined starches such as white bread and rolls). But you will not lose your taste for natural sweetness, and for this you will always have fruit and fruit-based desserts.

One of the most satisfying desserts I have found for my sweet and starch craver patients at Skinny School is Fruit Sherbet. (In posh restaurants this is called sorbet, to extract maximum revenue from a simple dish.) The recipe below works with all fruits. Try it with everything that comes into season.

FRUIT SHERBET

4 cups fresh fruit (strawberries, grapes, peaches, apricots, whatever you like) *or* fruit juice (orange juice, lime juice, pear juice, etc.)

1 tablespoon honey dissolved in 1 cup of warm water
Pinch of salt *if* desired

Clean the fruit and puree it in a blender. Add the honey-water mixture and place in an electric ice cream maker, following the manufacturer's directions. Or, if you do not have one, freeze the fruit mixture in ice cube trays for half an hour or until slushy. Take out and beat, then return to trays and freeze until firm. Makes eight servings.

A WEEK OF MEAL PLANS FOR SWEET AND STARCH CRAVERS

(* means the recipe for this dish appears in the recipe section of the food appendix.)

Monday:
Breakfast:
> one egg (poached, boiled, or fried in one teaspoon of a sweet vegetable oil)
> one slice of whole wheat toast
> one cup of coffee (use half or more decaffeinated)

Larger meal:
> Spiced Beef with Vegetables*
> Brown Rice*

Snacks: two small tangerines
Smaller meal:
> Sweet and Starch Cravers Vegetable Soup*
> sandwich made with three ounces fresh cooked tuna seasoned with a teaspoon of light mayonnaise and fresh dill, on whole wheat bread
> Lime Sherbet

Tuesday:
Breakfast:

>   glass of warm whole milk with a teaspoon of Ghee*
>   small bowl of whole grain cereal
>   one cup of half-decaffeinated coffee

Larger meal:

>   4-ounce Broiled Salmon Steak*
>   Braised Scallions and Jerusalem Artichokes*
>   2 pieces of rye krispbread

Snacks: one bunch of green grapes
Smaller meal:

>   Fresh Tomato Soup*
>   3 ounces Calves Liver with Herbs*
>   small baked potato

Wednesday:
Breakfast:

>   one egg (poached, boiled, or fried in one teaspoon of a sweet
>   vegetable oil)
>   one slice of whole wheat toast
>   one cup of coffee (use half or more decaffeinated)

Larger meal:

>   Spicy Tofu with Chicken* or
>   Stir-fried Tofu* (vegetarian)
>   steamed green beans
>   barley
>   Snacks: large apple

Smaller meal:

>   Chicken Burger*
>   *or* Lentil Burger*
>   whole wheat bun
>   Spinach and Grapefruit Salad*

Thursday:
Breakfast:

>   one cup plain yogurt
>   one slice rye bread
>   one cup half-decaffeinated coffee

Larger meal:

        Barbecued Shrimp and Scallops* on bed of millet*

        Baked Pepper and Potato*

        Chicory Salad*

Snacks: two small oranges

Smaller meal:

        Sweet and Starch Cravers Vegetable Soup*

        baked tomatoes with anchovies, tuna, and black olives

        ½ cup bulghur wheat

Friday:

Breakfast:

        one glass of warm milk with 1 teaspoon ghee

        one slice whole grain bread

        one cup of half-decaffeinated coffee

Larger meal:

        Spicy Sesame Noodles*

          with hard-boiled egg or tofu

        Roman-style Spinach*

Snacks: 2 slices of fresh melon

Smaller meal:

        Cabbage-Leek Soup*

        Boiled Potatoes with Green Olive Oil*

Saturday:

Breakfast:

        Coffee Egg or Tea Egg*

        1 slice pumpernickel bread

        1 cup half-decaffeinated coffee

Larger meal:

        Chicken with Tomatoes and Green Peppers*

        Green Rice*

        sauteed watercress

Snacks: 1 large pear

Smaller meal:

        Red Pepper Soup*

        Stuffed Tomatoes with Olives, Rice, and Tuna*

Sunday:
Breakfast:

>   one slice toast using whole grain bread and a small dollop of
>   molasses
>
>   one cup half-decaffeinated coffee

Larger meal:

>   Baked Red Snapper with Olives*
>   Brown Rice*
>   Ratatouille*

Snacks: one grapefruit
Smaller meal:

>   Sauteed Sliced Kidneys* *or* Sweetbreads*
>   Early Spring Salad*

12

THE GREASY AND SPICY FOOD CRAVERS DIET

YOUR TASTE PRINCIPLES

Satisfying tastes for greasy and spicy food cravers are astringent, umami, salt, and pungent/peppery.

Balancing tastes are sweet, sour, bitter, and pungent/peppery.

1. *Breakfast:* eat sweet, sour, or bitter tastes; sweet spices for seasoning.
2. *Lunch and dinner:* choose proteins from astringent end of protein list, grains and vegetables from sweet end of grain and vegetable lists.
3. Grains and vegetables should have an astringent second taste.
4. For snacks and dessert, eat fresh fruit with sweet tastes.
5. Eat more raw than cooked food, to increase astringency.
6. Eat only fresh, natural food.
7. Eat only delicious food.
8. Determine quantities with your fist.
9. Eat more grains than proteins.
10. Eat all of the eight tastes every day.

GREASY AND SPICY FOOD CRAVERS
SUPPLEMENT PROGRAM

Chapter 13 explains the Skinny School nutritional supplement program I have developed to eliminate deficiencies in greasy and spicy food cravers. *You should begin the supplements at the same time as the diet.* The supplements are designed to make it possible—and easy—to follow the diets. The supplements work to eliminate the massive chemical imbalances that drive the craving for greasy and spicy foods. For this reason, instructions on when to take your supplements are included along with the diet.

Many greasy and spicy food cravers (about 50 percent) have a secondary sweets or starches craving. If this is you, you should begin by taking the supplement program for the craving you have for greasy or spicy food and continue with it for at least four weeks. Then, if your primary craving is coming under control and you still have a sweets craving, you should *add* the Anti-craving Minerals for your secondary sweet and starch craving at that point.

Without the support of these supplements, you will find that your cravings will continue to make it very difficult to stay with your diet, especially at the beginning. I don't want you to have a repeat of the experience you've been through so many times in the past, when you are left alone with your cravings at times of stress. Take your supplements and make this experience different.

If you do have cravings at the beginning of the program, don't worry. This is natural—you've had them for so long, and the cure takes four to eight weeks. And above all don't feel guilty about them. What you should do is *notice* each craving, and refer to Chapter 13 for supplements that will cure it. Within four to eight weeks all *your* cravings will be at least 90 percent cured.

Don't forget, also, that you should begin using a technique of your choice to experience the M-State. Start this at the same time as the Skinny School diet and the supplement program. If you want to be naturally skinny, don't neglect this part of your education.

Note: With this as with any diet or supplement program, do not begin without consulting your physician.

The only part of Skinny School you *shouldn't* begin at this time is the "Lard" Lessons. They should wait until your cravings are at least 50 percent under control—about the third or fourth week of the program.

THE GREASY AND SPICY FOOD CRAVERS DIET

FIRST THING IN THE MORNING: Check your tongue in the mirror and scrape off any coating. Use a teaspoon and try not to gag yourself. The coating comes from toxic overload of your digestion and cravings. Removing it makes it easier to follow the diet.

If you are taking any amino acid supplements (Brain Food, Magic Pills, or Tri-Skinny), take them now, before eating. If you are taking the Graded Appetite Controllers, take your morning tablet now.

Breakfast:
One piece of fruit from the sweet end of the fruit list.

One grain exchange from sweet end of the grain list.

One cup of coffee. Nonfat milk okay, but *no cream*.

Supplements: Vitamin and mineral tablet (Skinny-All®).

WAIT 3 HOURS—LONGER IF YOU AREN'T YET HUNGRY.

Snack: Half piece of sweet fruit. Take Brain Food® and any Anti-craving supplements now.

WAIT 2 MORE HOURS.

Supplements: If you are taking the Graded Appetite Controllers, take your afternoon tablet one half hour before lunch.

Lunch:
CHOICE OF:
4 ounces of meat, fish, or poultry from the astringent end of the protein list. Vegetarians may substitute tofu, stir-fried or pan-fried. Use Greasy and Spicy Food Cravers Spice Mix or season with pungent/peppery spices.

You may also have steak tartare (raw chopped meat) but do *not* have any prepared meat or frozen food whatsoever. If you taste carefully, you will notice these have a bad second taste for you.

Two grain or legume exchanges.

Large salad made with fresh vegetables from the sweet end of the vegetable list, dressed with a little oil and lemon juice and seasoned with sweet herbs.

One cup of cooked vegetables, in addition to salad (optional).

Tea or coffee.

Supplements: First enzyme supplement (Grease Cutters®) now.

WAIT 3 HOURS.

Snack: One piece of fruit from sweet end of the fruit list.

WAIT 2 MORE HOURS.

Supplements: If you are taking the Graded Appetite Controllers, take your afternoon tablet one half hour before dinner.

Dinner:
CHOICE OF:
Greasy and Spicy Food Cravers Vegetable Soup (or soup made with other vegetables from the sweet end of the vegetable list). Two ounces of meat, fish, or poultry from the astringent end of the protein list or tofu.

One grain or legume exchange.

One teaspoon of oil from the astringent end of the oil list.

Tea or coffee.

Supplements: Second enzyme supplement (Grease Cutters®).

AT BEDTIME: 4-ounce glass of skim milk (optional).

Supplements: 500 mg. tryptophan.

MEALTIME NOTES

THE LARGER AND SMALLER MEALS

In the Skinny School plan, lunch is the larger meal and dinner is the smaller meal. If you study naturally skinny people, you'll see that they almost never eat a big meal at night. Skinny people know instinctively that your body doesn't digest a large meal as well at night as it does in the middle of the day. Much of the food you eat at night turns automatically into fat, and the toxic overload of your digestion shows up on your tongue the next morning.

When you are free of cravings, it's easy to eat a smaller meal at night. It also gives you more energy in the evening. A big meal turns into an evening of falling asleep in front of the TV.

Today, since the majority of people are working outside of the home, it's convenient as well as healthier to eat your larger meal at lunch. "Larger" doesn't mean *large*. You still should never exceed your fist size; the old theory that you need a lot of food to keep going is wrong. You need the right tastes to keep going. But you can have a more substantial meal at lunchtime and still digest it well.

If you eat out at lunch, find a restaurant that serves a selection of fresh, natural food. You can then make a smaller, simpler meal at home at night (saving time as well). If you are at home during the day, you can still make your bigger meal, and have more control over the freshness and deliciousness of the ingredients.

SUBSTITUTIONS

Since your Skinny School Anti-craving Diet is based on taste, all your *substitutions* should be based on keeping the same balance of tastes at each meal.

At breakfast you can substitute freely from the sweet fruits and sweet whole grains. But you must *never* have astringent foods, especially eggs, for breakfast, as this will make your cravings go wild all day.

At lunch or dinner you have great freedom to substitute within the taste categories given. As your ability to use your sense of taste grows, you will be able to make your own substitutions with confidence.

If you have read *Dr. Abravanel's Body Type Diet and Lifetime Nutrition Plan*, or are familiar with your Body Type Diet, you can see that the principles of taste can be applied to make these diets more flexible. Some foods become possible which weren't possible in the Body Type format. For example, Gonadal Types were not supposed to eat spicy foods at all in the Body Type Plan, because they were too stimulating for their sex glands. But using taste principles, Gonadal Types can choose pungent/sweet spices, and avoid the overstimulation.

SKINNY VEGETARIANS

Being a vegetarian on the Skinny School program is easy, too, using taste principles. Vegetarians who don't use taste balancing usually have too much sweet taste and not enough astringent and umami tastes in their diets. This is not usually a problem for greasy and spicy food cravers, however, because your natural attraction to the tastes of umami and astringency helps you to include these tastes in your diet even if you become a vegetarian.

Using the taste principles, simply be sure you include enough sources of astringency and umami, and maintain balance in this way.

THE MEAL PLANS AND THE SIMPLE MEAL

At the end of this chapter you'll find a week of suggested meal plans for greasy and spicy food cravers. I want you to look at these as suggestions, not as laws. Feel free to make up your own menus using the taste principles.

The meals I've suggested are not extremely elaborate, but they all involve some cooking and some time spent assembling ingredients. I want you to have some real *taste* in your meals, because taste is the key to satisfaction. Without satisfaction, you'll never be cured of your cravings.

But tasty meals do take time to prepare. And time is in chronically short supply. So you should have in your repertoire a simple meal that is tasty, that contains all the tastes, and that works for you as a greasy and spicy food craver.

You can always fall back on this meal; if you want, you can have it every day, with minor variations. It will work, it will satisfy you, and it will cure your cravings. Here it is:

GREASY AND SPICY FOOD CRAVERS SIMPLE MEAL

One small piece of fresh fish, brushed lightly with olive oil, sprinkled with fresh herbs or Greasy and Spicy Food Cravers Spice Mix, and broiled.

Or, for vegetarians, four ounces of tofu sauteed in one teaspoon of olive oil and sprinkled with your Spice Mix.

One-half cup of white or brown rice.

One large serving of vegetables from the astringent end of the vegetable list, lightly steamed.

DESSERT

Most greasy and spicy food cravers do not *need* dessert to live, but even greasy and spicy food cravers are sometimes struck with the need for something sweet. Almost everyone needs sweetness once in a while, if dieting and living are to be bearable.

If you have had a taste for the overly sweet taste of sugary desserts, you will find it disappearing after four to eight weeks on the Skinny School program. You will also find that your craving for rich, oil-laden desserts (pies with buttery crusts, mousse, or cheesecake) is leaving. But you will not lose your taste for natural sweetness—a taste you can satisfy without danger.

One of the most satisfying desserts I have found for my greasy and spicy food cravers patients at Skinny School is the Dried Fruit Compote. The recipe below works with many dried fruits.

GREASY AND SPICY FOOD CRAVERS DRIED FRUIT COMPOTE

Look for good quality dried fruit, avoiding those made with preservatives such as sulfur dioxide. Try your health food store, and read the labels. Choose from dried figs, peaches, pears, apples, apricots, prunes, or raisins. Let the fruits soak in water for a half hour, then cook until just tender. You can season them with a stick of dried cinnamon, some rose petals, or lemon or orange rind. Serve either warm or cold. A serving is a half cup. The compote is also very good for breakfast.

GREASY AND SPICY FOOD CRAVERS MEAL PLANS

(* means the recipe for this dish appears in the recipe section of the food appendix.)

Monday:
Breakfast:
>   one cup whole grain cereal with strawberries
>   and ½ cup nonfat (not low-fat) milk
>   coffee or tea

Larger meal:
>   Stir-fried Tofu*
>   ½ cup Brown Rice*
>   Tomato, Onion, and Herb Salad*
>   Stir-fried vegetables (optional)

Snacks: Large apple
Smaller meal:
>   Greasy and Spicy Food Cravers Vegetable Soup*
>   sandwich with one slice of whole grain bread
>   and two ounces of tuna fish

Tuesday:
Breakfast:
>   one cup oat bran cereal with ½ banana
>   coffee or tea

Larger meal:
>   4 ounces Saffron-broiled Chicken*
>   lettuce and raw mushroom Salad
>   baked potato (with 2 tablespoons yogurt if desired—no butter
>   or sour cream!)
>   Grated Zucchini with Nutmeg*

Snacks: Large, sweet pear
Smaller meal:
>   Root Vegetable Soup*
>   Chicken Burger*
>   *or* Lentil Burger*
>   one half whole grain roll

Wednesday:
Breakfast:
> one cup low-fat yogurt with fresh pineapple
> coffee or tea

Larger meal:
> 4 ounces Sole Ceviche*
> Tabouli Salad*
> steamed eggplant

Snacks: two plums

Smaller meal:
> Chicory Salad*
> Herbed Corn on the Cob*
> Three-Cabbage Cole Slaw*

Thursday:
Breakfast:
> one bunch of grapes
> whole grain toast
> coffee or tea

Larger meal:
> Ginger-Pear Soup*
> 4 ounces Curried Chicken with Vegetables*
> Brown Rice* with yellow lentils

Snacks: 2 slices of melon

Smaller meal:
> Mashed Sweet Potatoes with Tofu*
> Tomato and Mozzarella Salad*

Friday:
Breakfast:
> one orange
> one cup whole grain cereal with nonfat milk
> coffee or tea

Larger meal:
> Herb-stuffed Trout*
> 1 cup bulghur wheat
> Grated Zucchini*

Snacks: 2 fresh figs

Smaller meal:
>   Spicy Sesame Noodles*
>   Fresh Pea Soup*
>   seven grain bread, toasted

Saturday:
Breakfast:
>   one cup low-fat yogurt
>   one apple
>   coffee or tea

Larger meal:
>   Green Enchiladas*
>   Roman-style Spinach*
>   ½ cup white rice

Snacks: 2 tangerines
Smaller meal:
>   White Bean Soup*
>   carrot and orange salad

Sunday:
Breakfast:
>   whole grain pancakes with honey
>   bowl of strawberries
>   coffee or tea

Larger meal:
>   Halibut with Leeks*
>   Baked Pepper and Potato*
>   tomatoes on lettuce

Snacks: one large pear
Smaller meal:
>   sliced chicken sandwich on one slice of whole wheat bread
>   large Early Spring Salad*

13

ANTI-CRAVING
SUPPLEMENTS

The Skinny School supplement program is much more than a vitamin and mineral tablet added to your diet. It's a precise, *targeted* program of specific supplements designed to work *with* the Anti-craving Diets to cure specific cravings. Taking the right supplements can make all the difference between a complete cure and one more diet failure.

John and Maryanne L., a couple who came to Skinny School together, wanted to lose ten pounds each. Of the two, John had by far the worse cravings, even though their extra weight was the same. He was a sweets craver who bought Snickers in the economy-size pack. He was also a very high-strung, nervous person who exercised compulsively. His almost daily four-mile runs were the reason the Snickers hadn't resulted in any more than ten extra pounds.

Maryanne was a steadier kind of person, with a less "hyper" metabolism. Her cravings were for salty junk food of all kinds, especially potato chips and salted nuts. When she completed the Cravings Analysis Checklist, she turned out to be a greasy food craver. It was primarily the oils in these foods that she was using to change her brain state, not the starch. However, she did have a secondary craving for starches as well.

When I talked with them, I knew right away that Maryanne was going to do better than John. She understood cravings immediately. When I told her that her desire for junk food actually came from her need for inner calm and alertness (that is, for the M-State), she related to what I said. She could see it in her own life. So she was eager to do the entire Skinny School program—diet, supplements, and "Lard" Lessons.

John, on the other hand, seemed skeptical as we talked. His situation was different; his compulsive exercise was giving him a fake M-State "high," but he was convinced that his compulsive running every single day was extremely healthful and didn't want to hear anything different. His craving for sweets he thought of as something shameful, and didn't really want to talk about that either.

JOHN'S DOUBTS

John dealt with these conflicts by expressing doubts about the whole Skinny School program. His main doubt, he said, was that he needed to take vitamins. "I don't see why I should need them if I go on this healthy diet you're giving me," he argued. "I'll just stop the Snickers and that will be that. I don't need them." (Famous last words, I thought to myself.)

"Besides," he added, "you're telling me to take at least five vitamin pills every day. I don't think I can remember to take them. I'll just do the diet and forget the vitamins."

THREE WEEKS LATER

I knew that without the supplements John was simply not going to do as well as Maryanne. Sure enough, within three weeks of faithfully following the Greasy and Spicy Food Cravers Diet *plus* taking her supplements, Maryanne had almost completely lost her craving for potato chips and nuts—but John was still struggling.

He was having trouble staying on the Sweet and Starch Cravers Diet because of the intensity of his sweets craving. But he used the excuse that he needed the energy of the sweets for his running.

At this point Maryanne was nearly cured of her grease craving, but still having problems with starch. So I put her on the Anti-craving

Minerals for the starch craving. The supplements that cure the starch craving are similar to the ones that cure the sweets craving, so Maryanne was now taking a program similar to what John *should* have been taking.

THE TURNING POINT

I pointed this out to John and told him to watch what happened with his wife. By the end of the very first week on the minerals, Maryanne's starch craving was 85 percent controlled. That did it—John was finally convinced. He started to take the supplements. It took a full eight weeks, because he had massive deficiencies, but we did cure his craving. Snickers are a thing of the past, and the ten pounds are gone for good.

One interesting sidelight: Since John was getting a strong fake M-State from running, he found that as soon as he had his craving under control he needed to run much less. This was a relief to him, because in fact he was worn-out from running. Now he does three miles a day four times a week—a reduction of 16 miles per week. He feels much better. I told him that there is no evidence at all that running more than his present level would add either years to his life, or life to his years.

DEFICIENCIES

Over the twenty years that Skinny School has been in existence, I have become more and more convinced that *severe deficiencies* of vitamins, minerals, and enzymes are far more widespread than the medical establishment will admit. No matter how much of an effort you put into eating healthful food, if you have cravings, *you, too, have deficiencies,* deficiencies that have been undermining all your diets for years.

Deficiencies cause tremendous disruption at every phase of your digestion and utilization of food. But the most important disruption they cause is a *disruption of your ability to experience the M-State.*

DEFICIENCIES AND THE M-STATE

The M-State, as you know from Chapter 3, comes from a part of the brain called the *neuroglia*. Neuroglial cells are a type of brain cell; they surround and support the *neurons* (nerve cells) that make up the *neural brain*.

Neuroglial cells used to be considered merely the sanitation and food-service workers of the brain, simply providing support to the neurons. Today, neuroglial cells are thought to be the cells responsible for our underlying feeling of *continuity of the self*—that is, for the feeling of connected consciousness that makes sense out of all experiences, the "I" that experiences everything we do.

The M-State is the state of calm inner peacefulness and powerful alertness that provides us with inner refreshment and relief from stress. What happens in the M-State is that all the neuroglial cells of your brain become totally coherent and coordinated; they act as if they were one single cell. This is what gives the powerful sense of inner harmony that is part of the M-State.

When you're *not* in the M-State, the neuroglial cells are only partially connected, and the experience you have of "yourself," your sense of "I," is small and unsatisfying. The neuroglia is perhaps the seat of the craving for the fake M-State, because it wants to feel more of its own power.

When you are deficient in any vital nutrients, your ability to have the M-State is greatly weakened. The neuroglial brain cannot do its job without the nutrients it needs. If your deficiencies are *extreme*, you may lose the ability to have the M-State completely. There's barely any sense of "I" there—you're like a zombie.

If your deficiencies are less extreme, you will be able to experience the M-State using a reliable technique of meditation, but its stress-relieving effects will not last. You will finish your meditation period feeling much better, but find that you return to feelings of fatigue and stress almost immediately.

THE CRAVING CYCLE

Yet the more deficient you are, the more you *need* the M-State to relieve your stress. So your *cravings* for foods that mimic the M-State and give you an imitation of its calmness and alertness grow stronger and stronger.

With strong cravings, you become less and less likely to eat the kinds of foods that give you the nutrients you need. You become increasingly deficient, and your cravings just keep on growing.

As cravings grow, your need for the M-State becomes more desperate, yet you become increasingly unable to get it. This is why I have designed the Skinny School supplement program. It is a strong program of intense intervention in the cycle of cravings and deficiencies.

Deficiency-free nutrition is the key to the fully functioning brain that can have and maintain the M-State. With deficiencies, your cravings may prove stronger than any diet.

WHERE DEFICIENCIES COME FROM

Deficiencies in vitamins, minerals, and other vital nutrients have three main causes. You will have deficiencies when:

1. You are not getting an adequate *supply* of any nutrient, or,
2. You have a high *demand* for any nutrient, or
3. Your body is not able to *use* the nutrients it is getting.

THE SUPPLY SIDE

The fact that your *supply* of nutrients is inadequate is because food today is much less nutritious than it has ever been in history.

Your body didn't evolve for the kind of environment we're all living in today. It has spent millions of years organizing itself to live in the "natural environment."

In nature, plants draw nutrients from the soil, and the soil is replenished in turn by these plants. There is a state of balance among all the parts of the natural world—the soil, the vegetation, the animals, and the people who grow and live there.

Modern food processing, chemical fertilizers, and the creation of new, hybrid plant species all combine to disrupt this process. Which means that your food is missing the natural abundance of nutrients that it should contain.

Chemical fertilizers, for example, stimulate plants to grow more quickly than they normally would. They don't get time to draw all the minerals from the soil that naturally grown food does. Simultaneously, growing greater *quantities* of plants in the same soil causes the soil to lose its minerals and become depleted. So our vegetables have fewer minerals than they should have.

Hybridization has also seriously compromised our supply of nutrients. "New, improved" strains of wheat, for instance, have protein contents of 8 percent—down from 18 percent in the "bad old" wheat. The protein in natural wheat used to buffer the brain stimulation of the starch; whole wheat flour from the old kind of wheat was a good source for protein. Today, wheat is a craving food.

Then, after all this industrial interference, food processing—industrial cooking, canning, or freezing—takes away even more of the nutrients. So you end up eating a zucchini, for instance, with about one fifth as much magnesium as it would normally have.

But your digestion is set up for the "old zucchini," with all the magnesium zucchini should have. It *needs* that magnesium to digest the zucchini. If the magnesium doesn't come in the zucchini, your body will have to draw magnesium from its own stores, which start running an overdraft, just like your bank account at holiday time.

The result: ever-increasing deficiencies.

THE DEMAND FACTOR

Yet even as your *supply* of nutrients decreases, your *demand* for them is constantly increasing.

Modern life is extremely stressful, especially in comparison with the lives of our hunter-gatherer ancestors, who worked an average fourteen-hour week. Stress increases your body's need for *all* the nutrients.

For example, suppose you stress your body by cooking your food on aluminum cookware. Tiny amounts of aluminum enter your system: this is a stress. Your body now requires a greater supply of another mineral, selenium, in order to eliminate the aluminum, which is otherwise poisonous. Thus stress has increased your body's *demand* for selenium.

Another example: Suppose you spend time at night in bright light. This is a stress, because your body actually evolved in an environment where it's dark at night. The invention of artificial light was one of humankind's better moves, but it has the effect of causing your body to burn vitamin A and the B vitamins at a greater rate than before. The *demand* for A and B vitamins is greater in you than in your ancestors, who either sat up reading by candlelight when it got dark, or just went to sleep.

In fact, almost everything you do increases your body's demand for nutrients. Smoking, alcohol, and all drugs, prescription or recreational, increase your need for nutrients. Exercise (and the hundreds of microinjuries to muscles and joints that go along with exercise) also increases your nutrient needs.

If you are fatigued or depressed, your body's need for a wide spectrum of nutrients increases manyfold. Stress, fatigue, worry, and anxiety are such common features of our lives that today our nutritional needs are far higher than at any time in history.

THE ABILITY TO USE NUTRIENTS

Finally, the ever-increasing deficiencies that come from decreased supply and increased demand mean that your body becomes increasingly *less able to use what nutrients it does receive.*

If your body is working well—digesting your food efficiently and well—you will be able to extract every possible nutrient from anything you eat. But if you're at less than peak efficiency, even those nutrients you do get will be partially wasted, because your body won't be working well enough to extract them from the food.

Your body's efficiency depends very largely on taste and smell (see Chapters 8 and 9). The tastes and smells of food carry the "instructions" to your brain and body: they tell it what the food is and how to use it. This means that the same lack of natural tastes and smells that disrupts your digestion *also disrupts your body's ability to use the nutrients in your food*. It even disrupts your body's ability to *use any nutritional supplements you may be taking now*.

The way nutritional deficiencies come out of this lack of taste and smell is one of the largest uncharted areas of knowledge in the entire field of scientific nutrition. When taste, smell, and human health are fully understood, the entire food-growing and -processing industry will have to change radically.

There will have to be a total return to natural farming methods in order to restore the right tastes and smells to food. Because it is only when food has the right tastes and smells that the massive deficiencies that haunt today's world can be eliminated.

The Skinny School Anti-craving Diets will give you the tastes and smells your body needs to *use* the nutrients in the Skinny School supplement program. That's why I repeat yet again: You must follow the entire program, because you need the supplements to follow the diet, and you need the diet to be able to use the supplements.

THE RETURN TO TASTE

I am very happy with my Skinny School supplement program. It has helped tens of thousands of patients eliminate their cravings, and this is totally gratifying to me as a physician and as a person. But I still feel that taking nutritional supplements is *not* the ideal way to get your nutrients.

The ideal is for every nutrient you need to come inside the food it is supposed to come in, packaged right along with the right tastes and smells, in nature's own convenient package.

Until farming and food-producing methods change completely, however, this is simply not possible. In time it may be; today, it is not.

There are a few slight indications that our growing concern with health might lead in the right direction. In December 1988, for example, Europe banned the import from the United States of meat grown with growth hormones. Their move has been widely interpreted as an economic move against the United States, but it can also be viewed as a positive health measure.

Europeans believe that growth hormones given to animals are harmful to health, and have banned them on their own farms. On the basis of the evidence, it is not entirely clear how much harm the growth hormones actually do; but it *is* clear that growth hormones reduce the taste and smell of meat, which has already been much reduced by so-called scientific animal feed.

Another positive sign is the fact that in California, organic farming methods are being used on a larger scale and are becoming more profitable. People want organic food and are willing to pay for it.

Yet another positive indication is in the movement headed by the World Health Organization and supported by certain far-thinking seed companies to find, preserve, and begin to grow again some of the old, nonhybrid varieties of vegetables and grains. These varieties have been almost completely replaced in the commercial marketplace. Yet these older vegetables—ones with wonderful, evocative names like Aunt Mary's sweet corn and Thelma Sanders's sweet potato squash—have the kind of tastes you haven't had in years.

They are also a rich reservoir of genetic diversity. Today, so few varieties are grown commercially that a single disease could conceivably wipe out a large percentage of the world's food supply. We need to maintain a "bank" of different genes in order to prevent this kind of disaster. And better-tasting, better-smelling vegetables will be the great side effect.

"PURE FOODS AND DRUGS"

The idea that taste and smell carry "instructions" to the body and brain is, to say the least, strange to modern science. It appears illogical. Science takes a far more simplistic view of nutrition. The tiny traces of various chemicals that give food its taste and smell are considered insignificant. All that's "important" are the proteins, carbohydrates, and fats—the more obvious components of the food.

In exactly the same way, modern medicine is biased against using complex chemical compounds, such as herbs, and prefers to use drugs that contain simple elements whose effects can be isolated.

Medicine is constantly seeking to purify its drugs. It wants only the "active ingredient." The thinking is, why give a sick patient extra chemicals that might cause trouble, when you can give a pure drug?

THE CASE FOR WHOLE HERBS

There is a growing body of evidence to suggest that "instructions" for the use of the "active ingredient" are found in the other, supposedly "nonactive" parts of medicinal herbs.

These so-called "nonessential" parts of the medicinal plants add tremendously to their effectiveness. In the case of very powerful addictive drugs, the nonactive ingredients help the body prevent overdosing.

For example, natives of Colombia and Bolivia who chew coca leaf (called "aculli") instead of using refined cocaine or "crack" never use more than one fourth the actual cocaine (the "active" ingredient) that addicts in the United States use.

They get their effect largely from the "instructions" contained in the "nonessential" parts of the leaf. So even their addiction to medicinal herbs is softer than is the case with refined drugs. The same is true of opium, a medicinal herb, as opposed to heroin, a refined drug.

The chemical instructions carried in the taste and smell of the herb have tremendous effect even independently of the active ingredient. The popularity of Coca-Cola, which gets much of its taste from a strain of coca leaf (from Ecuador, called *Trujillo coca*), is based on the efficacy of the taste and smell in the leaf. Naturally, all the cocaine is removed before the Coca-Cola is made, but what remains—the wintergreen and other flavors—still give a lift. Otherwise there would be *no* reason for anyone to drink caffeine-free Diet Coke over plain water.

THE TASTES AND SMELLS OF DRUGS

Today science does not know whether the taste and/or the smell of an herb, or of a purified drug, has any effect on the drug's efficacy. If a drug or a food is "purified" so that it no longer has the natural taste and smell nature gave it, it still has *some* taste and *some* smell.

Even antibiotics have some taste. What are the effects? What instructions are being carried to your brain with these drugs? What basic chemical and energetic differences are there, what subtle messengers that might be making the same drug effective for one individual and ineffective for another with the same disease?

Vitamins and minerals also have tastes and smells; but as anyone who has had a vitamin pill "repeat" knows, they are not the natural smells of real food. This is still another reason for coordinating your supplement program *with* a diet designed for the right tastes and smells. This lets you fill in the (inevitable) nutrient gaps of your diet with supplements, on the one hand, and fill in the lack of natural taste and smell "instructions" in the supplements from the food at the same time.

HOMEOPATHY

Many of my Skinny School supplements have instructions actually *built in,* because I have designed them using a system of medicine that is actually entirely built around the "instructions." *Homeopathy,* or homeopathic medicine, is a system of medicine that uses *only the minute taste elements that carry instructions to your body and brain.*

In the nineteenth and early twentieth centuries, homeopathy was widely used and known to be very effective. In the later part of our century, however, it has lost ground to allopathic medicine (our present system of "pure drugs" against diseases). And in fact homeopathy has become today quite ineffective, because it relies on the patient to eat a balanced diet (with taste and smell intact) and to live a balanced life-style.

Homeopathic remedies are very subtle, but they work *with food* to activate the curative and balancing qualities in the food. When used in this way they are extremely effective in a way that allopathy is not; they create balance and do not have harmful side effects. Homeopathy lost ground simply because food stopped containing enough nutrition and enough taste and smell to make the homeopathic remedies work. It relied for its effectiveness on a natural food source that, today, no longer exists.

Homeopathic remedies work in the opposite way from allopathic (or modern western) remedies. Where allopathic drugs work directly against a disease, homeopathics work to stimulate the body to throw off the disease itself. For instance, if you are nauseated you would be given an herb called *nux vomica* that in normal doses would make you feel nauseated. The assumption is that along with the nausea-producing effect, *nux vomica* would also contain "instructions" to your body on how to overcome the nausea.

Homeopathic remedies are diluted many times (ten thousand times is common). When you take this very diluted dose of *nux vomica,* it gives your body *only the instructions* of how to overcome nausea. It is, simply, a messenger.

Homeopathy assumes that your body has within it the natural balance and resources to heal itself; it needs only the messenger to stir it up to do this. The homeopathic medicine doesn't cure the condition, but it acts, in the concert of the body, as a conductor that tells the right musicians how and what to play so that the right music comes out.

If you are on the Anti-craving Diet for your cravings and are taking the supplements for your cravings, then homeopathic medicine will have the raw materials to work in your system.

THE SKINNY SCHOOL ANTI-CRAVING SUPPLEMENTS

On the next pages you will find a complete listing of the supplements you need to cure each of your cravings. Every item listed is available in health food stores, although you will have to look carefully at labels in order to be sure of what you are getting. You should consult your physician before beginning this program, especially if you are taking any medications.

The Skinny School program has three parts:

1. The foundation program, which consists of those vitamins, minerals, and trace elements needed by *everyone*.
2. The specific *additional* supplements that cure each craving.
3. Special supplements for specific situations that you may have, such as weight loss plateaus, the need to increase muscle strength, and many others.

PART I: THE FOUNDATION

The Skinny School supplement program to cure deficiencies begins with a basic vitamin/mineral supplement. Everyone, regardless of cravings, should be taking these nutrients.

At Skinny School they are combined into a tablet called Skinny-All®. You will be able to find all these nutrients at a good health food store, although you may have to combine more than one product to get all your requirements.

VITAMINS	AMOUNT	% USRDA*
A (water soluble)	10,000 I.U.	200
D-3	400 I.U.	100
E (d-alpha tocopherol succinate, water soluble)	30 I.U.	100
K (water soluble)	79 mcg.	70
C (ascorbic acid)	100 mg.	166
B-1 (thiamine mononitrate)	15 mg.	1000
B-2 (riboflavin)	15 mg.	882
B-3 (niacinamide)	40 mg.	200
B-6 (pyridoxine HCl)	25 mg.	1250
B-12	25 mcg.	416
Folic acid	400 mcg.	100
Pantothenic acid	25 mg.	416
Biotin	300 mcg.	100
Choline bitartrate	10 mg.	
Hesperidin complex	10 mg.	
Citrus bioflavonoids	10 mg.	
Inositol	10 mg.	
Rutin	10 mg.	
Para-aminobenzoic acid	8 mg.	
MINERALS		
Calcium	100 mg.	10
Magnesium	100 mg.	25
Iron	20 mg.	111
Manganese	6 mg.	150

VITAMINS	AMOUNT	% USRDA*
Iodine	100 mcg.	66
Copper	2 mg.	100
Potassium	25 mg.	
Zinc	30 mg.	200
Phosphorus	52 mg.	5
Chromium (GTF factor, chelate)	500 mcg.	
Molybdenum (sodium molybdate)	100 mcg.	
Selenium (chelate)	10 mcg.	

*USRDA—recommended daily allowance for adults and children 12 years of age or older.
   Your tablet, like Skinny-All®, should contain no yeast, soya, corn, wheat, phenol, preservatives, sugar, chlorine, or added salicylates.

PART II: ADDITIONAL SUPPLEMENTS FOR SPECIFIC CRAVINGS

1. To Cure Sweets Cravings:
In addition to the nutrients listed above, you need:

- 500 mg. of magnesium three times per day. The magnesium should be chelated (bound to protein). We recommend magnesium gluconate. To increase effectiveness, add 10 mg. vitamin B6, which enhances absorption.
- 1500 mg. tryptophan, taken at bedtime.

   Curing a sweets cravings requires replenishing deficiencies of the trace minerals magnesium, zinc, and chromium, and replenishing brain neurotransmitters.
   Additional chromium and zinc are not required, as the amounts listed in the foundation program are sufficient to cure the deficiency. Studies done on rats indicate that it requires large amounts of supplemental zinc to cure a sweets craving, but research at Skinny School has shown that this is not generally the case in humans.
   Extra magnesium, however, is absolutely necessary. Processed carbohydrates contain only about one third of the magnesium present in whole grains, so sweets cravers generally have massive deficiencies of this

mineral. Blood levels of magnesium often remain normal even in the presence of fairly severe tissue deficiencies. For this reason blood tests are often of very little use in detecting magnesium deficiencies until they have become extreme.

Magnesium is a *neuromodulator*—which means that it modulates your brain's sensitivity to the brain chemicals (including serotonin) that are involved in feelings of satisfaction. When you are deficient in magnesium, your brain becomes less sensitive, and needs *more* serotonin to get the same effect.

When you crave sugar, your brain is actually craving the serotonin that is stimulated by eating sugar (see Chapter 5). If you are magnesium deficient, you will need *much* greater amounts of sugar to get the effect you are seeking. Eliminating this deficiency weakens sugar cravings *dramatically* within a very short period.

Clinical symptoms of magnesium deficiency include:

1. Type-A behavior
2. Cardiac rhythm abnormalities
3. Migraines
4. Muscle spasm
5. Depression and apathy
6. Premenstrual syndrome

These symptoms are gross manifestations that you may or may not have along with severe sweets cravings, but I see them often in people who do have these cravings. If you have any of these symptoms, you may find that the extra magnesium helps greatly.

Along with the magnesium, the 1500 milligrams of tryptophan at bedtime will help restore your brain levels of serotonin.

2. To Cure Starch Cravings:
In addition to the nutrients listed in the foundation program, you need:

• 15 mg. elemental manganese three times per day. The manganese should be chelated (bound to protein). We recommend manganese gluconate.
• 1500 mg. tryptophan, taken at bedtime.

Manganese deficiency is a classic deficiency caused by stress and pollution of the environment. Fifty years ago it was impossible to be deficient in manganese; today, polluting chemicals (such as lead, aluminum, and hydrocarbons) that compete with manganese in your body for absorption have created widespread manganese deficiencies.

In nonindustrialized countries, manganese deficiency is caused by hybridized plants that have lost their ability to pull manganese from the soil. But in really primitive cultures, where natural farming methods still exist, manganese deficiency is unknown.

Manganese plays a key role in the creation of neurotransmitter chemicals such as serotonin. Manganese deficiency has similar symptoms to those caused by magnesium deficiency (see page 173), and it is difficult to tell the two deficiencies apart on a clinical basis. And indeed they often appear together.

Zinc and chromium deficiencies also play a role in starch cravings, but you will get a sufficient supply of these minerals in Skinny-All.

The tryptophan works to restore brain levels of neurotransmitters, specifically of serotonin.

3. To Cure Cravings for Starchy Sweets:
In addition to the foundation program, you need:

- A combination tablet containing 5 mg. manganese and 13 mg. magnesium, three times per day. Both the manganese and the magnesium should be chelated (bound to protein). Adding 10 mg. vitamin B6 aids absorption. (In Skinny School this combination is called Vitomag.)
- 1500 mg. tryptophan, taken at bedtime.

Starchy sweets are combinations of sweets with starches, such as cake. This cure is also for people who have mild cravings for *both* starches and sweets.

If you are more than 25 pounds overweight, this is *not* you. More than 25 extra pounds indicates that you should take the supplements for either sweets or starches, depending on which craving is stronger. Once the stronger craving is under control, you should begin the program to cure the less intense craving.

4. To Cure Cravings for Greasy Foods:

- 200 mg. amylase
- 50 mg. lipase. These are digestive enzymes that enable you to digest greasy foods. At Skinny School they are combined in capsules called Grease Cutters®.
- 500 mg. tryptophan, taken at bedtime.

Greasy food cravers have a different class of deficiency from sweet and starch cravers. Instead of trace minerals, they are deficient in gastrointestinal enzymes.

This means that the digestive juices work slowly and inefficiently. When you have a craving for greasy food, you are seeking a specific brain effect that comes from oils, but since your digestion is slow, your brain doesn't get to experience the effect it wants until you have eaten much too much of the most caloric kind of food.

The signal that you are "full"—the *satiety signal*—is given to your brain by the hypothalamus, a glandular nerve center located deep inside the brain. But your hypothalamus relies on your digestion to tell it that you have had enough food. When your digestion is very slow, the signal comes much too late. In fact, your hypothalamus may never even get the message from your digestion. Many greasy food cravers eat until the stomach itself sends messages that it is too stuffed to accept any more food.

Because of this deficiency, you may also have incomplete and toxic digestion of your food. Greasy food cravers have a habit of eating even though they are still full from the previous meal, because eating *activates* their digestive enzymes. Eating again is an attempt to digest the *previous* meal—to process food they ate before.

Basically, they are attempting to get the food they've eaten to move through their digestive system. This does work, in a way, but the effect is brief, because it adds even more food to an already overburdened system.

5. To Cure Cravings for Spicy Foods:
In addition to the foundation program, you need:

• A digestive enzyme combination with the following enzymes:

Pancreatin	300 mg.
Pepsin	75 mg.
Amylase	5 mg.
Diastase	50 mg.
Papain	50 mg.
Glutamic acid HCl	10 mg.
Betaine HCl	10 mg.

At Skinny School these are combined into a tablet called Prevenzyme.

• A mineral tablet containing the following amounts of minerals:

	AMOUNT	% USRDA
Calcium (amino acid chelate)	500 mg.	50
Magnesium (amino acid chelate)	210 mg.	52
Iron (amino acid chelate)	15 mg.	83
Iodine (kelp)	.75 mg.	50
Copper (amino acid chelate)	1.5 mg.	75
Zinc (amino acid chelate)	11.25 mg.	75
Manganese (amino acid chelate)	5 mg.	
Chromium (amino acid chelate)	100 mcg.	
Vitamin D (fish liver oil)	200 I.U.	50
Betaine HCl	500 mg.	
Glutamic Acid HCl	50 mg.	
Selenium (kelp)	5 mcg.	
Potassium (potassium proteinate)	47.5 mg.	

At Skinny School these are combined into a tablet called Multi-Min.

• A combination of the following diuretic herbs: buchu leaves, juniper berries, and couch grass.
  At Skinny School these are called Herbal Diuretics.
  All these nutrients are available in health food stores.

Spicy food cravers have a combination of deficiencies. They are deficient in digestive and pancreatic enzymes just as greasy food cravers are; they also have a deficiency in minerals that comes from their poor digestions. In addition, they have toxic bloat and tend to retain fluid.

The digestive enzymes listed above work to cure the deficient enzyme system. The mineral tablet cures the mineral deficiency, and the toxic bloat is relieved by the herbal diuretic. These herbs help remove excess fluids and toxins from your body.

PART III: SPECIAL NUTRIENTS FOR SPECIAL PROBLEMS

These Skinny School nutrients are designed to help with problems that occasionally come up during a weight loss program. If you have any of these symptoms, you should also consult your physician before taking any of these supplements.

1. **Problem:** Fatigue, dullness, or depression.
   Solution: 500 mg. d,l phenylalanine (DLPA) twice a day, in the morning and evening. DLPA, as it is commonly called, is available at most health food stores.

   At Skinny School we call DLPA our Magic Pills, because their effect in restoring alertness and reducing depression is like magic. Magic Pills eliminate the kind of eating that you do to relieve depression—which is a *lot*.

   Magic Pills also reduce appetite, especially in sweet and starch cravers. DLPA is a chemical similar to the one found in chocolate, and often cures a chocolate craving *overnight*.

2. **Problem:** Weakness and lack of muscle mass and strength, especially in sweet and starch cravers.
   Solution: A combination of the following amino acids:

   300 mg. argenine
   300 mg. lysine
   225 mg. ornithine

   All these amino acids are available at most health food stores. At Skinny School we call this combination Tri-Skinny, because of its effect in building up your muscles and making you look skinnier.

   If you are a sweet and starch craver, you have spent your life eating too many refined carbohydrates—too much sugar and/or white flour. The excessive sugar in your bloodstream stimulates the production of insulin, which in turn causes your body to store fat. Insulin also counteracts another hormone called growth hormone. Growth hormone is responsible for growth in young people and for muscle strength and buildup in adults. If you don't have enough growth hormone, you will lack muscular strength and look flabby.

Tri-Skinny stimulates your body to produce growth hormone, and counteracts some of the negative effects of the insulin. It helps your body mobilize and burn fat, while at the same time encouraging the accumulation of lean body mass and muscle. In effect, you exchange fat for muscle.

3. **Problem:** Memory loss, mental fatigue, general reduction in mental energy. All cravings that come from a desire to have more mental or psychological energy.
   Solution: A combination of the following nutrients:

   500 mg. L-glutamine
   400 mg. choline bitartrate
   50 mg. inositol, in a base of lecithin

   All these nutrients are available in health food stores. At Skinny School we call this combination Brain Food®. L-glutamine is a general neurotransmitter used throughout the nervous system. Choline, inositol, and lecithin are nerve-cell nutrients that facilitate the utilization of the glutamine.

   The phenomenal effectiveness of Brain Food® in enriching brain function must be experienced to be believed. It generally takes about two weeks to work.

4. **Problem:** "Plateaus" in weight loss.
   Solution: A combination of the following nutrients:

   100 mg. vitamin B6
   50 mg. niacin
   50 mg. hypthalamic substance
   50 mg. trimethylglycine

   These ingredients are available in most health food stores. At Skinny School we call this combination our Plateau Pill. A plateau is defined as a time when your weight loss slows or stops for more than one week, even though your cravings are controlled and you are staying with your Skinny School Anti-craving Diet.

Plateaus are normal, and occur for several reasons. One reason is that as you lose weight, your new, lower-weight body needs less food to maintain its weight. The same amount of food that would let you lose weight when you were heavier is now enough to maintain your skinnier weight.

Another reason is that your body is becoming more efficient on the Skinny School program. Eating the right tastes and smells and curing your deficiencies make your digestion much more efficient, which is associated with longer life span. So again, you need less food to maintain your weight. In addition, it takes your body time to break through various "set points"—weights it has been programmed to maintain. Plateaus may occur for any of these reasons, or for a combination of them.

Plateau Pills work to help your body break through its set points. To break through plateaus caused by lower weight or a more efficient body, you also must eat less to adjust to your new, skinnier reality.

5. **Problem:** Headache, gnawing feeling in your stomach, or bad taste in your mouth between meals.

   Solution: Protein, fructose, or vitamin C tablets. All of these problems may come up when you first begin your Anti-craving Diet. They occur because you have been used to eating your craving foods, and are used to having something to help you last between meals. Reducing caffeine may also produce a headache for 3 to 4 days. Protein tablets, fructose tablets, or a good chewable vitamin C tablet will help. Most health food stores can help you with them. At Skinny School we use all of these, depending on your individual preference.

6. **Problem:** Hunger.

   Solution: Graded appetite controllers.

   Appetite control by means of mild appetite suppressants has a bad name in some circles. But there is ample new research that tells us that not only are mild appetite suppressants not bad, they are *positive* and helpful.

   Many Skinny School patients have told me that they understand the way the program works and have every intention of following the Anti-craving Diet, taking the supplements, and curing their cravings.

But, they say, they are *also* very hungry between meals and have a hard time beginning the program. For them I recommend a graded series of varying amounts of phenylpropanolamine (PPA).

PPA is a mild appetite suppressant that is available over the counter under various names (simply read the labels of the "diet" preparations in your drugstore). I recommend beginning with a dose of 25 mg. twice a day, taken before breakfast and before lunch. Look for the gradual-release kind. If this amount controls your hunger, simply stay with it. If not, you can gradually increase the amount until your hunger is under control. Do not go higher than 75 mg. of PPA twice a day. Be sure to check with your physician before taking PPA.

At Skinny School, I use a series of Grade Packs, which are supplement packs containing the foundation program of vitamins and minerals, and varying strengths of PPA. My nurses and I watch each patient and work with him or her to find exactly the right amount of PPA to control their hunger.

In greasy and spicy food cravers, PPA works to stimulate and reprogram the dopamine system (see Chapter 14) while it suppresses their appetite—the same effect that is achieved by Magic Pills in sweet and starch cravers. In other words, it has a balancing effect that is helpful.

Sweet and starch cravers also do well with PPA. In the Body Type books, I said that thyroid and pituitary types (who are sweet and starch cravers) should not take PPA for appetite control because it would be overstimulating. But subsequent research has shown that it is perfectly safe for them to take.

An occasional side effect of PPA is to increase hypertension; but again, recent research shows that this side effect is extremely rare and also very mild.

RETRAINING YOUR FOOD HABITS

A fascinating effect of taking PPA has recently emerged: the fact that taking it *facilitates retraining of your reward circuits*. The "reward circuits" are the circuits in your brain that reward you when you eat good food or do other positive, healthy actions.

All addictions work by "taking over" the reward circuits (see Chapter 5)—in other words, a food that you crave makes you feel "rewarded" even though it is not healthy or ultimately good for you. Taking PPA, by stimulating the dopamine system, contributes to a general sense of arousal that makes changing your food habits *easier*. It also helps any changes you make become *permanent* more easily.

For this reason, I recommend the Grade Packs as a valuable part of the Skinny School program. If you take the right amount of PPA for the first eight weeks on the program *while you are on your diet and taking your supplements,* you will make tremendous progress in curing your cravings.

Taking PPA will also make the food-behavior modification exercises— the "Lard" Lessons—that appear in the next chapter, easier and more effective. "Lard" Lessons are techniques for getting rid of those old eating habits you developed when you had cravings, and creating new reward circuits for your new, craving free self. They work, of course, all by themselves; but many patients find that the difference made by taking PPA is helpful. And the research bears this out: long-term studies (three years) on people who have taken PPA while dieting show that they actually do *better* at keeping off the weight they've lost than people who just dieted, without taking PPA.

14
THE "LARD" LESSONS

I had a delightful patient years ago named Lily whom I loved talking with whenever she came to my Beverly Hills Skinny School. One day she said to me, "You know, El, I'm doing really well with my cravings. I don't feel like I *need* that clam dip I used to dip into every night. But whenever I sit down to watch TV, I get such an urge to eat clam dip anyway. It's like TV equals clam dip. Can't you give me some lessons on how not to do that?" She looked down at her stomach in dismay, and added, "I've just *got* to get rid of this lard!"

From that moment on, we've always called our food behavior modification exercises "Lard" Lessons. A "Lard" Lesson is a way of looking at some of your old habits that have given you your extra pounds—and changing them for the better. In other words, *retraining your reward circuits*.

Habits develop under circumstances where they are appropriate. If, in the past, you *needed* sugar at five in the afternoon to get some tranquillity—some fake M-State—into your brain, then it made sense for you to get in the habit of stopping at the convenience store on the way home and picking up a candy bar. But once you don't need the sugar anymore, it's time to change that habit for something appropriate to your new, skinny self.

The trouble is, the act of buying a candy confers its own rewards. When you fork over your dollar, you are preparing your body with anticipation and preactivating the chemicals you will feel in your brain when you eat the candy. This is why we sometimes speak of anticipation itself as "delicious."

As long as these reward circuits are half lit up by anticipation, there will be a *behavioral* part of your craving that will still remain even when the *physiological* part of them is fully cured.

HOW TO TELL YOUR BRAIN YOU'RE SKINNY

Satisfying a craving is *rewarding*. It feels good. Even though temporarily and at a high cost, the foods you crave (or *used* to crave) give you a feeling that is pleasurable for you and has genuine survival value. This fact automatically creates a reward circuit for that food.

Reward circuits are actual, existing pathways in the way your brain is hooked up. Every animal has them. A goat gets them from eating junk, just as you do. Since you have established pathways in your brain, it requires additional work to reroute these pathways and create new ones, even though the *cause* of the reward circuit, the craving, is now gone.

The reward circuits in your brain run on a brain chemical called "dopamine." When you do something that you're in the habit of doing, your brain produces dopamine, and the dopamine fires off the "feel good" circuitry. These circuits are similar in all mammals—but what triggers them off is different. When a cow eats grass or a cat eats a mouse, the reward circuits are the same. When Lily sat down to watch TV, falling into her old habit of eating clam dip gave her the same sort of reward, even though she wasn't interested in the clam dip itself anymore.

In other words, she was ready to act like a naturally skinny person, but her brain didn't quite know it yet. The "Lard" Lessons are about getting the message to your brain that the old habits can give way to something better.

LOOSENING UP THE CIRCUITS

In the last chapter I discussed the recent finding that a chemical called phenylpropanolamine, or PPA, a common, over-the-counter appetite suppressant, is helpful in changing the dopamine reward circuits.

This effect of PPA is independent of its appetite-suppressing qualities. It appears that it makes your brain more malleable in some way. When you are taking fairly small doses of PPA (25 to 150 mg. per day), your brain becomes more "willing" to give up its old reward circuits and establish new ones.

Studies show that this effect, and the appetite-suppressing effect of the PPA, are *stronger for overweight people* than for skinny ones. Which is fine, since naturally skinny people are doing fine with their reward channels. Skinny people get as much reward out of their good eating habits as people with cravings get out of their bad habits.

ARE YOU READY?

Before you begin the Lessons, you should be sure that your cravings are *at least 50 percent controlled*. This means that you want your craving food half as often as you did when you began the program, or that your cravings are only half as strong as they were when you started Skinny School.

Don't try to do the lessons before that, or you will feel frustrated. You need this degree of freedom in order to make genuine inroads into your established reward circuits.

For most people, this point is reached after two to four weeks following the Anti-craving Diet and taking the Skinny School supplements.

LESSON 1: USE NOVELTY.

Novelty will help retrain your reward circuits. Eat in new situations to make eating a constantly new experience.

For example, I knew Lily always wanted clam dip when she sat down to watch TV in the evening; this was a habit, fixed in her brain by a dopamine-driven reward circuit. I told her that the whole *gestalt* of the habit hung together in her brain circuits: the TV, the chair she always sat in, the look of her room at night, even the old pair of jeans she always put on in the evening. So she could use *novelty* to change the habit simply by watching TV in a different room.

I asked her if she had another TV. She did—a little one in her bedroom. "Go in there," I said, "and watch it wearing your best silk negligee. Absolutely no jeans. Drink a good-tasting herb tea. Do everything differently. And very nicely. You'll have new reward circuits created in no time."

You can use novelty to change habits; you can also use it to increase satisfaction with your food. Eat your meals in novel situations—different rooms, outside, off plates you don't usually use. Research has shown that novelty increases the impact of anything you do. Patients who are given painkillers like morphine every day in the same situation quickly become tolerant to a dose and need more to get the same effect; but if you can change the situation in which it is given, the *same* dose of morphine will remain effective for *much* longer.

If you have a craving and can't help giving in to it, use novelty to keep the craving "unusual," and not let it become a fixed habit. If you used to eat Fritos in the kitchen before dinner, and you find you have to have a Frito, go eat it on the roof or in the bathtub. Always do it in a different place; your reward circuits won't know what to do. And you won't develop a tolerance for Fritos and need more each time.

LESSON 2: PUT DOWN YOUR FORK BETWEEN BITES.

After each bite you take, put down your fork. Actually let go of it and put your hand in your lap. This lesson is to learn to eat more slowly. You may not be aware how quickly you eat. The more overweight you are, the greater the chances are that you eat alarmingly rapidly. Naturally skinny people almost always eat very slowly. An informal study at Skinny School showed that the average meal is consumed in four to five minutes; six with dessert.

We're all busy, and fast eating of fast food is an American way of life. But remember that it takes about twenty minutes for the message to reach your hypothalamus that you have eaten enough food. If you've finished with your meal in five minutes, you will still feel hungry for fifteen more minutes, and will want to continue eating.

Putting down your fork between bites is a way of getting you to slow down. It will also help you taste. If you concentrate on each bite rather than on the next one, you have to experience your tastes more fully. So try to stretch each meal out to twenty minutes *minimum*. If you finish eating too soon, you must sit at the table until your twenty minutes are up, drinking hot water or herbal tea.

If you can begin eating more delicious meals more slowly, your food experience will change completely.

LESSON 3: PAY ATTENTION TO EATING.

Give your full attention to your meals, which are the main activity of your body at that time. In other words, don't eat while watching TV, reading, or listening to the radio intently. You can have on soft background music, but that's all.

Perhaps you eat breakfast with the morning talk shows, lunch over a magazine, and dinner with the evening news. You might even have special foods to eat with certain shows: like popcorn with *thirtysomething,* chocolate cookies with *L.A. Law,* or coffee with Regis. But even if you say you watch only PBS operas and nature shows, and eat only "health food" cookies, it still counts. Turn off the TV until you are *finished eating*.

What's wrong with TV, you might ask. Isn't it company? Why can't we have coffee and toast with Willard Scott, lunch in the *General Hospital* cafeteria, and a TV dinner with Dan Rather? Followed by ice cream with Olivia de Havilland on the late movie?

What's wrong is it's a way to be completely unconscious of what you're eating and oblivious to the taste, smell, and brain effects of your food.

Don't worry if this is a difficult lesson to do. Many people find it hard. I ask patients to try it for a week, but often it takes three or four weeks before they are even ready to give it a chance. People who live alone have an especially hard time, because they watch TV for company. But people who live and eat with their families have a problem with this, too, because it is such a fixed habit.

If you turn off the TV and your family just sits there in stunned silence, you should realize that you don't have to suddenly transform your family into the one you remember from *Leave It to Beaver*. Your offspring will complain, but don't mind. Just sit there. It's even okay to eat in silence; in fact, it's nice. Don't turn the TV back on just to get some conversation into the room.

When your family realizes they can talk if they want to, or just sit and enjoy their food, you'll know you've made a very positive change in all your eating habits.

LESSON 4: PAY ATTENTION TO YOUR BRAIN STATE.

Now that you're putting down your fork between bites, and you've turned off the TV and put away the magazines, what is it that you *do* while you're eating? Pay attention to your inner feelings and how the food you are eating is affecting them. In other words, pay attention to your brain state. That will tell you how the food is contributing to your M-State and exactly when you have had enough.

Since your fork is down, you're in a position to stop eating at any time. Check your feelings after every single bite. And when your brain tells you you're full stop. Don't swallow that last bite if it feels wrong. You'll feel better about yourself, because you are following your own best interests.

In the olden days you would eat until you felt full—maybe even until you felt stuffed. That's because it took a sledgehammer feeling to get through to you in your distracted way of eating. If you had been paying close attention to your brain state, it would have told you you were full long before you had eaten those last twenty bites, the ones that included the chocolate mousse cake.

Following this lesson may involve throwing away some food, at least at the beginning. We have all been taught to clean our plates, but if you want to stay in the Clean Plate Club, buy a spatula. You may have been in the habit of preparing more food than your brain and body really need. That's okay. Don't worry about it. The waste will only last for a few days—a couple of weeks at the max.

LESSON 5: CHANGE YOUR "RITUAL EATING."

"Ritual eating" is eating to mark off the passage of time or at fixed "occasions." It can be as simple as marking the halfway spot through the morning with a doughnut, or a more elaborate ritual, such as always having chicken soup whenever you see your daughter-in-law.

Whatever your eating rituals, you should look at them and change them to reflect what you've learned about cravings. Don't do away with the ritual itself; they're important. Vary the actual *eating* part of the ritual.

For example, if you mark your progress through the morning with a doughnut, you need to get rid of the doughnut but keep the satisfaction of being half done with your morning's work. You should take the break you're used to taking, but have some hot water, consommé, or herbal tea. Close your eyes and rest for a minute. Get some real M-State instead of doughnut-fake. Do everything except eat the doughnut. Remember, the doughnut isn't the reward, the break and the sense of completion are the reward.

If you and your daughter-in-law usually get together over food, look for something else to share to show your love. Hugs are good. Words of affection are good. Both are much less fattening than fat chicken soup.

LESSON 6: STOP IMITATING.

Stop imitating some other overweight person in your life. Being heavy like them is not proof of love.

This is a lesson in awareness that may lead to important changes in your behavior, and it is interesting for most people. We all look like someone; and many people are told from childhood that they look like, "are the very image of . . ." their mother, father, uncle, grandparent, or some other relative.

If you had this kind of conditioning, you may be making a conscious or unconscious attempt to *imitate* that person. This happens if you try to emulate them or become very identified with them.

It can become a problem, though, because the person you admire and identify with may be overweight. If your mother was heavy, you can become fat in the same way, with the same kind of habits and quirks. If she ate ice cream every day, you may find yourself doing the same thing. It can be a very powerful psychological habit, and it can be quite destructive. You may feel on a deep level that if you don't eat ice cream, you don't love your mother. Many people begin imitating after a loved parent has passed away, in an unconscious attempt to keep that person with them. Yet you can be different from your role model, and still love and admire them.

Your model may get sick and even die. People have been known to get the same diseases as their parent, and even to die at the same age as a parent died. This is not the same as genetics; you need to live out the full genetic potential of *your* life, which may be much longer and healthier than that of anyone else in your family. You do come from two sides of the family, not just one. You don't have the same genetic combination as *any* member of an older generation.

The way to do this lesson is to look at yourself (preferably naked) in the mirror and ask yourself who you see. Who do you look like? Is that person overweight or unhealthy? If so, consciously think that you can be different. It doesn't mean you don't love that person; you still love them, but you also love yourself.

Make a conscious practice of eating *differently* from that person. If your mother eats eggs every morning, you eat something else. Show your love by being yourself, and doing what you know is right for you. Taking good care of yourself is a sign of love.

LESSON 7: STOP "PREVENTIVE EATING."

Preventive eating is conditioned anticipation designed to ward off an uncomfortable craving. Because it is conditioned, it is a reward pattern that can continue even when your craving is gone.

Miss Piggy calls preventive eating "nipping hunger in the bud." You eat something not because you want it now, but because it's there now, and you might want it later.

You eat because you're going to be in the car for a while, and what if you get hungry? You eat because you're going to need your strength. You eat because you might be getting sick. You eat because you are planning to exercise, and you might get hungry in the middle.

To make this lesson work, give yourself permission to eat just what you want and are hungry for *now*. Tell yourself that if you are hungry later, you will definitely be able to find something to eat; later on can take care of itself. You won't be stranded in the jungle with nothing to eat. In our civilization, lack of food isn't the problem. It's the opposite.

LESSON 8: TRY A FASTING DAY.

Fast one day each week on just liquids. This is a change in behavior that you will find very rewarding. You may be afraid of fasting, but you'll find if you try it that a fast lasting one day is quite a pleasure.

Be sure to check with your doctor before fasting. Also, you shouldn't fast until you have been on the Skinny School program for four weeks. By that time your body will be running more like the body of a naturally skinny person—and they often skip meals without even realizing it.

Your fasting day can run either throughout the entire day (you skip breakfast, lunch, and dinner on the same day), or from afternoon to afternoon (you skip dinner the first day and breakfast and lunch the second day; some people find this easier).

Drink plenty of water (hot and/or cool) all day, along with herbal tea. Be sure to take all your Anti-craving supplements.

Fasting is a very liberating way to change old food habits. You acquire confidence that you don't have to eat constantly to live. "I skipped three meals and didn't die!" In some religions, fasting is associated with repentance, and perhaps it does provide a sort of antidote to old eating habits. Patients who have tried it usually love it. They always tell me how light and free they feel at the end of the fast.

Make your fasting day a resting day too, as much as possible. Fasting gives your body a real rest (digesting food is work). The lining of your digestive tract, the enzyme-secreting mechanism, the colon—all receive an opportunity to recover from what may be years of misuse.

Even though you will feel wonderful after your fast is over, you may find yourself uncomfortable during the fast. You may have occasional symptoms such as headaches, fatigue, and irritability, especially during the first few fasts. These symptoms are caused by substances you previously consumed (such as pesticides from food and toxic by-products of incomplete digestion) which your body couldn't deal with. These substances have been stored away in fat. When you fast, they enter your bloodstream on their way to being eliminated, and this causes the symptoms.

Drinking liquids during your fast will help. Resting will help even more. If your symptoms persist, you should see your physician and be checked. Do not fast more than a single day without being under the care of a physician, and even for a single day, check with him or her.

LESSON 9: PRACTICE COMMUNICATING ABOUT FOOD.

If you have been overweight, you may be very ashamed of your feelings about food. Talking about how you think and feel has big rewards.

You will find, as you become naturally skinny, that there are a few people in your life who are threatened or upset by your change. Lily told me that her husband, who had urged her to get rid of her "lard," started to get worried as she became skinny. He was a little insecure, and was afraid she might make him jealous.

People who are worried about your change may try to sabotage your eating. Lily's husband started pressing her to eat in the evenings with him, just as she was successfully changing her eating habits. She was angry at first, but then she realized that her husband had dopamine reward circuits associated with *her*. The sight of Lily companionably eating clam dip at his side was a habit of his that made him feel good. He needed her help to change that habit.

Lily started telling him openly what she was doing, and sharing with her husband how important it was to her to be skinny. And he soon became more supportive. She involved him in her progress, and he became interested in Skinny School as well. But to achieve this, Lily had to practice communicating.

She also had to practice with her mother. Her mother had a habit of having coffee and a danish with her whenever they saw each other. Lily had to practice saying no without hurting her mother's feelings. It wasn't easy, but she was able to do it, and now she and her mother just have coffee and enjoy each other even more than before.

LESSON 10: EXERCISE.

I don't believe in having my patients start exercising right at the beginning of Skinny School. If you are overweight and haven't exercised for a long time, you can hurt yourself by starting an exercise program when you aren't prepared.

But when you are ready, you will find that exercise is great. The pleasure of movement will create new, healthy reward circuits that will help you stay skinny. Exercise conditions your body and provides cardiovascular benefits. It also reduces stress and anxiety and improves your body's ability to maintain the benefits of the M-State during times of activity.

The best exercises are swimming, yoga exercises, and brisk walking. I have seen too many people with exercise-related injuries to be in favor of extreme, high-impact exercise. And studies show that gentler exercise in smaller amounts confers great benefits.

You should begin to create a routine of exercising for half an hour three or four times a week. I strongly recommend that if you want to do aerobics, you find an exercise class where the instructor has a lot of experience with people who are heavy or who are losing weight.

Everyone needs to be reminded to warm up by stretching before beginning to exercise, then go on to movement exercise and only then to aerobics. You also need to be reminded to cool down for at least five minutes after twenty minutes of exercise.

As for yoga, the best thing about it is that even though it isn't aerobic, it removes stiffness, increases flexibility, and enhances the M-State.

LESSON 11: STOP NONFOOD CRAVINGS TOO.

Stop smoking, excessive drinking, and taking any recreational drugs. If you are doing any of these things, you will find that the same things you have learned in Skinny School about food cravings will help you stop them as well.

Take a moment to look back at your M-State substitution score on the Cravings Analysis Checklist. If your score is more than 50, you have a tendency to make substitutions for the M-State, and both smoking and drinking are good examples of M-State substitutes. Both are highly addictive.

Studies have shown that as little as one alcoholic drink per week (this includes just one glass of wine or a single beer) significantly increases anger and depression in women. It may be that you are ready to stop drinking entirely. Many people who have become naturally skinny have done this, and feel very good about it.

LESSON 12: CULTIVATE A NEW IMAGE.

You have permission to release yourself from the bondage of the old you and be your new self.

Lily said one day, when she was almost finished with the lessons she had inspired, "You know, everything I do that's like what skinny people do helps me stay skinny."

I realized that she was telling me that she constantly reinforced her new image of herself as a naturally skinny person. Among the things she did was to take pictures of herself at every ten-pound interval, wearing her cutest outfit. She started to buy sexier clothes than she used to; she painted her toenails and showed off her feet and legs in sandals; and in general she simply acted the way she saw confident, skinny women act.

She completely stopped talking about dieting (skinny people never do), and she tried to forget totally how many calories anything had. Whenever the word "calorie" came into her mind, she said to herself, "Yes, but what does that food taste like? Is it good? Do I want it?"

Everything she did for her new image actually created new, pleasurable reward circuits in her brain. She gave up the habit of being heavy, got real satisfaction rather than fake M-State from her food, and acquired an unbreakable habit of being skinny. She had completed Skinny School.

15

QUESTIONS AND ANSWERS: FOLLOWING THE SKINNY SCHOOL ANTI-CRAVING PROGRAM

Skinny School is different from every other diet program. You aren't allowed to count calories—but suddenly you have to pay attention to taste and smell and choose only food that tastes and smells good. You're supposed to meditate for the M-State, and are required to notice your feelings. You don't eat specified portions or weights—but must judge everything by the size of your fist. Is this weird, or what? Yes, maybe, but very interesting.

The most radical difference of all is that your cravings for foods that aren't on the diet—the shameful little secret on every other program—are suddenly the very center of the Skinny School approach. Instead of ignoring what you crave, or trying to beat your cravings into submission by force, you're told to pay close attention to your cravings, become aware of them, listen to them—and treat them so that they are cured.

If you're like my Skinny School patients, you have *questions*. This chapter gives you the answers to my most commonly asked questions; we should cover yours. If not—feel free to write. We do answer. Write to Skinny School, 355 East Beach Avenue, Inglewood, CA 90302, or call us at (800) 622-4449. We'll either help you ourselves, or refer you to one of the physicians across the country who use the Skinny School program in their medical practices.

I understand there are doctors around the country who use the Skinny School system. I don't think I have a doctor in my area who has a Skinny School, but I do want to do the program. Is there any problem? Can I find the vitamins and other supplements I need to cure my cravings anywhere else?

You can follow the complete program from this book. Here's what you do. First, follow the steps of the Cravings Analysis Checklist to discover your cravings. Then, when you know what you crave, go into the best health food store in your area with this book in your hand. Go down the list of the supplements I recommend for your cravings. Pick out what you need.

You may need to buy several different types or brands of vitamins to get everything you want, but keep on looking until you have put together the complete program.

You may have a little trouble finding all the trace minerals I recommend. Many vitamin/mineral tablets do not have selenium, vanadium, or silicon. Keep looking until you find these minerals. Some multimineral tablets have them. Also, if you are a sweet and starch craver, do not be content with less than the recommended amounts of magnesium, manganese, chromium, or zinc, as these are vital in curing your craving. *Read the labels carefully*.

If you have trouble finding any of the supplements, call or write to Skinny School, and we will try to assist you in your search.

Also, look for the supplements that cure any special problems you have with dieting. Be sure to take your supplements while you are following the right diet for your craving.

If you were attending a Skinny School, we'd work with you from week to week to make sure we had uncovered all your cravings and brought them under control. So you should be attentive to yourself each week, and be sure to notice what foods you are craving.

When you are satisfied that your cravings are coming under control, start in on the "Lard" Lessons, to help you change any old habits or behavior patterns that your cravings might have created in you.

THE MEDICAL SETTING

Everything we would do, and everything you need, is in this book. The only differences between this book and the Skinny School office program lie in a few procedures that just can't be done outside of a medical setting. A physician would supervise your weight loss from a medical point of view. You should be sure to get your physician's okay to follow any diet in any case.

One thing we do at Skinny School that is strictly medical in nature is that we help our patients with a weekly injection of a few vitamins that aren't absorbed as readily by mouth, along with some extra minerals for cravings. These injections are helpful, but not absolutely necessary. You can have complete success without them.

We have squeezed the benefits of the injection into the supplement program in Chapter 13. Perhaps with the injection the cravings will be cured a bit more quickly. Also, we've found over the years that the injection helps patients with their energy while they are dieting. The injection also helps burn fat.

In addition to the regular weekly injection, Skinny School also uses a special injection to burn fat from specific locations such as thighs and rear. These are called Spot Shots®, and they can be taken only under special circumstances—when your cravings are controlled and you've lost most of your weight but still have "pockets" of fat on your body.

Since we can't give you the injections, I've used every possible avenue to give you all the benefits of the program. I've come very, very close. Except for the fact that I don't see you each week, and that I can't prescribe anything that is strictly medical, I've given you the complete Skinny School program. Nothing has been held back. It's just up to you to use it on yourself. I've given you all the results of my decades of research and practice, and if you use it in your own life, I feel absolutely confident you will get the results you want.

I'm really excited about the Skinny School program, but I have one problem. I eat out a lot, and I just don't know how I'm going to be able to eat all this great-tasting, fresh, natural food with the right tastes and smells. Any advice?

My first piece of advice is to choose restaurants where you can get fresh, delicious food. This doesn't have to mean very expensive places. It simply means that you can and should choose your restaurants with *taste* in mind. Remember, it's your body, and your brain, and what you choose to feed it with is vital to your health and weight, not to mention your peace of mind.

In California, many restaurants pride themselves on freshness. I know we Californians are considered nutty by some, but—what can we do? We like fresh, natural food, and with our abundance of fresh fruits and vegetables all year, it's possible to indulge that taste.

But anywhere in the country, salads can be found on the menu year-round. If you're eating out, it's a good idea to order a salad for your first course. Ask for oil and vinegar or lemon to be brought to the table, and dress the salad yourself. Start with the oil, and use just enough to coat the salad vegetables lightly. If there is any oil in the bottom of the bowl, you used too much.

Then, after you've tossed the salad with the oil, sprinkle a little vinegar or lemon juice, and toss again. You can use just a *touch* of salt and pepper, or bring your Spice Mix. Do this rather than using so-called "diet" dressings, which are much too heavy.

The salad will take the edge off your hunger, and you'll be in a much better position to choose the foods you really want from your Anti-craving Diet. With the Skinny School Anti-craving Diets, you have a tremendous range of foods to choose from; and remember, the basis of your choice should be taste.

SWEET AND STARCH CRAVERS EAT OUT

If you are a sweet and starch craver, remember to choose protein foods that are sweet and vegetables and grains with an astringent or pungent/peppery taste. A good choice in a restaurant is a small, spicy pasta dish accompanied by a sweeter fish or chicken dish.

Your biggest problem comes at the beginning and the end of the meal. The beginning problem is the bread basket. You should take a roll if you want one (you don't have to finish it), but then ask to have the rest of them removed. This is the time to ask for hot water and whip out an herbal tea bag. Sip your tea and you'll never miss the extra bread.

The end problem is dessert. If you've chosen your tastes correctly, you may not want or need anything sweet, but if you do feel you need something, it's better to order something than to go home feeling deprived and eat an entire box of Oreos. Ask for a fresh fruit dish, or cooked fruit such as baked apple, stewed figs or prunes, or the ever-popular sorbet. And yes, you can even split a sorbet.

GREASY AND SPICY FOOD CRAVERS AT THE RESTAURANT

For greasy and spicy food cravers, a good restaurant meal should be a light but spicy protein dish (a simply broiled piece of fish, chicken, or meat) with a sweeter grain dish on the side.

Your worst temptation will be to order a typical restaurant-type dish that you don't usually get at home because it's too much trouble to make, like beef Stroganoff or some other grease-over-meat concoction. Avoid it by eating a piece of bread or a bread stick before your sweets-craving companion sends away the bread basket. The sweet taste of bread will calm you down and reduce your craving for something greasy.

QUANTITY

Whatever your cravings, quantity of food in restaurants is always a problem. Unless you eat in very expensive places, you almost always get more than you need. It's ironic that the more expensive the restaurant, the smaller the portions they serve.

We have a restaurant in Santa Monica that is equally famous for the deliciousness of its food and the minute size of its servings. This fits in very well with Skinny School. If food is very delicious, you feel satisfied with much less—it's the magic of good tastes and smells and the satisfied brain state they give you.

But less expensive restaurants often serve huge portions. Another restaurant in my area is locally known as "a lot for cheap." It must have another name, but no one uses it. Its fame rests on the size of its portions. I can hardly advise you to stay away from places like that (I've been there myself), but it's best to stay out of them until you've been following your Skinny School program for at least four weeks. By this point your cravings will be controlled enough to handle the quantity of food you'll be given; but before this point your cravings may go wild.

But if your cravings are controlled enough to give you some free will, here's a tip for you. Eat half the meal and ask for a doggie bag, and eat the rest for lunch the next day—if you still feel like it then and if it still smells good. This is plenty of food, so don't be embarrassed. You can throw it away yourself if you don't want it the next day.

I guess I can never eat fast food again, right?

Oh, come now. Let's get real. You, I, and everyone else eats a meal in a fast food restaurant once in a while, so it's best to have a strategy in mind when you do.

Here is your best bet: First, choose a place that uses a grill rather than fries the burgers. Then, order a fish sandwich, chicken sandwich, or hamburger. Do not have the "meal deal," whatever the bargain price. When your sandwich comes, first throw away the top slice of bread. Then throw away (or don't order) the "special sauce," the tartar sauce, or whatever goopy grease comes on top of the sandwich. Finally, blot the sandwich with a napkin.

Eat slowly, chew, and enjoy. Notice the first and second tastes. Just because it *comes* fast doesn't mean you have to *eat* it fast.

My question is about snacking. I know you've built a midmorning and a midafternoon snack into the Anti-Ccaving Diets. But what happens if I freak out? What if I come home and have an incredible desire to start eating something unauthorized, at some unauthorized hour? What should I do?

First of all, you should take note of what it is that you want at these "unauthorized" times, because these are definitely your craving foods. Be sure to follow all the recommendations in this book to cure your craving. If you're going to a Skinny School, you should be sure to tell the nurse about them.

Then, give yourself a break by remembering that it takes four to eight weeks to cure cravings, and everyone has an occasional lapse, so don't feel too guilty. You are still normal.

To limit damage on a serious craving attack, try this:

1. *Drink some water.* Many times you are feeling discomfort from thirst, and that makes you think you need food. This is especially true in the late afternoon. Drink a full glass of room-temperature water, even two glasses. If it's cold out or you feel particularly stressed, try hot water, which is extra-comforting.

2. *Try to rest.* Take your glass of water, go to the couch, and sit down. You'll be out of the kitchen, and you'll be giving your system a chance to right itself naturally and even kick into the M-State. Which is what you're trying to achieve with the snack.

3. *Let yourself have your feelings.* If you have just come into the house after doing battle in the world (this is when most craving attacks strike), you might be trying to keep from feeling something (frustration, anger, depression) by eating the craving food. Keep in mind that it's okay to feel that way, and that if you do feel the feeling for a little while, it will go away by itself.

4. *Feel your body.* Many people find that if they feel particularly frustrated or aggravated, it helps to sit down, close their eyes, and feel what is happening in their body. Usually there will be some sensation somewhere. Simply feel the sensation for a few minutes. You will find that it will change and become less intense. If you take the time to do this, it will surprise you how much less craving you feel.

5. *Make a little noise.* It also helps to let out your aggression by beating your feet on the floor, hitting a pillow, or in general do something physical. Try not to scare the children, but if you do this, there's a good chance you may not have to eat.

6. *Have some fruit.* If you know you're prone to craving attacks (and who isn't?), be sure to have fruit available at all times. Even if you've already eaten your official half piece of fruit from the diet, it won't be the end of the world if you eat another half bunch of grapes. And by the way, buy the *smaller* fruit at the market. The giant fruit

are usually mushy. Use your nose to select, not your eyes. That way, when you have an attack, you'll just have a small, tasty piece of fruit around.

7. *Less is more.* If you get really desperate and nothing has worked, keep this in mind: If you have a craving and you can't resist it, try to actually satisfy it with the least damage to your diet. If you have to have something sweet, remember Dr. Wurtman's research finding that you don't get any more of those calming brain chemicals out of more than an ounce and a half of chocolate. Have that much, stop, and wait for the effect, which will come within ten minutes. It's a short enough time, but you can get through a lot of chocolate in ten minutes if you don't wait!

If you are desperate for something spicy-rich, again, know that a small amount of fat will give you all the brain effects you are going to get out of it. So don't send out for a large pepperoni pizza; make a piece of toast and butter it *lightly,* eat, and wait. You'll feel better, and you will have practiced effective damage control. But remember— this is only for when you've tried everything else first, not permission to pig out whenever you want to.

Doctor, I've read both of your previous books, the ones on Body Type. I'm a total Thyroid Type; I feel like you had to know me personally to write those sections. I did great on the Body Type Program, too—lost my fifteen pounds and I've kept them off. But now I'm reading all about the Skinny School program and the cravings cure. Is there any conflict between body types and Skinny School?

No conflict at all. They are different angles, but my vision of your health and your body's innate ability to be naturally skinny is at the heart of both of them.

The Body Type Program looks at weight control (and many other health issues as well—see *Dr. Abravanel's Body Type Program for Health, Fitness, and Nutrition*)—from the point of view of differences among people. People are different; that is the great discovery of the Body Type Program, and it has helped many people figure out why their diets have gone wrong in the past, and how to find the right one for themselves.

Knowing your Body Type tells you what you were born with. It's about your individual type of metabolism, the one built into your genes. It gives you a strong indication, too, of what foods you are most likely to crave, based on your genetic makeup. From this angle it is very valuable, and if you haven't yet become familiar with your Body Type, you may want to do so.

The Skinny School program is not so much about *differences* as about *what all cravings have in common*. Your Body Type is just *part* of the picture of your cravings. It tells you about the way your glands are involved in cravings, but doesn't cover the entire story of cravings.

BODY VS. BRAIN

One of the causes of your cravings is that you are trying to stimulate your dominant gland. You're a Thyroid Type, and you've been working with the Body Type Program, so you know that when you eat sugar or starch, or drink caffeine drinks, you are stimulating your dominant thyroid gland. This makes you feel (temporarily) better: more alert, calmer, better able to deal with stress. It gives you a fake M-State. It seems to revive you—though at a tremendous cost, because you end up exhausting your thyroid gland.

The effect on your body is what the Body Type books were about. The effect of craving foods on your *brain* is what this book is about.

When you use thyroid-stimulating foods to get the fake M-State, in time you will develop a craving for those foods. If you weren't a Thyroid Type you would have chosen different foods to use to increase your calm and alertness. And with a different choice of foods, a different craving would have developed.

If you were one of the other types—an Adrenal Type, a Pituitary Type, or a Gonadal Type—you would have chosen other foods: greasy or salty foods if you were an Adrenal Type, dairy or fruit if you were a Pituitary Type, or spicy/greasy food if you were a Gonadal Type.

The foods you would choose would be different—and Body Types explain the differences. But the *way* you'd be using your craving food would be the *same*. The Skinny School program is about cravings and brain states, the basic mechanics of which are the same in everyone.

I understand that these two programs are complementary and relate to each other. But I don't know which one to go on! I bought your first two books but I never went on the program. I guess I wasn't ready to

*lose my weight yet. Should I go on the Body Type Diet now, or should
I do the Skinny School program?*

You should follow the Skinny School program. The principles of
dieting that I have developed in my two million patient visits at Skinny
School are the most comprehensive diet thinking that exists anywhere in
the world today. Using taste and smell to balance your own food intake,
analyzing your cravings and curing them with food and targeted supplements, and changing your food habits with the "Lard" Lessons—these
are the principles of weight control that will help you the most.

*And if I already have done well on the Body Type Program? Should I
change to Skinny School?*

If you've lost weight and balanced your metabolism with the Body
Type Program, what you should do is add the vital Skinny School
concepts to the way you think about weight control.

Taste and smell must become part of your life. Go for the best tastes,
the most satisfying and freshest food, the most natural food you can
find. If you're at your best weight, you don't need the Skinny School
program for weight control, so you can stay with your Body Type
maintenance program—just make it even more delicious.

Use the Food Lists in the Appendix of this book to help you make
substitutions in your body type diet. If you want to be a vegetarian, use taste to make the right substitutions for the protein sources in
your diet.

Also, use your Anti-craving Spice Mix to add the right tastes to your
diet. Pituitary and Thyroid types should use the Sweet and Starch Cravers
Spice Mix. Adrenal and Gonadal types should use the Greasy and Spicy
Food Cravers Spice Mix.

If you do this, you'll notice how accurate the Body Type Diets are.
You'll find that when you are using taste and smell, you'll naturally
want the foods that are on your Body Type Diet. And if you have
questions about any of the foods, use the guidelines of taste and smell
from Skinny School to make your decisions.

*The Skinny School cravings analysis has helped me with something I
always wondered about on the Body Type program. I am a Gonadal Type
woman, and I do mainly crave spicy Thai food, but I also have
cravings at times for sweets. I wasn't sure why I would have a sweets*

craving if I was trying to stimulate my dominant gland with greasy and spicy foods. Why do I?

This is one of the questions that I, too, felt was not fully resolved by the Body Type Program. Such questions are behind my ongoing research at Skinny School.

Part of the reason that you have a secondary sweets craving is that all human beings have an *intrinsic*, slight craving for the sweet taste. It is genetically built in, and goes back to the taste of mother's milk, which is sweeter than cow's milk and is intended as our first food. It may also be related to our backgrounds as food gatherers. This is one reason that greasy and spicy food cravers often have a secondary sweets craving.

Also, you may be creating a fake M-State in yourself with a mosaiclike approach. You use oils to feel stronger and more stable, but you added some of the sugar effects to your fake M-State in order to feel more of the tranquillity that sugar gives. So you have a secondary sugar craving.

Your Body Type tells you your main craving, but you can also have other cravings as well. I like the flexibility I get with my Skinny School approach in dealing with people like you, who have multiple cravings. I cure the main craving with diet (you'll be on the Greasy and Spicy Food Cravers Diet), but then I can use Skinny School nutritional supplements to cure your sweets craving.

Is there a difference between the Body Type vitamins and the Skinny School nutritional supplements?

If you remember from my Body Type books, the vitamins I recommend for each Body Type actually come from Skinny School. If you've taken Body Type vitamins, you know that special supplements like Brain Food and Magic Pills are Skinny School supplements.

The Skinny School supplements are even more *targeted* than the Body Type vitamins. At Skinny School, you take just what you need to cure your cravings. The basic program is more streamlined than the Body Type Program, and then you add supplements to cure specific cravings. But for the most part, my recommendations are the same.

I hope you know, Doctor, that if I follow your recommendations I'm going to end up changing my entire life-style. I haven't cooked for years; I've heated things up, but that's different, I think. What tips do you have for cooking that will help me ease back into real food?

My first tip is, set aside some time. Shopping, cooking, and eating all take time and are supposed to take time. They are inherently enjoyable as long as you aren't too rushed to appreciate them, and they are part of the process that will give you the satisfied brain state you need out of your food.

Ideally you should shop every few days and buy just enough fresh food for those days. Frequent markets where the produce is good; make this your priority, even over price. Often the pricier markets have better produce for more money, but you'll make up the difference in what you save on those crummy cookies you used to buy, and on waste (the bad strawberries at the bottom of the box, etc.).

Once you have all this lovely fresh produce at home, my next tip is to learn to stir-fry. This is the Oriental method of quickly cooking fresh vegetables, seasoned with spices and a small amount of animal protein or tofu, in a teaspoon or so of hot oil. It works with all kinds of vegetables and all kinds of meat, and it doesn't get monotonous because you are always changing the ingredients. The complete directions are in the recipe section; I just want to add that you might find it more fun if you invest in a real wok. Regular frying pans work, but woks are especially good for stir-frying because the round bottom concentrates the heat in a smaller area for quicker, faster cooking.

Stir-frying a handful of vegetables and a chicken breast (skin on), and making some brown rice on the side, hardly takes longer than "heating up," as you put it. It's quicker than getting dressed and driving to a restaurant. And it will make you feel very good.

I'm very ready to go on the Skinny School program, but I'm wondering one thing: How will I know when I'm actually at my ideal weight? I've never actually believed in those height-weight charts, and I'm just not sure how much I'm supposed to weigh.

You're right about the weight charts. I have a collection of them, from insurance companies, medical texts, and magazines, and they are hardly definitive. Many have you in heels, dressed—how much do your clothes weigh? Also, you're supposed to just somehow know whether you have a small, medium, or large "frame" (are you a picture?). We all like to think we have petite frames when buying clothes, but large ones when we check the weight charts. What if we are wrong?

Here is a sample weight chart. Try to see if you can tell from this chart whether you are overweight or not.

Women Aged 25 Years and Over (in indoor clothing)

Height	Small frame	Medium frame	Large frame
5′0″	105–113	110–122	118–134
5′1″	108–116	113–126	121–138
5′2″	111–119	116–130	125–142
5′3″	114–123	120–135	129–146
5′4″	118–127	124–139	133–150
5′5″	122–131	128–143	137–154
5′6″	126–135	132–147	141–158
5′7″	130–140	136–151	145–163

Do you see what I mean? Take a woman of 5′4″—an average height. If she weighs 150 pounds, she is pretty round, even if she does have on "indoor clothes" (in what climate?) and has a "large frame." In Beverly Hills, she'd consider herself definitely overweight, if not obese. Most of the women who come to Skinny School are not obese—or even extremely overweight. But according to this chart, she is at her right weight, as is a woman of the same height who weighs 118. Is this helpful?

Since the charts are useless, we might try looking to scientific research; but here again the results are inconclusive. There are studies showing that a very low body weight is healthy, but there are also studies showing that, especially in older people, it is beneficial to be a little heavier. Smoking throws a curve into all the studies, because people who smoke are generally a little lighter, and a good deal unhealthier, than nonsmokers. Again, there are no clear-cut guidelines.

If you feel that you are overweight, you probably are, but feelings can mislead—think of the young girls with anorexia nervosa who are convinced they are obese when they are tragically thin. Also, some cultures in this country value thinness very highly—too highly. Fortunately, there are other American cultures in which a more relaxed and reasonable standard is maintained.

Your right weight also depends on your Body Type. Generally, Adrenal and Gonadal types have a higher "best weight" than Pituitary or Thyroid types.

Tables, Body Type, numbers, your culture, how you look, your health—all are factors in determining your best weight, but no single one is conclusive. The bottom line for you is how you feel and function.

So, the answer is, *your best weight is the one at which you look and feel your best*. It is the weight at which you don't worry about yourself, and at which your mind feels at peace. To find it, cure your cravings with the Skinny School program, and follow your Anti-craving Diet. Let your body gradually adjust to the satisfied feeling it will have on this program, and let your weight gradually come down by itself. When you reach your best weight, you will know. You will look good, but know that if you went lower you would not look as good. People will tell you, and you'll know it yourself.

Doctor, I know in your other books you gave specific exercises for each of the four Body Types. Are there special exercises to cure each of the different cravings?

I'll answer your question, but first you need a little background on the way exercise works in curing cravings. Exercise is not an unqualified good; it must be placed in the right context if it is to be really useful, healthy, and in your best interests. You'll notice that even Jane Fonda has modified her views in recent years.

I have long been against my patients just going out and starting an exercise program, because I have seen too much of the negative consequences—and I don't want them to happen to you. The most common effect of exercise is simply that by choosing a form of exercise that doesn't relate to your needs, you simply abandon it. Despite the fitness "boom" (or fad), the majority of people who have problems with food still don't exercise; most have started programs, sometimes many times, but haven't stayed with it. This is a pity, because it promotes a negative self-image ("I have no willpower, I just can't stay with anything . . ." and so on), and doesn't get you any benefits.

OVEREXERCISING

The other negative result, which is actually at the opposite extreme, is that a small percentage of people get too caught up in their exercise, and begin to use it as an M-State substitute. Exercise can be addictive, and if you start using it to get a fake M-State, you aren't any closer to a cure than you were before.

Overexercising also produces a lot of injuries. If you're using exercise for the "high," you'll tend to keep right on even though your muscles, back, or joints are protesting that they've had enough. It's just one more example of the way cravings lead you away from your best interests.

Even noncompulsive exercise still carries a risk of injury, and at best gives you a trade-off between increased fitness and increased wear and tear on your body. And if you are overweight, the risk is greater, the wear and tear on your joints more pronounced. The books on exercise all say to "get your doctor's permission before starting this program," but who ever does? Besides, what is the doctor going to say? "Sure, but take it easy," right? So most people just put on the leotards, get out there, and, all too often, do themselves more harm than good.

NATURAL EXERCISE

This doesn't mean you shouldn't exercise. It simply means that before you start, you have to do a little thinking. Engage brain before donning leotard.

If exercise carries dangers, so does inactivity. Being a couch potato has many more risks than just the chance of falling off the sofa. Your heart and lungs, your circulation, your digestion, even your mood, are improved by physical activity; this has been extremely well documented.

But there is, actually, something unnatural about *just* exercising. It has a rather pointless feeling about it. If I drive down San Vicente, a major jogging thoroughfare here in Santa Monica, I can't help wondering where all these people are running to in the smog.

Our bodies didn't evolve around aerobics classes any more than they evolved around taking vitamin supplements. In the natural environment, vitamins come in food, and exercise comes in activity.

The author Laurens Van der Post tells of seeing bushmen of the Kalahari Desert run literally for days, as tirelessly as gazelles, in pursuit of food. It's a long way from this effortless, natural running and what I see on San Vicente. The bushmen are running as part of their job, as it were—for a purpose. The people on San Vicente are adding exercise to their day because their jobs give them no chance to be physically active.

You do need to exercise—but it should go along with an effort to become more active in your life itself. Exercise alone fills only a partial function. Your body and mind will respond in a more integrated way to purposeful activity than to nonpurposeful activity. So have a purpose.

In practical terms, here are some strategies to give point to your exercising:

1. If you walk or run, go somewhere. Walk to the store or to a friend's house. Or, if you have nowhere you need to go, head for a special tree a mile away or a house in your neighborhood with a pretty flower garden. Or go bird-watching, or fly a kite. Don't just run up the street and back, or round and round the track.
2. If you do aerobics or work out in a gym, dance. Don't just jump up and down; relate to the music and to your inner feelings. Feel your body and relate to what it is doing.
3. If you play a sport, enjoy it. Don't just work out, play to excel. And remember, it's supposed to be fun.
4. And while you do these things, also think about bringing more real activity into your life. Leave the car at home as often as you practically can. When you go to the mall, park at the far end of the lot, and never use a "disabled" space. Buy a bike and ride it. Walk. Move around. Get rid of the remote.

Go out into your vegetable garden and dig. This has two benefits: tastier vegetables and excellent exercise. One study actually showed that working in a garden several times a week had as many health benefits as aerobic exercise.

THE BEST EXERCISES

To choose the best exercise for you, keep in mind:

1. If you are a sweet and starch craver, your main need is to increase your endurance and relieve your tendency toward depression.

   To achieve these goals, your best exercises are ones that require sustained energy output: walking, running, aerobics, sports like swimming.
2. If you are a greasy and spicy food craver, your main need is to increase your flexibility and coordination, relieve your anxiety, and blow off excess steam.

   To achieve these goals, your best exercises are ones that require good eye–hand coordination and make use of strong bursts of concentrated energy: tennis, basketball, Ping-Pong, jazz dancing, karate, and racquetball.

16

BEYOND THE
CRAVINGS CURE

I had a strange experience while I was finishing this book. I went into a bookstore here in Los Angeles called the Bodhi Tree that specializes in books that most people would call *weird*. The Bodhi Tree sells books from the East, tomes full of ancient wisdom, treatises on Chinese and Tibetan and Indian philosophy, books on American Indian medicine— strange and very interesting books of that kind.

I consider the Bodhi Tree a valuable resource. My own research draws on many branches of learning, including ancient medical systems. Hence I drop by the Bodhi Tree at times to buy, for instance, a copy of the *Charaka Samhita,* Charaka's ten-thousand-year-old textbook of Indian medicine. (It's relevant today, by the way.) But there in the Bodhi Tree, among many a quaint and curious volume of forgotten lore, I saw, of all things, my Body Type books.

I felt pleased even beyond the pleasure writers always feel on seeing their books out there on the shelves instead of in a barrel labeled ''Books Near Fifty Cents.'' Because seeing it there told me that the transcendental dimension that I always sense behind the seemingly all-too-physical subject of weight control was finding a response.

Whenever we eat, and certainly whenever we have a craving, there is a spiritual dimension as well as a physical one. I have alluded to it constantly throughout this book, but in this last chapter I want you to know that I consider it as important as the diet, the supplements, or the Food Lists.

Unless we make room for the need we all share for some inner spiritual feelings in our lives, we won't be able to understand what cravings are all about, and we certainly won't be able to proceed with a genuine cure.

THE SPIRITUAL ICEBERG

Those inexplicable, irresistible cravings that you and everyone else feel for "bad" foods, the same ordinary, everyday longings for your down-fall foods that have sabotaged so many of your diets in the past, are the tip of a huge spiritual iceberg. Beneath every craving is the universal longing to be in touch with deeper and more essential feelings of connection with your inner self and with the universe.

When I talk about the M-State, I am simply giving my own name to the most important experience of life. The most important point I want you to take away from this book is that if you don't have this experience, nothing else will really satisfy you.

Food certainly can't deliver the M-State—just a pale imitation. And we haven't been put on this planet just to feed our bodies anyway. We're here to unfold our consciousness and contribute to the moral fabric of our world.

I don't see any reason why you should take my word for this, but I do want you to ask yourself whether it makes sense, and whether it strikes a responsive chord.

THE CRAVING FOR LIFE

Many of the books in that "weird" bookstore seem to support this idea, that there is a connection between the longing for inner spiritual fulfill-ment and cravings of all kinds. The most effective of all self-help programs, Alcoholics Anonymous, says that addictions are basically cured by spirituality.

All seemingly "bad" habits and actions are easy to understand when you realize that they are attempts to feel better, stronger, and more a part of the universe. Our culture and way of life tend to devalue spiritual experiences, and so people are turning anywhere—especially to drugs of all kinds—to fill the void.

The term "M-State" is neutral and "scientific," and I chose it for that reason (this is a diet book after all), but inner experiences are also referred to in more poetic and romantic terms. Often they are called "mystical," meaning mysterious, although in reality they are quite comprehensible and only seem mysterious because we've been ignoring the inner side of life for so long. But whatever you call them, these kinds of experiences are vital to life.

I recently saw this quotation:

A civilization that denies the mystic is no civilization at all. It offers no hope and no adventure, no challenge worthy of sacrifice and joy to its youth or its artists. It offers no festivity, no sabbath, no living ritual to its people. And no deep healing. Such a culture actually promotes negative addictions: drugs, crime, alcohol, consumerism, militarism. It encourages us to seek outside stimulants to provide meaning for life and defense from enemies because it is so woefully out of touch with the power inside.*

THE BIOCHEMISTRY OF MYSTICAL EXPERIENCES

I was struck by this connection between addictions and the denial of inner experiences. Since I am a physician, I think in terms of what goes on inside the brain and the body and how it impacts on health and disease.

My contribution to the discussion of cravings (or addictions) here is to say that there is a biochemical connection between the brain state associated with inner calm and alertness (the M-State), and the brain state produced by particular foods. The biochemical similarity of these brain states helped me see that there is a link between such seemingly unrelated acts as eating chocolate and seeking inner fulfillment.

What happens in your brain is just a reflection of what is going on

*Matthew Fox, *The Coming of the Cosmic Christ*, quoted in the *New York Times Book Review*, January 15, 1989.

inside your mind (or your soul). Calling the M-State a biochemical event or a state of the brain doesn't make it more real or more "scientific." But it does seem to make it more acceptable in these skeptical times.

THE INNER GAME OF DIETING

Even though I developed Skinny School and consider it the best and most complete way to cure overweight, I would rather have you pay attention to my recommendation about the M-State and ignore my diet advice than the other way around.

I'd prefer that you do both. Skinny School has been thoroughly tested and it really works. If you take my recommendations seriously, and pay attention to the taste and smell of your food, you will find that the natural mechanisms of the chemical senses will make you naturally skinny.

Also, if you follow my supplementation recommendations, you will get over your deficiencies, and you will find your food cravings losing their intense hold on you.

But if you don't add the M-State to your life, you will continue struggling with some kind of cravings, because you won't have dealt with their real cause.

Many people who give up smoking gain weight for this reason—the craving has not really been cured, just transferred to something else. In the same way, people who lose weight without curing their cravings often find themselves shopping compulsively, or gambling, or taking pills, because they still need something to give them a fake M-State.

MEDITATION

So you must bring the M-State into your life. There are many ways. My own way is through practicing Transcendental Meditation, and I recommend it to all of you. But choosing your way of turning within is a personal decision only you can make.

I like TM, among other reasons, because it has been studied extensively; most of the studies done on meditation are actually about TM, and this gives me confidence that it's a technique that works.

But that doesn't mean other, less thoroughly investigated forms of meditation don't work; my educated guess is that most of them do. Exactly how much, I can't say.

If the thought of meditating is too strange, then don't call it that, but still take time for yourself. Begin to pay attention to your inner life, call it what you will. If you give yourself time, you're sure to find a way to get in touch with yourself, because it's you—your own self—and nothing is closer to you than that. And if you don't seem to be able to do it on your own, then go ahead and learn to meditate. You owe this to yourself.

Studies have shown that people who meditate regularly are much more likely to be at their best weight, and the truth is that most of them have never heard of Skinny School. Some TMers maintain their best weight on diets that I don't consider ideal. But since they don't have cravings, and they don't eat to create the fake M-State, they do fine. If you have the M-State, any reasonable diet will at least have a chance to work for you. But if you don't, no diet will be truly effective.

SKINNY SCHOOL GRADUATE WORK

Skinny School begins with the Anti-craving Diets, the supplements, and the "Lard" Lessons. But it doesn't end when you've reached your best weight. Your "graduate work" will continue.

As you continue with the program over time, a series of changes, gradual but predictable, will occur. Although some of these changes may seem distant and even impossible now, you should be aware of them so that as they occur you will have a sense that everything is happening the way it is supposed to.

The stages you'll experience are:

1. Weight loss and balancing
2. Weight loss and behavior changes
3. Principles, not program

THE BEGINNING DAYS OF SKINNY SCHOOL

The first stage, weight loss and balancing, begin when you start Skinny School. Your task is to first identify whether you are mainly a sweet and starch craver or a greasy and spicy food craver, and then begin the Anti-craving Diet for your main craving.

As you continue following the diet and taking the supplements you need, your weight will normalize.

But more important than the weight loss will be the regaining of your body's natural ability to regulate what and how much you eat. You will get used to *choosing* both the quantities and the kinds of food you eat, not by rule but by your feelings.

At this stage you will still be referring to the diets, the meal plans, and the Food Lists, but as you continue with the program you will learn to identify any food's value for yourself. This stage is complete when you are fully in touch once again with your tasting and smelling ability, and can choose the foods you need yourself without referring to this book.

This stage takes between four and eight weeks in most people, as long as you give it your full attention, follow the Anti-craving Diet for your main craving, and take your supplements.

AS YOU CONTINUE SKINNY SCHOOL

The second stage, weight loss and behavior change, begins in earnest when your cravings begin to be controlled. Depending on how much weight you want and need to lose, you may still be losing weight when you complete the first stage. But even if you do go on to lose more weight, it becomes much easier at the second stage, because of the ability you've acquired to choose the right foods to nourish and satisfy you.

At the second stage, food becomes your ally, not your enemy. You begin to be able to *use* food, rather than *being used by* your cravings and compulsions. Your cravings are no longer daily companions—but they may still pop up at this stage if you are under stress.

It's important to continue with the supplements at this time, *including your Anti-craving supplements.* If you stop taking your extra minerals or enzymes, your cravings will return quickly.

"I don't crave chocolate anymore," a patient who had been on the program about six weeks told me, "but every once in a while I get a sort of strong memory of my old craving. I start to think, 'A chocolate bar would be nice about now.' It's usually when I'm stuck in traffic, which I hate. But now I know what to do, and I don't feel so out of control. So even when my craving tries to get me back, I'm safe."

This is the stage to start the "Lard" Lessons. When your cravings stop pressing you so hard, you can begin to change the habits and routines you have that are destructive to your health and well-being.

At this stage, also, you will begin to see benefits from your M-State experiences. You will find that a calmer, restorative wind starts to blow gently through your whole life. The change is subtle. You might not notice anything beyond feeling less frazzled as you go about your daily round; very often it is *other people* who remark that you seem more relaxed, happier, less irritated.

It is a very good sign when you notice this, because it means that you are starting to feel the comfort that the M-State will give you—more and more as time goes by.

PRINCIPLES, NOT THE PROGRAM

This third stage arrives gradually; you may not even notice its arrival, but the change is definite and unmistakable. You will have lost all your extra pounds and been stable at your best weight for some time, usually six months to a year, sometimes more. You are well established with your M-State experiences. By this time you feel you would just as readily skip a night's sleep or your favorite music as you would your regular time to enjoy the M-State.

What happens at this stage is that you forget the program. You literally stop thinking at all about your weight, which (as my patients have told me) has been an obsession for years, sometimes for nearly an entire life. You don't have to follow the program anymore because it has become part of your life. You are still on it, though; it's just that you are using the principles for yourself.

If you eat foods you used to crave, it's because your own inner sense of what you need tells you to, not because you're "off the Skinny School diet." At this stage there is no diet; just the central principle of trusting and following your inner instincts.

You should continue with the foundation program supplements, but you may be able to stop your Anti-craving supplements. Many people continue to take Brain Food® at this stage, and others keep a supply of their Anti-craving minerals or enzymes on hand for times of food stress, such as holidays.

Remember, it may happen that stresses come along from time to time that are large enough to overwhelm your M-State and cause cravings. They will never be as bad as before, but it may happen under such strong stresses as losing a job. When we have our Big Earthquake in California, a lot of people may get their cravings back. But it will be temporary, because now you know what to do, and you *will* restore your balance and your cravings will depart again.

YOU ARE EVOLVING

Something important is happening at this stage. Time and the M-State are helping you to evolve. Your body is changing in a very positive direction under the influence of the M-State. Just as the biochemistry of the M-State has been studied in detail in the past twenty-five years, the changes that take place with regular experiences of the M-State are beginning, today, to be studied and understood in scientific terms.

What you will experience is a continuation of what you felt in the second stage: an increasing sense that the calmness and alertness you feel in the M-State are becoming part of your daily life.

The changes that take place are simply those changes that are necessary for your system to remain calm and alert (as in the M-State) along with activity. The studies that would show us all these effects are not yet available, but researchers such as Dr. Alaric Arenander have theorized that there is a gradual change in the neuroglial part of the brain.

Glial cells, the nutritive cells in the brain, are apparently central in

M-State experiences. Dr. Arenander suggests that the neuroglial cells gradually "learn" to retain their M-State activation even while the neural brain is busy processing all your activity.

THE FEELING OF CONSCIOUSNESS GROWING

More important than what is happening in the brain is what you feel like at this stage, and what the effects of the M-State continuing into activity are. The feeling is that inner calm coexists with all your activity. It will make you feel much more creative, as well as more "centered" and more in control of your life.

You'll feel more inner freedom and sense of personal stability that frees you in a very real sense. When you have this sense of inner calm, you will never be able to become addicted to anything. You will have moved beyond the reach of all addictions.

The Euphoria Scale that you saw in Chapter 6 appears again on the next page. This time I have drawn in a new set of axes with a new starting point to illustrate the way you will feel at this point in the program. As you change, your natural state of calmness and alertness becomes greater, reflecting your new higher level of M-State, so the various things that you might have used to change your inner state don't have anything at all to offer you. You are already beyond what they can give. The substances that fall in the shaded area no longer have any charm for you. As time passes, the shaded area in the chart will become greater.

Even before you began the program, you were probably beyond the reach of many addictions. For instance, if you already sleep well, you can never become addicted to sleeping pills. There is no lack in your life for them to fill. You already have more restfulness than they can give you. So you are beyond that addiction.

In the same way, if you become calmer and more alert than sugar, coffee, or cigarettes could make you, these substances will never have the same hold on you again.

Yet those things that are natural and healthful for you actually grow with you as you change. The M-State is the best example: As you become calmer and more alert, the M-State continues to give you even

15. EUPHORIA SCALE II

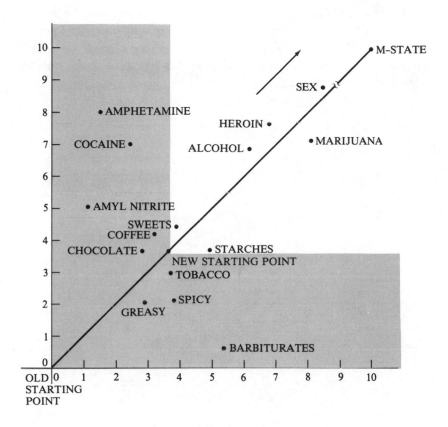

If you look at the Euphoria Scale after your brain has developed some ongoing M-State, an interesting thing happens.

At the beginning you started out at the old starting point on the scale as a reference. From there everything looks good to you because it raises either your arousal level, or increases your relaxation, or both. From this point you're always looking up. But once the M-State gets established, you have a new starting point and many of the things that looked good before and which you could have craved are now in the "gray zone" below and behind. So their effect is now negative and the chances of craving them are zero because they reduce even your *fake* M-State.

What used to be a euphoriant is now a dysphoriant—it makes you feel worse.

The more M-State you have in your life the more your 0,0 moves up and to the right, leaving all the things you craved far behind. That's how you finally cure cravings.

more of a sense of inner peace. You grow, but it grows too, because it is a natural part of who you are.

In the same way, Skinny School will grow with you. You will always eat. The more you grow and evolve, the more pleasure you will be able to take from everything you eat—yet the less will any food be able to have a power over you. You will move into increasingly greater fields of inner power, happiness, and peace, and I will take great joy in the thought that my weight control program has played a small role in helping you along that path.

APPENDIX

FIRST TASTES

The Food Lists below give the *first taste* of the most common foods. Use the lists to make the right choices in your Anti-craving Diet. Within six to eight weeks you will not need these lists because your tasting ability will grow and you will be able to determine the tastes of foods for yourself.

Each list gives you the *basic taste* of the type of food—for example, proteins are *basically* astringent, grains are *basically* sweet. Then, within each category, the foods are listed beginning with the *sweetest* food of that category and ending with the *most astringent* food in that category.

1. Meat/Protein List
Basic taste: astringent

The list begins with the sweetest protein and goes to the most astringent.

Sweet and starch cravers should choose proteins beginning at the *sweet end of the list*.

Greasy and spicy food cravers should choose proteins beginning at the *astringent end of the list*.

(Sweet end)
beef
lamb
shellfish
tofu (fried)
pork
tofu (raw or steamed)
fish
eggs
chicken
squab
(Astringent end)

2. Dairy List

Basic tastes: astringent and sour

The list begins with the sweetest dairy foods and goes to the most astringent.

Sweet and starch cravers should choose dairy from the *sweet end of the list*.

Greasy and spicy food cravers should choose dairy from the *astringent end of the list*.

(Sweet end)
eggs
cheese
whole milk
skim milk
goat's milk
yogurt
(Astringent end)

3. Oil List

Basic taste: umami

The list begins with the sweetest oils and goes to the most astringent.

Sweet and starch cravers should choose oils from the *sweet end of the list*.

Greasy and spicy food cravers should choose oils from the *astringent end of the list*.

(Sweet end)
corn oil
sunflower oil
olive oil
safflower oil
sesame oil
(Astringent end)

4. Legume List
Basic taste: combination of sweet and astringent

The list begins with the sweetest legumes and goes to the most *astringent*.

Sweet and starch cravers should choose legumes from the *sweet end of the list*.

Greasy and spicy food cravers should choose legumes from the *astringent end of the list*.

(Sweet end)
black lentils
red lentils
peas
garbanzos
kidney beans
mung beans
(Astringent end)

5. Nut List
Basic taste: combination of sweet and astringent

The list begins with the sweetest nuts and goes to the most astringent.

Sweet and starch cravers should choose nuts from the *sweet end of the list*.

Greasy and spicy food cravers should choose nuts from the *astringent end of the list*.

(Sweet end)
almond
cashew
peanut
sunflower seed
walnut
pumpkin seed
(Astringent end)

6. Grain List
Basic taste: sweet

The list begins with the sweetest grains and goes to the most astringent.

Sweet and starch cravers should choose grains from the *astringent end of the list*.

Greasy and spicy food cravers should choose grains from the *sweet end of the list*.

(Sweet end)
pasta (noodles, spaghetti, macaroni, etc.)
potato, sweet
potato, white
corn
white bread
white rice
millet
whole wheat
whole wheat bread
whole wheat crackers
oats
toasted grains—only granola without nuts
brown rice
barley
buckwheat
rye
(Astringent end)

Note: the following are *equivalent* servings of grain. Each one is considered to be one "grain exchange." Modify the amounts according to the amount you can hold in your fist.

bread, one slice
dry cereal, one cup
all grains, ½ cup cooked
tortilla, one
white potato, one small
sweet potato, ½
pasta, ½ cup cooked

7. Vegetable List
Basic taste: Vegetables may be sweet, sour, pungent, or astringent.

Whatever you crave, you may eat *any* vegetables that are fresh and in season. No vegetables are forbidden.

Sweet and starch cravers should eat more astringent vegetables, and greasy and spicy food cravers should eat more sweet vegetables.

Also, sweet and starch cravers should eat more cooked vegetables than raw, and greasy and spicy food cravers should eat more raw vegetables than cooked.

Sweet vegetables:
beets
carrots
sweet potatoes
onions (cooked)

Sweet/astringent vegetables:
broccoli
cabbage
cucumber
zucchini

Sweet/sour vegetables:
tomatoes

Astringent vegetables:
spinach
sprouts

Pungent vegetables:
onions (raw)
garlic
radishes

8. Fruit List
Basic taste: sweet

The list begins with the sweetest fruit and goes to the most astringent.

Sweet and starch cravers should choose fruit from the *astringent and sour end of the list*.

Greasy and spicy food cravers should choose fruit from the *sweet end of the list*.

(Sweet end)
dried fruit
coconut
melon
banana
peach
pear
pomegranate
apple
grapes
plum
fig
tangerine
orange
grapefruit
lemon
(Astringent end)

9. Spice List
Basic taste: pungent

The list begins with the most pungent/sweet spice and goes to the most pungent/peppery. Cinnamon is the sweetest spice and cayenne pepper is the most pungent.

Sweet and starch cravers should choose spices from the *sweet end of the list*.

Greasy and spicy food cravers should choose spices from the *most pungent end of the list*.

(Sweet end)
cinnamon
allspice
cardamom
coriander
saffron
turmeric
sesame seed
fenugreek seed
poppy seed
anise
cumin
ginger
black pepper
cayenne pepper
(Pungent end)

10. Herb List
Basic taste: pungent

The list begins with the most pungent/sweet herb and goes to the most pungent/peppery. Basil is the sweetest and garlic is the most pungent.

Sweet and starch cravers should choose herbs from the *sweet end of the list*.

Greasy and spicy food cravers should choose herbs from the *pungent end of the list*.

(Sweet end)
basil
thyme
dill
oregano
cilantro
parsley
garlic
(Pungent end)

11. Sweetener List
Basic taste: sweet/bitter

The list begins with the sweetest sweetener and goes to the least sweet. I do not recommend artificial sweeteners. If you must have something, sweet and starch cravers should choose aspartame. Greasy and spicy food cravers should not take any artificial sweeteners but should use sugar in very small amounts.

(Sweetest)
white sugar
maple syrup/sugar
brown sugar
molasses
(Least sweet)

FIRST AND SECOND TASTES

Food	First Taste	Second Taste
MEATS		
alligator	sweet	sweet
beef	sweet	sweet
chicken	sweet/astringent	pungent
fish/seafood	sweet	sweet
lamb	sweet/astringent	sweet
pheasant	sweet/astringent	pungent
pork	sweet/astringent	sweet
rabbit	sweet/astringent	pungent
squab	sweet/astringent	astringent
squirrel	sweet/astringent	sweet
DAIRY		
cheese (unsalted)	sweet/sour	sweet
milk	sweet	sweet
eggs	sweet/astringent	pungent
goat's milk	sweet/astringent	sweet
yogurt	sour/astringent	sour

Food	First Taste	Second Taste
OILS		
butter (unsalted)	umami/astringent	sweet
coconut oil	umami	sweet
corn oil	umami	sweet
ghee (clarified butter)	sweet	sweet
oil (general)	umami	sweet
safflower oil	umami/pungent	pungent
sunflower oil	umami	sweet
white mustard oil	umami/pungent	pungent
sesame oil	umami/bitter/astringent	sweet
SWEETENERS		
aspartame	sweet/bitter	bitter
honey	sweet/astringent	bitter
maple syrup	sweet/bitter	bitter
saccharine	sweet/bitter/salty	bitter
sugar	sweet	sweet
LEGUMES		
black lentils	sweet	sweet
garbanzos	sweet/astringent	sweet
kidney beans	sweet/astringent	sweet
lentils (general)	sweet/astringent	sweet
mung beans	sweet/astringent	sweet
red lentils	sweet/astringent	sweet
soybeans	sweet/astringent	sweet
VEGETABLES		
beets	sweet	sweet
broccoli	sweet/astringent	pungent
cabbage	sweet/astringent	pungent
carrot	sweet/bitter/astringent	pungent
cauliflower	astringent	pungent
celery	astringent	pungent
cucumber	sweet/astringent	sweet
lettuce	astringent	pungent
okra	sweet/astringent	pungent

Food	First Taste	Second Taste
onion (raw)	pungent	pungent
potato	sweet/salty/astringent	sweet
radish	pungent	pungent
spinach	astringent	pungent
sprouts	astringent	sweet
tomato	sweet/sour	sour
zucchini	sweet/astringent	pungent

FRUITS

apple	sweet/astringent	sweet
banana	sweet/astringent	sour
coconut	sweet	sweet
fig, fresh	sweet/astringent	sweet
grapes, purple	sweet/sour/astringent	sweet
melon (general)	sweet	sweet
orange	sweet/sour	sweet/astringent
peach	sweet/astringent	sweet
pear	sweet/astringent	sweet
plum	sweet/astringent	sweet
pomegranate	sweet/sour/astringent	sweet

HERBS/SPICES

aniseed	pungent	pungent
black pepper	pungent	pungent
cardamom	sweet/pungent	sweet
celery seed	pungent	pungent
cinnamon	sweet/bitter/pungent	sweet
clove	pungent	pungent
coriander	pungent/astringent	sweet
cumin	bitter/pungent/astringent	pungent
fenugreek seed	bitter/astringent	pungent
garlic	pungent	pungent
ginger	pungent	sweet
mustard seed	pungent	pungent
saffron	sweet/astringent	sweet
salt	salty	sweet
sesame seed	sweet/bitter/astringent	pungent
soy sauce	sweet/salty/astringent	sweet
turmeric	bitter/pungent/astringent	pungent

Food	First Taste	Second Taste
GRAINS		
barley	sweet/astringent	sweet/pungent
white rice	sweet	sweet
brown rice	sweet/bitter	sweet
buckwheat	sweet/astringent	sweet
corn	sweet	sweet
millet	sweet	sweet
oats	sweet	sweet
rye	sweet/astringent	sweet
wheat	sweet	sweet
NUTS/SEEDS		
almond	sweet	sweet
cashew	sweet	sweet
peanut	sweet/astringent	sweet
pumpkin seed	sweet/bitter/astringent	pungent
sunflower seed	sweet/astringent	sweet
walnut	sweet/astringent	sweet

RECIPES

These recipes are used in the meal plans for the Sweet and Starch Cravers Diet (Chapter 11) and the Greasy and Spicy Food Cravers Diet (Chapter 12).

SWEET AND STARCH CRAVERS VEGETABLE SOUP

This soup uses vegetables with *astringent* tastes, which are balancing and reduce your cravings. The soup also supplies minerals to correct the deficiencies that lead to sweet and starch cravings. Use the freshest vegetables you can find—organically grown if possible. Or—grow your own. They will be tastier.

green beans   leeks
celery with tops   zucchini
parsley   green pepper

Cut vegetables into 1-inch slices. Use as much as you wish, using more zucchini and green beans than the other vegetables. Place in a pot with either water or chicken or beef stock from which you have previously removed all fat. (The best way to do this is by cooling the stock in the refrigerator until the fat hardens at the top, and then removing it.) Cook the vegetables until they are just tender—about 5 minutes. You may eat as is or puree in the blender if you prefer. Use salt and pepper to taste.

GREASY AND SPICY FOOD CRAVERS VEGETABLE SOUP

This soup uses vegetables with *sweet* tastes, which are balancing and will reduce your cravings. Use the freshest vegetables you can find— organically grown if possible. Or—grow your own. They will be tastier.

carrots	yellow squash
beets with tops	mushrooms
sweet onion	

Cut vegetables into 1-inch slices. Use as much as you wish, using more carrots and yellow squash than the other vegetables. Place in a pot with either water or chicken or beef stock from which you have previously removed all fat. (The best way to do this is by cooling the stock in the refrigerator until the fat hardens at the top, and then removing it.) Cook the vegetables until they are just tender—about 5 minutes. You may eat as is or puree in the blender if you prefer. Season with fresh herbs. Use only a tiny pinch of salt.

SWEET SPICE AND HERB MIX

This spice mix is to be used on protein foods by sweet and starch cravers. Greasy and spicy food cravers may use it on vegetables and grains.

cinnamon	dried basil
allspice	dried dill (leaves and/or seeds)

Mix equal quantities of the herbs and spices together and grind in a blender. Keep in a shaker and use whenever you wish.

PUNGENT SPICE AND HERB MIX

This spice mix is to be used on protein foods by greasy and spicy food cravers. Sweet and starch cravers may use it on vegetables and grains.

anise   dried cilantro (coriander)
ginger   dried parsley leaves
black pepper   onion powder

Mix equal quantities of the herbs and spices together and grind in a blender. Keep in a shaker and use whenever you wish.

SPICED BEEF WITH VEGETABLES

8 oz. flank steak, sliced ⅛ in. thick across the grain

Marinade: 2 T soy sauce
          1 t cornstarch
          1 T peanut oil
          ½ clove garlic, minced

Sauce: 1 t fresh ginger, minced
          1 T soy sauce
          1 T vinegar
          pinch of sugar
          1 t hot pepper, chopped
          ¼ cup water or chicken broth

1 T peanut oil, for frying   ½ cup celery, sliced
½ cup bamboo shoots, sliced   ½ cup onion, sliced

Stir flank steak in marinade mixture and let stand in refrigerator for several hours. Heat a wok or frying pan and heat half the peanut oil. Add the vegetables. Stir-fry for 2 minutes and remove from pan. Add remaining oil to pan and heat. Add the meat. Stir-fry until half done, add vegetables, and toss together until meat is cooked. Add sauce. Serves 2.

BROWN RICE

For one serving, take the amount of rice you can hold in your closed fist. Wash the rice carefully. Place in a saucepan with twice as much water as rice. Bring to a boil. Reduce heat, cover, and cook over a very low flame for about 45 minutes, or until all the water is absorbed.

BROILED SALMON STEAKS

juice of 1 lime   2 salmon steaks
2 t soy sauce

Preheat broiler. Combine lime juice and soy sauce. Put salmon on a baking sheet and baste. Broil for about 5 minutes on one side. Turn, brush again with marinade, and cook 5 minutes on the other side. This recipe is good with fresh tuna as well. Serves 2.

BRAISED SCALLIONS AND JERUSALEM ARTICHOKES

8 to 10 Jerusalem artichokes   sprig of fresh parsley, chopped
  (also called sunchokes)   2 T dry vermouth (optional) or
1 bunch green onions   chicken stock
1 T butter   salt and pepper

Steam the artichokes in the top of a steamer or boil in a quarter cup of water for 5 minutes. Meanwhile, trim the green onions. When the artichokes have cooled, peel them. Heat the water and butter together in a small frying pan and add the peeled artichokes and the green onions. Cook together for 5 minutes. Allow the vegetables to brown. Remove the vegetables and add the vermouth or stock, swirl it around in the frying pan for a moment, and pour it over the vegetables. Salt and pepper lightly. Sprinkle with parsley. Serves 2.

FRESH TOMATO SOUP

1 T olive oil
1 small pat butter
1 carrot, peeled and diced
1 stalk celery, chopped
½ large onion, chopped
4 large fresh tomatoes, peeled, or
  1 16-oz. can of tomatoes (fresh is
  preferable, but only if you can get
  tomatoes that have some taste—
  not easy)

sprigs of fresh parsley and basil
salt and pepper

Heat the oil and butter together in a heavy pot. Cook carrots, celery, and onion until tender. Add tomatoes and continue cooking for 25 to 30 minutes more. Stir in herbs. Salt and pepper to taste. Serves 2.

CALVES LIVER WITH HERBS

Liver is sweet in itself, and is very good for sweet and starch cravers when seasoned with fresh herbs. However, it is wise to search for organic meats in your health food store when serving organ meats.

2 T olive oil
1 onion, sliced
6 oz. baby beef liver (or calves liver),
  sliced less than ¼ in. thick

herbs to taste: a handful of dried sage,
  2 large sprigs of fresh rosemary,
  and a handful of fresh parsley are
  all good

Heat half the oil in a heavy frying pan, and cook the onion until tender. Remove from pan, and heat the remaining oil. Quickly toss the liver in the hot oil until golden brown, about 5 minutes. Do not overcook the liver, as this quick cooking will keep it very tender. Remove the liver from the pan and quickly toss the herbs and onion in the oil that remains in the pan. Spoon the herbs and onion over the liver. Serves 2.

SPICY TOFU WITH CHICKEN

This recipe and the one that follows are examples of the way you can use tofu as a protein food. This recipe includes chicken; the next one is vegetarian.

2 T peanut oil
1 garlic clove, minced
1 minced green onion
1 T fresh ginger, minced
2 cakes tofu cut into ½-inch squares
1 T soy sauce

¼ lb. ground chicken or turkey
½ t cornstarch
¼ cup chicken stock or water
½ t chili oil (optional—a peppery oil from Oriental markets)

Heat the oil in a wok or frying pan and stir-fry the garlic, green onion, and ginger briefly. Add the tofu, soy sauce, and chicken. Cover and cook for 3 to 5 minutes. Dissolve cornstarch in stock or water and add to the mixture. Sprinkle with chili oil. Serves 2.

STIR-FRIED TOFU (VEGETARIAN)

2 cakes tofu cut into small cubes
1 T peanut oil

2 green onions, cut into 1-in. lengths

Dipping sauce:
1 t chili oil
1 t Oriental sesame oil
1 T light soy sauce

1 T sesame seed paste (tahini) or peanut butter

Pat tofu cubes with paper towel to dry. Heat the oil in a wok or frying pan and stir-fry the green onions 1 minute. Add tofu and gently stir-fry until golden. This will take longer than you think. Serve with sauce. Serves 2.

CHICKEN BURGERS OR LENTIL BURGERS

1 lb. ground chicken or
  1 lb. cooked lentils

Seasonings:
Chinese plum sauce   salt, black pepper
soy sauce   fresh parsley
Hoisin sauce

Mix the seasonings to taste with the chicken or lentils. Form into 5 burgers and fry in a *small* amount of vegetable oil. You can also wrap these burgers and freeze them, then cook them in the microwave. Serves 5.

SPINACH AND GRAPEFRUIT SALAD

1 bunch fresh spinach   1 grapefruit, sectioned
  (washed carefully)

Dressing:
1 T white wine vinegar   3 T vegetable oil
1 T honey   1 T olive oil
juice of ½ lemon   2 T poppy seeds

Combine dressing ingredients. Toss together with spinach and grapefruit. Serves 2.

BARBECUED SHRIMP AND SCALLOPS

¼ lb. medium shrimp, peeled and   1 t chopped fresh cilantro (coriander)
  deveined   ¼ lb. scallops
juice of ½ grapefruit   juice of ½ orange
1 T safflower oil   1 t chopped fresh mint

Marinate the shrimp in a glass or stainless steel bowl with the grapefruit juice, half the oil, and the cilantro. At the same time, marinate the scallops in the orange juice, the rest of the oil, and the mint. Stir both mixtures, cover, and refrigerate for half an hour. Preheat the broiler. Alternate shrimps and scallops on skewers and broil for 2 minutes. Brush with marinade (you can combine the two together) and broil again until the shrimp and scallops are lightly browned. Serves 2.

STUFFED TOMATOES WITH OLIVES, RICE, AND TUNA

Note: Use this recipe only if you can get hold of some nice firm ripe tomatoes with *taste*. With the usual supermarket cardboard tomatoes, it won't be very good.

2 tomatoes	½ can tuna fish
salt	2 T chopped parsley
1 T olive oil	6 black olives, chopped
½ small onion, chopped fine	1 T capers, washed and drained
½ clove garlic, chopped fine	(optional, but they add astringency)
½ cup brown rice, cooked	Parmesan cheese

Preheat the oven to 375 degrees Fahrenheit. Slice off the tops of the tomatoes and scoop out the pulp and seeds, leaving a shell (your finger works great for this). Salt the insides of the tomatoes very lightly and leave them upside down on a paper towel to drain.

Heat the olive oil in a frying pan and cook the onion and garlic, stirring constantly, until onion is transparent. Add rice and tuna and cook, stirring, for several minutes. Remove from heat and add parsley, olives, and capers if you are using them. Spoon the mixture into the hollowed tomatoes and top with a tiny sprinkling of Parmesan cheese. Place in a baking dish and bake for 20 to 30 minutes. They should be tender but not limp, and the rice on top should be browned and crisp. Serve hot or cold, and sprinkle a little more chopped parsley on top. Serves 2.

CHICORY SALAD

1 medium head chicory

Dressing: (makes one cup; use 1 to 2 t per serving)

½ cup vegetable oil	1 T mustard
¼ cup olive oil	1 T honey
3 T white wine vinegar	salt and pepper to taste

Chicory is a slightly bitter green whose taste is very satisfying to sweets cravers. It helps cure your sweets cravings through taste balancing. Prepare the salad by washing and tearing the leaves. Blend the dressing ingredients together and toss with the chicory.

SPICY SESAME NOODLES

4 oz. buckwheat pasta

Dressing:
1½ T rice vinegar   sprinkling of sesame oil
½ T sesame paste (tahini)   1 T vegetable oil
1 T peanut butter   1 T orange juice
½ T honey mustard   2 green onions, slivered
1 T soy sauce   1 T roasted sesame seeds
1 t chili oil

Cook the buckwheat noodles in a large pot of water. Drain and cool off with cold water. Combine the dressing ingredients and whisk them together. Toss the noodles with the dressing, green onions, and sesame seeds. Serves 2.

ROMAN-STYLE SPINACH

1 bunch spinach, washed carefully   pinch of salt and pepper
2 cloves garlic, crushed   1 T vegetable oil
2 T pine nuts

Put washed but not dried spinach in a frying pan and cook until it collapses, stirring constantly. Remove to a colander and set aside. Heat the oil in the pan and brown the garlic, then remove it. Put the pine nuts in the oil and cook them, watching carefully, until they turn brown. Return spinach to the pan and cook a few more minutes. Season with salt and pepper. Serves 2.

POTATOES IN GREEN OLIVE OIL

3 red-skinned new potatoes   2 T green olive oil
3 white-skinned new potatoes   salt and pepper

In simmering water (not boiling), cook potatoes until just tender, about
10 minutes. Drain. Place in a serving bowl and drizzle with the olive oil.
Sprinkle with salt and pepper. Serves 2.

CABBAGE SOUP WITH LEEKS

4 small leeks   2 T olive oil
1½ cups red cabbage   2 cups chicken or vegetable stock
1 turnip

Set aside one leek and a half cup cabbage, and shred them very fine.
Chop the remaining leeks, cabbage, and turnip and saute in one tablespoon of the oil until tender, about 15 minutes. Add stock and simmer
30 minutes. Puree. Saute the shredded cabbage and leeks in the remaining oil for just three minutes. Stir into the pureed soup. Serves 2.

COFFEE EGGS OR TEA EGGS

4 eggs   available in Oriental food stores
2 T dark soy sauce   or Oriental section of grocery)
1 whole star anise (optional—   3 T tea or ground coffee

These eggs are simply hard-boiled eggs slightly flavored with coffee or tea.
But the preparation makes them extremely pretty and unusual. Prepare them
by hard-boiling the eggs for 20 minutes. When they are cool, drain and
tap the shells all over with a spoon, or else roll them around until the
shell is cracked all over. Then put them in a pan and cover with cold
water. Add soy sauce, anise if you are using it, and the tea or coffee.
Simmer slowly for 2 to 3 hours, then leave them in the liquid overnight.
Keep them, refrigerated, in their shells until you are ready to eat them,
at which point you peel them and admire your beautiful marbleized eggs.

CHICKEN WITH TOMATOES AND GREEN PEPPER

1 T olive oil
2 pieces of chicken, breasts or thighs
½ onion, sliced

1 clove garlic, minced
3 large tomatoes
1 green pepper, sliced

Heat half the oil in a heavy frying pan and quickly brown the chicken for 5 minutes on each side. Remove from pan. Heat the rest of the oil and cook the onion and garlic until just soft. Add tomatoes and green pepper and cook for 5 more minutes. Add the chicken, cover the pan, and simmer together for 20 to 25 minutes, or until done. Serves 2.

GREEN RICE

1 cup of brown rice
2 T olive oil

⅓ to ½ cup each fresh chopped dill
    and parsley
1 or 2 green onions (optional)

Cook rice according to directions. When it is ready, place in a serving dish and add the oil and the fresh herbs. You can also add a chopped green onion or two, softened by cooking briefly in the oil.

RED PEPPER SOUP

4 red peppers
2 carrots
½ small onion
1 clove garlic
1 small pear

2 T olive oil
2 cups chicken or other stock
½ t dried red pepper
salt and pepper

Slice three of the peppers, the carrots, the onion, the garlic, and the pear. Cook in the oil in a large skillet until tender, 8 to 10 minutes. Add the stock, dried red pepper, and salt and pepper to taste and simmer, covered, for 30 minutes. Meanwhile, roast the remaining pepper over a gas flame or under the broiler, carefully turning it until it is blackened all over. Then put in a paper bag for 5 minutes. Wash off the blackened skin and remove seeds. Add half the pepper to the soup, and puree all of it in a blender. Cut up the remaining half of the roasted pepper and use it to garnish your soup. Serves 4.

BAKED RED SNAPPER WITH OLIVES

2 T olive oil
3 T capers (optional, but their strong taste is a good antidote to sweets or starches cravings)
2 T black olives, cut up into small pieces

1 t dried oregano or 1 T fresh oregano
black pepper
2 pieces of red snapper, mullet, or ocean perch, about ¼ lb. each one
1 T lemon juice
1 T chopped parsley

This dish can be prepared with any fresh, firm fish that looks good to you in the market—the ones mentioned are all good. Preheat oven to 425 degrees Fahrenheit. In a heavy ovenproof skillet, heat 1 T of olive oil and stir in the capers and olives. Remove and put in a small dish. In the same skillet, heat the remaining tablespoon of oil and add the oregano and a sprinkle of black pepper. Roll the fish in this, and place in the oven. Bake, basting the fish in the oil every 5 minutes, for 20 to 30 minutes, or until fish is done. Rewarm the caper and olive sauce, add the lemon juice and parsley, and brush over fish. Serves 2.

RATATOUILLE

1 small eggplant
1 medium-size zucchini
4 ripe tomatoes, hopefully with taste
½ red pepper, seeded
½ green pepper, seeded
½ yellow pepper, seeded

1 onion
1 clove garlic
2 T olive oil
fresh herbs: marjoram, thyme, oregano, parsley
salt and pepper

Cut all the vegetables into fairly large chunks; mince garlic.
   In a large casserole or skillet, heat ½ T oil. First saute onion and garlic for 5 minutes. Set aside. Take another ½ T of oil and saute the eggplant chunks for 5 minutes. Set aside. Keep cooking the various

vegetables in a small bit of oil, cooking each one separately and just until they begin to soften. When all have been sauteed, layer them in the casserole and sprinkle with the herbs and salt and pepper to taste. Cover and cook together over low heat until all are tender, about 20 minutes.

SAUTEED KIDNEYS

4 lamb kidneys, or one veal kidney   1 T parsley, chopped
1 T olive oil   1 T lemon juice
½ clove garlic   salt and pepper

Most of us are not familiar with kidneys; but they are not difficult to prepare and they are extremely helpful for sweets cravings. However, be sure to find organically grown lamb or calves. With a small sharp knife, carefully peel away the thin membrane that covers a veal kidney and cut away the knob of fat under it. Lamb kidneys do not need to be peeled. Cut them crosswise into very thin slices. Heat the oil in a heavy skillet. Cook the kidneys in the hot oil, stirring constantly, for 2 minutes. Add the garlic and parsley and continue stir-frying another minute or two, until the kidneys are browned. Pour in the lemon juice and let it boil up once, then turn off the heat. Season to taste with salt and pepper and serve at once. Serves 2.

EARLY SPRING SALAD

Choose a combination of these greens: dandelion, chicory, spinach, escarole, Swiss chard. Make a delicious, tangy dressing by combining a tablespoon of vinegar with two tablespoons of olive oil and a teaspoon of Dijon mustard. Toss the greens with the dressing and add a sprinkling of salt and pepper.

TOMATO, ONION, AND HERB SALAD

2 large ripe tomatoes, hopefully with   ½ mild red onion
   taste   sprigs of fresh thyme, parsley, or basil
2 T olive oil   1 scant T vinegar

Slice the tomatoes and onion and arrange on salad plates. Sprinkle with
fresh herbs and dress with oil and vinegar.

SAFFRON-BROILED CHICKEN

2 chicken quarters (either legs or   ¼ t saffron
   breasts), *skin not removed*   juice of ½ lemon
salt and pepper

Preheat your broiler. Put chicken on a foil-covered baking sheet and
sprinkle with salt, pepper, half the saffron, and half the lemon juice.
Broil for 8 to 10 minutes. Turn and season with the remaining lemon
juice and saffron. Broil another 8 to 10 minutes or until chicken is done.
Serves 2.

GRATED ZUCCHINI

1 T butter   nutmeg
1 clove garlic   salt and pepper
2 small zucchini, grated

In a heavy skillet, melt the butter and saute minced garlic until just soft.
Add the zucchini and toss in the garlic butter for just two or three
minutes, or until hot and tender. Season with nutmeg and salt and
pepper.

ROOT VEGETABLE SOUP

1 yellow onion
2 shallots
1 small leek
1 clove garlic
1 parsnip
1 large carrot
1 celery root (celeriac), if available
  (optional)

2 small boiling potatoes
1 turnip
2 T vegetable oil
3 cups chicken or vegetable stock
salt and pepper
fresh herbs: cilantro (coriander),
  parsley, or chervil

Chop all the vegetables into small chunks.

In a large, heavy saucepan, heat the oil and cook the onion, shallots, leek, and garlic until tender, about 5 minutes. Add the root vegetables and stock. Simmer until all are soft, about 35 minutes. Puree in a blender until smooth. Return to the pan and add water if the mixture is too thick. Heat through and season with salt and pepper to taste. Garnish with fresh herbs. Serves 2.

SOLE CEVICHE

1 lime
1 fillet of sole (about ½ lb.)
1 T white wine vinegar
1 clove garlic, minced
1 T walnut oil

1 T vegetable oil
fresh chives
salt and pepper
1 pink grapefruit, sectioned

Remove the zest (the green part) from the lime and set it aside. Squeeze the juice from the lime, strain, and save. Slice the sole thinly and put in a shallow dish. Combine lime juice with zest, vinegar, garlic, oils, chives, and salt and pepper to taste. Pour over fish and refrigerate 2 to 3 hours or longer (overnight is good). The lime juice and vinegar actually "cook" the fish, so it is ready to eat. This can also be done with scallops, as in a classic ceviche, or with other very fresh white fish. Arrange grapefruit sections on top when serving. The fresh tart tastes are very good cures for greasy food cravings. Serves 2.

TABOULI SALAD

1 cup bulghur wheat
1½ cups water
1 stalk celery, sliced
½ onion, sliced

fresh parsley
2 T olive oil
1 T lemon juice or vinegar

Bulghur wheat is a cracked wheat which is prepared much like rice. Place the bulghur in a pot with 1½ cups water, bring to a boil, cover, and cook for 15 to 20 minutes or until all the water is absorbed.

Cool the bulghur in the refrigerator, and then toss in a bowl with the sliced celery and onion, the parsley, and the oil and vinegar. Serves 4.

HERBED CORN ON THE COB

2 ears fresh corn, as fresh as you
  can get
1 T butter

fresh herbs: oregano, parsley, thyme,
  or a combination

Place the corn in rapidly boiling water and cook until just tender (5 to 10 minutes, depending on the freshness of the corn). Soften the butter and mix with the fresh chopped herbs. Serve with the corn.

THREE-CABBAGE COLE SLAW

Shred a combination of red, white, and green cabbage with two green onions and one shredded carrot. Toss with a dressing made of 1 tablespoon of mayonnaise flavored with a few drops of Worcestershire sauce.

GINGER-PEAR SOUP

3 ripe pears, peeled and cored
2 cups water
1 T sugar
1 vanilla bean

1 stick cinnamon
2 cloves
1 small slice fresh ginger
powdered ginger

Cook the pears in water with the spices until soft, about 40 minutes. Drain and save the pears; discard vanilla bean, cinnamon stick, and cloves. Puree the pears and ginger slice in a blender or food processor. Pour back in saucepan. Add 1 cup of the liquid, or just enough to get a souplike consistency. Heat over medium flame until just hot. Serve sprinkled with powdered ginger. Serves 2.

CURRIED CHICKEN WITH VEGETABLES

2 T vegetable oil
2 chicken thighs, with skin
1 onion, sliced
1 clove garlic

2 boiling potatoes, cut into cubes
2 large carrots
1 large tomato
1 teaspoon curry powder

Heat 1 tablespoon of the oil in a pan and quickly brown the chicken. Remove from pan. Cook the onion and garlic in the remaining oil, then add the other vegetables, the seasoning, and the chicken. Add a little water to the pan, cover, and cook until the chicken and potatoes are done—about 30 minutes. Serves 2.

MASHED SWEET POTATOES WITH TOFU

2 sweet potatoes
1 cup tofu, cut into 1-in. cubes
2 T vegetable oil

fresh thyme
salt and pepper to taste

Cook the sweet potatoes in lightly salted water for 20 minutes. Drain and place in the oven for another 30 minutes or until done. Halve the potatoes and scoop out the flesh. Mash it together with the tofu, leaving the tofu cubes mostly intact. Add the oil and the fresh thyme (you can use other fresh herbs if you prefer), and salt and pepper. Return to the potato skins and serve. Serves 2.

TOMATO AND MOZZARELLA SALAD

2 large ripe tomatoes with taste, sliced   1 T olive oil
1 large sweet onion, sliced   salt and pepper to taste
4 oz. fresh low-fat mozzarella, cut   sprigs of fresh basil
   into thin slices

Arrange the slices of tomato, onion, and mozzarella alternating on a plate. Sprinkle with olive oil, salt, pepper, and fresh basil and serve. This salad is found all over the Mediterranean in the summer, and is an extremely satisfying taste combination. But it works only with good tomatoes!

HERB-STUFFED TROUT

bunches of fresh herbs: sage, dill,   2 T safflower oil
   parsley, thyme, or combinations   lemon wedges
   of these
2 trout, frozen or fresh, boned but
   left whole

Place the bunches of fresh herbs inside the fish and tie them with bits of twine to hold the herbs in place. Heat the oil in a heavy frying pan and cook for about 5 minutes on each side, depending on thickness. Serve with the lemon wedges. This is an excellent way to add wonderful flavoring to fresh fish. Serves 4.

FRESH PEA SOUP

2 T vegetable oil
1 cup fresh peas (use frozen if fresh aren't available)
1 small head of lettuce, chopped
2 green onions

3 cups chicken or vegetable stock
salt and pepper
fresh herbs (tarragon, thyme)
yogurt (optional)

Heat oil in a pot and add peas, lettuce, and green onions. Cook over low heat for 5 minutes, but do not brown. Add stock, bring to a boil, reduce heat, and simmer 10 to 15 minutes or until peas are tender. Puree in a blender or food processor. Season with salt and pepper to taste and add herbs. If you wish, add a dollop of yogurt to heighten the fresh tart flavor.

GREEN ENCHILADAS

2 chicken breasts, with skin
2 T vegetable oil
½ small onion, chopped fine
½ lb. fresh spinach
1 cup yogurt

1 4-oz. can green chilies, drained and chopped
½ t cumin
4 flour tortillas
2 oz. low-fat Monterey Jack cheese

Preheat oven to 350 degrees Fahrenheit. Poach chicken breasts in a saucepan with just enough water to cover, about 15 to 20 minutes. (Save stock for use in making soup, if you wish, but be sure to refrigerate until fat has congealed on top, and remove the fat from the stock.)

Meanwhile, heat the oil in a skillet and saute the onion about 5 minutes. Add spinach to onion and saute briefly, then chop. Add yogurt, chilies, cumin, and a small amount of water to moisten the onion-spinach mixture. Shred chicken and add to *half* the sauce mixture. (Reserve the other half.) Soften tortillas in the oven for a few minutes, then divide the mixture among the tortillas and roll up. Place seam side down in a lightly oiled casserole dish. Cover with remaining half of sauce mixture and sprinkle with cheese. Bake 30 minutes. Serves 2.

WHITE BEAN SOUP

With most of the other recipes in this section I have been giving servings for two, but with a bean soup recipe it is worthwhile to make a large pot, as it is a certain amount of trouble, and the soup can be frozen very well for later.

1 pound navy beans	2 bay leaves
6 cups chicken stock	3 T olive oil
1 large onion, chopped	1 large head escarole
3 cloves garlic, chopped	salt and pepper

Soak the beans overnight, or boil for 3 minutes, discard water, boil again, and soak 1 hour. Simmer the beans in soaking water and stock with onion, garlic, and bay leaves until tender, about 1 hour. When beans are cooked add escarole leaves, separated into individual leaves. Simmer for 2 minutes and season to taste with salt and pepper. Makes 6 servings.

HALIBUT WITH LEEKS

1 T vegetable oil	2 fresh leeks, cut into thin strips
2 green onions	juice of one lemon
2 small halibut steaks, about 1 in. thick	salt and pepper

Preheat oven to 375 degrees Fahrenheit. Lightly oil a shallow baking dish. Sprinkle the dish with green onions and place the halibut steaks on top. Arrange leek slices over the fish, sprinkle with remaining oil, lemon juice, and salt and pepper to taste. Bake 10 minutes, remove from oven, and brush with baking juices. Return to oven and cook 10 minutes more, or until fish is done. Serves 2.

SPINACH-WRAPPED FISH FILLETS

2 fish fillets (such as fillet of sole)	lemon juice
salt and pepper	large, washed spinach leaves

Sprinkle each fillet with salt and pepper and lemon juice, and fold in half crosswise. Place in a steamer and cook 5 to 7 minutes. Remove and cool until you can handle them. Wrap each one in one or more spinach leaves, and secure with a toothpick. Return them to the steamer and cook just 2 minutes, until spinach is just tender. Serves 2.

BAKED PEPPER AND POTATO

8 spicy cherry peppers   1 T olive oil
4 small waxy potatoes   fresh marjoram, basil, or oregano

Preheat the oven to 450 degrees Fahrenheit, and lightly oil a shallow baking dish. Slice the vegetables thinly and arrange prettily. Drizzle the remaining olive oil over them and sprinkle with fresh herbs. Bake for 15 to 20 minutes, then reduce the heat to 400 degrees and continue baking until the potatoes are cooked and browned, about 15 minutes more. Serves 2.

NOTES

Chapter 3
Figure 3. Benefits of the M-State
1. Sugi, Y., Akutsu, K. (1968). Studies on respiration and energy-metabolism during sitting in Zazen. *Research Journal of Physical Education,* 12:190–206.

2. Wallace, R. K., Benson, H. (1972). The physiology of meditation. *Scientific American,* 226(2): 84–90.

3. Ibid.

4. Ibid.

5. Orme-Johnson, D. W. (1973). Autonomic stability and transcendental meditation. *Psychosomatic Medicine,* 35(4): 341–349.

6. Jevning, R., Wilson, A. F., VanderLaan, E., and Levine, S. (1975). Plasma prolactin and cortisol during transcendental meditation. *The Endocrine Society Program 57th Annual Meeting,* New York City, 18–20 June 1975, p. 257.

7. Kasamatsu, A., Hirai, T. (1966). An electroencephalographic study of the Zen meditation (Zazen). *Folio Psychiatry Neurology Japonica,* 20:315–366.

8. Banquet, J-P., Sailhan, M. (1974). EEG analysis of spontaneous and induced states of consciousness. *Revue d'Electroencephalographie et de Neurophysiologie Clinique,* 4:445–453.

9. Levine, P., et al. (1975). EEG coherence during the transcendental meditation technique. In D. W. Orme-Johnson, J. T. Farrow (eds.), *Scientific Research on the Transcendental Meditation Program, Collected Papers,* 1:187–207. West Germany: MERU Press.

10. Werner, O., et al. (1986). Long-term endocrinologic changes in subjects practising the transcendental meditation and TM-sidhi program. *Psychosomatic Medicine*, 48(1-2):59–66.

11. Wallace, R. K., et al. (1983). Modification of the paired H-reflex through the transcendental meditation and TM-sidhi program. *Experimental Neurology*, 79:77–86.

12. Pirot, M. (1973). The effects of the transcendental meditation technique upon auditory discrimination. Victoria, British Columbia, Canada: University of Victoria.

13. Pelletier, K. R. (1974). Influence of transcendental meditation on autokinetic performance. *Perceptual and Motor Skills*, 39:1031–1034.

14. Ibid.

15. Tjoa, A. S. (1975). Meditation, neuroticism, and intelligence, a follow-up. *Gedrag, Tijdschrift voor Psychologie* (the Netherlands), 3:167–182.

16. McCallum, M. J. (1975). *Meditation and Creativity*. Long Beach: California State University.

17. Blasdell, K. S. (1977). *The Effects of Transcendental Meditation upon a Complex Perceptual-motor Task*. Los Angeles: University of California.

18. Appelle, D. S., Oswald, L. (1974). Simple reaction time as a function of alertness and prior mental activity. *Perceptual and Motor Skills*, 38:1263–1268.

19. Frew, D. W. (1974). Transcendental meditation and productivity. *Academy of Management Journal*, 17(2):362–368.

20. Abrams, A. I. (1974). Paired associate learning and recall: a pilot study of the TM technique. Berkeley: University of California.

21. Collier, R. W. (1973). The effect of meditation upon university academic attainment. *Pacific Northwest Conference on Foreign Languages*, Seattle, Washington.

22. Reddy, M. K. (1976). The role of transcendental meditation in the promotion of athletic excellence: Long- and short-term effects and their relation to activation theory. In R. A. Chalmers, G. Clements, H. Schenkluhn, M. Weinless (eds.), *Scientific Research on the Transcendental Meditation Program: Collected Papers, Vol. 2*. Vlodrop, The Netherlands: MERU Press.

23. Hjelle, L. A. (1974). Meditation and psychological health. *Perceptual and Motor Skills*, 39:623–628.

24. Ferguson, P. C., Gowan, J. C. (1976). TM—some preliminary psychological findings. *Journal of Humanistic Psychology*, 16(3).

25. Seeman, W., Nidich, S., Banta, T. (1972). Influence of transcendental meditation on measure of self-actualization. *Journal of Counseling Psychology*, 19(3):184–187.

26. Goldman, B. L., Domitor, P. J., Murray, E. J. (1979). Effects of Zen meditation on anxiety reduction and perceptual functioning. *Journal of Consulting Clinical Psychology,* 47(3):551–556.

27. Orme-Johnson, D. W., Clements, G., Haynes, C. T., Badaoui, K. (1977). Higher states of consciousness, EEG coherence, creativity, and experiences of the sidhis. *MERU Report 7701,* Center for the Study of Higher States of Consciousness. Seelisberg, Switzerland: MERU Press.

28. Shapiro, J. (1974). *The Relation of the TM Program to Self-actualization and Negative Personality Characteristics.* Los Angeles: Department of Psychology, University of Southern California.

29. Benson, H., Wallace, R. K. (1972). Decreased blood pressure in hypertensive subjects who practice meditation. Supplement II to *Circulation,* 45 and 46:516.

30. Kita, Y., Yokode, M., Kume, N., Ishii, K., et al. (1988). The concentration of serum lipids in Zen monks and control males in Japan. *Jpn. Circ. J.,* 52(2):99–104.

31. Cooper, M. J., Aygen, M. M. (1979). Transcendental meditation in the management of hypercholesterolemia. *Journal of Human Stress,* 5(4):24–27.

32. Wilson, A. F., Honsberger, R., Chiu, J. T., Novey, H. S. (1973). Transcendental meditation and asthma. *Respiration,* 32:74–80.

33. Benson, H., Wallace, R. K. (1972). Decreased drug abuse with transcendental meditation: a study of 1,862 subjects. In Chris J. D. Zarafonetis (ed.), *Drug Abuse: Proceedings of the International Conference.* Philadelphia: Lea and Febiger, pp. 369–376.

34. Weldon, J. T., Aron, A. (1974). *The Transcendental Meditation Program and Normalization of Weight.* Fairfield, Iowa: Department of Psychology, Maharishi International University.

35. Miskiman, D. E. (1975). *Long-term Effects of Meditation on the Treatment of Insomnia.* Edmonton, Alberta, Canada: University of Alberta.

36. Ogata, M., Ikeda, M., Kuratsune, M. (1983). Mortality among Japanese Zen priests. *Journal of Epidemiology and Community Health,* 38(2):161–166.

37. Wallace, R. K., Jacobe, E., Harrington, H. (1982). The effects of the transcendental meditation and TM-sidhi program on the aging process. *International Journal of Neuroscience,* 16(1):53–58.

38. Toomey, M., Pennington, B., Chalmers, R., Clements, G. (1982). *The Practice of the Transcendental Meditation and TM-Sidhi Program Reverses the Physiological Ageing Process.* MERU Research Institute in Mentmore, Buckinghamshire, England, and Department of Biology, University of York, Yorkshire, England.

Chapter 5
Figure 9. References Real M-State vs. Fake M-State
1. Wallace, R. K., Benson F., and Wilson, A. F. "A Wakeful Hypometabolic Physiologic State," *American Journal of Physiology*, 221, no. 3 (U.S.A.: 1971) 795–799.

2. Farrell, O. J. "Changes in Metabolic Rate and Heart Rate During Meditation," *Proc. Nutr. Eoc. Aust.* 4:136.

3. Levine, P. H., Herbert, J. R., Strobel, V. (1975). "EEG Coherence During the Transcendental Meditation Technique." In D. W. Orme-Johnson, J. T. Farrow (Eds.): *Scientific Research on the Transcendental Meditation Program: Collected Papers, Vol. 1* (pp. 187–207). West Germany: MERU Press.

4. Banquet, J. P. (1973). "Spectral Analysis of the EEG in Meditation. *Electroencephalography and Clinical Neurophysiology* 35: 143–151.

5. Bujatti, M., and Reiderer, P. (1976). "Scrotonin, Noradrenalin, Dopamine Metabolites in Transcendental Meditation Technique," *Journal of Neural Transmission* 39: 257–267.

6. Walton, K. G., et al. " 'Substance M,' a Serotonin Modulator Candidate from Human Urine?" In Y. H. Ehrlich et al., *Molecular Mechanisms of Neuronal Responsiveness: A volume of advances in experimental medicine and biology.* Plenum Press, 1987.

7. Appelle, S. and Oswald, L. E. "Simple Reaction Time as a Function of Alertness and Prior Mental Activity," Perceptual and Motor Skills, vol. 38 (1974), pp. 1263–1268.

8. Blasdell, K. S. "Effects of the Transcendental Meditation Technique upon a Complex Perceptual-Motor Task." In Collected Papers, pp. 322–325.

9. Pelletier, K. R. "Influence of Transcendental Meditation on Autokinetic Perception," *Perceptual and Motor Skills* vol. 39 (1974), pp. 1031–1034.

10. Orme-Johnson, D. W. "Autonomic Stability and Transcendental Meditation," *Psychosomatic Medicine* 35: 341–349.

11. Williams, P. W., West, M. "EEG Responses to Photic Stimulation in Persons Experienced at Meditation." *Electroencephalography and Clinical Neurophysiology* vol. 39 (1975), pp. 519–522.

12. Wandhofer, A., Plattig, K. H. "Stimulus-linked DC-shift and Auditory Evoked Potentials in Transcendental Meditation." *Pfluegers Archiv.* (1973), 343, R79.

13. Banquet, J. P., Lesevre, N. "Event-related potentials in altered states of consciousness—Motivation and sensory processes of the brain." *Progress in Brain Research* (1980) vol. 54, pp. 447–453.

14. Maslow, A. H. *Toward a Psychology of Being.* New York: Harper and Row, 1968.

15. van den Berg, W. P., Mulder, B. "Psychological Research on the Effects of the Transcendental Meditation Technique on a Number of Personality Variables," *Heymans Bulletins*, Psychologische Instituten R. V., Groningen, N.R.: H.B.-74-147-*ex.*

16. Shapiro, J. "The Relationship of Meditation to Self-Actualization and Negative Personality Characteristics." Ph.D. thesis, Department of Psychology, University of Southern California, Los Angeles, California (1974).

17. Weldon, J. T. and Aron, A. "The Transcendental Meditation Program and Normalization of Weight." In Coll. Papers.

18. Sandman, C. A., Kastin, A. J., Schally, A. V. "Neuropeptide Influences on the Central Nervous System." In P. D. Hridina, Singhal, R. D. *Neuroendocrine Regulation and Altered Behavior.* New York, Plenum Press (1981).

19. Singhal, R. D., Rastogi, R. B. "Thyroid Hormone in the Regulation of Neurotransmitter Function and Behavior." In Hdrina.

20. Cox, B. M., Baizman, E. R. "Physiologial Functions of Endorphins." In J. B. Malik, Bell, R. M. S. *Endorphins*, Marcel Dekker, New York (1982).

21. Orme-Johnson, D. W. (1986). Reduced health insurance utilization through the Transcendental Meditation program. (Prepublication manuscript).

22. Wallace, R. K., Jacobe, E., Harrington, B. (1982). The effects of the Transcendental Meditation and TM-Sidhi program on the aging process. *International Journal of Neuroscience* 16(1):53–58.

23. Cooper, M. J., Aygen, M. M. "Effect of Transcendental Meditation on Serum Cholesterol and Blood Pressure." *Harefuah, the Journal of the Israeli Medical Association* (1978) vol. 95(1), pp. 1–2.

24. Shafii, M., Lavely, R. Jaffe, R. D. "Meditation and the Prevention of Alcohol Abuse." *American Journal of Psychiatry* Vol. 131 (1975), pp. 942–945.

25. Nutrition and Diseases. Parts 1–3. Hearings Before the Select Committee on Nutrition and Human Needs of the United States Senate. Washington: U.S. Government Printing Office, 1973.

26. Jeanes, Hodge (1975). Physiological effects of food carbohydrates. *ACS Symposium Series #15.* American Chemical Society.

27. Schandler, S. L., Cohen, M. J., McArthur, D. L. "Event-related Brain Potentials in Intoxicated and Detoxified Alcoholics during Visuospatial Learning." *Psychopharmacology (Berlin)* 1988; 94(2): 275–283.

28. Srinivasan, D. P, "Trace Elements in Psychiatric Illness." Br. J. Hosp. Med., 1984 Aug; 32(2): 77–79.

29. Dillbeck, M. C., Bronson, E. C. "Short-term Longitudinal Effects of the Transcendental Meditation Technique on EEG Power and Coherence." *International Journal of Neuroscience* vol. 14 (1981), pp. 147–151.

30. Orme-Johnson, D. W., Clements, G., Haynes, C. T., Badaoui, K. "Higher States of Consciousness: EEG Coherence, Creativity, and Experiences of the Sidhis." In D. W. Orme-Johnson, J. T. Farrow (Eds.): *Scientific Research on the Transcendental Meditation Program: Collected Papers, Vol. 1* (pp. 705–712). West Germany: MERU Press, 1977.

31. Clements, G., Milstein, S. L. "Auditory Thresholds in Meditation." In Collected Papers, pp. 719–722.

32. McEvoy, T. M., Frumpkin, L. R., Harkins, S. W. "Effects of Meditation on Brain Stem Auditory Evoked Potentials." International Journal of Neuroscience vol. 10, 1980 (2–3) pp. 165–170.

33. Pivik, R. T., Mercier, L. "Motoneuronal Excitability during Wakefulness and non-REM Sleep: H-reflex Recovery in Man." *Sleep* vol. 1 1979, (4) pp. 357–3676.

34. Wallace, R. K., et al. "Modification of the Paired H-reflex through the Transcendental Meditation and TM-Sidhi Program." *Experimental Neurology* vol. 79 1983, pp. 77–86.

35. Wallace, R. K., et al. "The Effects of the Transcendental Meditation and TM-Sidhi Program on the Aging Process." *International Journal of Neuroscience* vol. 16 1982, pp. 53–58.

36. Toomey, M., Chalmers, R., Clements, G. "The Transcendental Meditation and TM-Sidhi Program Reverses the Physiological Aging Process: A Longitudinal Study. In R. A. Chalmers, G. Clements, H. Schenkluhn, M. Weinless (eds.): *Scientific Research On the Transcendental Meditation Program: Collected Papers, Vol. 3*. Vlodrop, the Netherlands: MIU Press. 1983.

37. Glaser, J. L., Brind, J. L., Eisner, M. J., Wallace, R. K. "Elevated Serum Dihydroepiandrosterone Sulfate Levels in Older Practitioners of an Ayurvedic Stress Reduction Program," (1986). Sixteen Annual Meeting of the Society for Neuroscience, Washington, D.C.

38. Werner, O., et al. "Long-term Endocrinologic Changes in Subjects Practicing the Transcendental Meditation and TM-Sidhi Program." *Psychosomatic Medicine* 48(1–2):59–66, Jan.–Feb. 1986.

39. Hedge, G. A., Huffman, L. J. "Vasopressin and Endocrine Function." In D. M. Gash, G. J. Boer (Eds.): *Vasopressin, Principles and Properties*. Plenum Press, New York, 1987.

40. Bohus, B., de Kloet, E. R. "Behavioral Effects of Neuropeptides." In M. T. Jones, Gillham, B., Dallman, M. F., Chattopdhyay, S. (Eds.): *Interaction Within the Brain-Pituitary-Adrenocortical System*. Academic Press, London, 1979.

41. Wurtman, R. J., Cohen, E. L., Fernstrom, J. D. "Control of Brain Neuro-transmitter Synthesis by Precursor Availability and Food Consumption." In E. Usdin, Hamburg, D. A., Barchas, J. D. (Eds.): *Neuroregulators and Psychiatric Disorders*. Oxford University Press, New York, 1977.

42. Sandman, C. A., Kastin, A. J. "Neuropeptide Influences on Behavior: A Possible Treatment for Disorders of Attention." In *Neuroregulators and Psychiatric Disorders*.

43. Grossman, A., Sutton, J. R. "Endorphins: What are they? How are they Measured? What is their Role in Exercise?" *Med. Sci. Sports Exerc*. 1985, Feb; 17(1):74–81.

44. Steinberg, H., Sykes, E. A. "Introduction to Symposium on Endorphins and Behavioral Processes; Review of Literature on Endorphins and Exercise." *Pharmacol. Biochem. Behav*. 1985, Nov; 23(5):857–62.

45. Morgan, W. P. "Affective Beneficence of Vigorous Physical Activity." *Med. Sci. Sports Exerc*. 1985, Feb; 17(1):94–100.

46. Schiffman, S. S. "Taste and Smell in Disease" (second of two parts). *N. Engl. J. Med*. 1983, Jun; 308(22):1337–43.

47. de Wied, D. "Central Actions of ACTH and Related Peptides, Introduction." In D. de Wied (Ed.): *Central Actions of ACTH and Related Peptides*. Fidia Research Series, Symposia in Neuroscience-IV, Liviana Press. Padova, 1986.

48. Morley, J. E., Levine, A. S., Gosnell, B. A., Billington, C. J. "Neuropeptides and Appetite: Contribution of Neuropharmacological Modeling." *Fed. Proc*. 1984, Nov: 43(14):2903–2907.

49. Lieberman, H. R., et al. "Mood, Performance, and Pain Sensitivity: Changes Induced by Food Constituents." *J. Psychiat. Res*. Vol. 17, No. 2, pp. 135–145 (1982/1983).

50. Temple, N. J. "Refined Carbohydrates—A Cause of Suboptimal Nutrient Intake." *Med. Hypotheses*. 1983, Apr; 10(4) pp. 411–424.

51. Hill, A. J., Blundell, J. E. "Nutrients and Behavior: Research Strategies for the Investigation of Taste Characteristics, Food Preferences, Hunger Sensations, and Eating Patterns in Man." *J. Psychiat. Res*. 1982–1983; 17(2):213– 21.

52. Adams, H. B. "Studies in REST.III.REST, Arousability, and the Nature of Alcohol and Substance Abuse." *J. Subst. Abuse Treat*. 1988; 5(2):77–81.

53. Trulson, M. E. "Disassociations between the Effects of Hallucinogens on Behavior and Raphe Unit Activity in Behaving Cats." *Pharmacol. Biochem. Behav*. 1986, Feb; 24(2):351–357.

54. Gelenberg, A. J., Wojcik, J. D., Gibson, C. J., Wurtman, R. J. "Tyrosine for Depression." *J. Psychiat. Res*. 1982–1983; 17(2):175–80.

55. Growdon, J. H., Wurtman, R. J. "Dietary Influences on the Synthesis of Neurotransmitters in the Brain." *Nutr. Rev.* 1979, May; 37(5):129–36.

56. Wurtman, R. J. "Food Consumption, Neurtransmitter Synthesis, and Human Behavior." *Experientia [Suppl]* 1983, 44:356–369.

57. Wurtman, J. J., Wurtman, R. J. "Studies on the Appetite for Carbohydrates in Rats and Humans." *J. Psychiatr. Res.* 1982–1983, 17(2):213–221.

58. Wurtman, R. J. "Research Strategies for Assessing the Behavioral Effects of Food and Nutrients. Introduction." *J. Psychiatr. Res.* 1982–1983, 17(2):103–5.

59. Wurtman, R. J., Wurtman, J. J. "Carbohydrate Craving, Obesity, and Brain Serotonin." Appetite [Suppl] 1986, 7:99–103.

60. Hoebel, B. G. "Brain Reward and Aversion Systems in the Control of Feeding and Sexual Behavior." *Nebr. Symp. Motiv.* 1975, 22:49–112.

61. Any checkout-stand calorie counter will give you this information.

62. Louis-Sylvestre, J. ["Mechanisms of Dietary Selection in Man Preferences and Aversions."] *Ann. Nut. Aliment.* 1976, 30(2–3):331–339.

63. Hoebel, B. G. "Brain Reward and Aversion Systems in the Control of Feeding and Sexual Behavior." *Nebr. Symp. Motiv.* 1975, 22:49–112.

64. Lepkovsky, S. "Regulation of Food Intake." *Adv. Food. Res.* 1975, 21: 1–69.

65. Wurtman, R. J. "Dietary Treatments that Affect Brain Neurotransmitters. Effects on Calorie and Nutrient Intake." *Ann. N.Y. Acad. Sci.* 1987, 499: 179–190.

66. Ksir, H. C., Hakan, R. L., Kellar, K. J. "Chronic Nicotine and Locomotor Activity: Influence of Exposure Dose and Test Dose." *Psychopharmacology (Berlin)* 1987, 92(1):25–29.

67. Ksir, H. C., Hakan, R., Hall, D. P. Jr., Kellar, K. J. "Exposure to Nicotine Enhances the Behavioral Stimulant Effect of Nicotine and Increases Binding of [3H]acetylcholine to Nicotinic Receptors." *Neuropharmacology* 1985, Jun; 24(6):527–531.

68. Markesbery, W. R., Ehman, W. D., Alauddin, M., Hossain, T. I. "Brain Trace Element Concentrations in Aging." *Neurobiol. Aging.* 1984, Spring; 5(1): 19–28.

69. Metropolitan Life Insurance Company, 1975. New Weight Standards for Men and Women.

70. U.S. Department of Health, Education, and Welfare, Public Health Service, National Center for Health Statistics. "Weight, Height, and Selected Body Dimensions for Adults" (1985). Washington, D.C., Government Printing Office.

71. Morley—see S2.

72. Mattes, R. D. "Salt Taste and Hypertension: A Critical Review of the Literature." *J. Chronic Dis.* 1984, 37(3):195–208.

73. Bartoshuk, L. "Influence of Chemoreception and Psychologic State on Food Selection." *Int. J. Obes.* 1980, 4(4):351–355.

74. Pirot, M. "The effects of the Transcendental Meditation Technique upon Auditory Discrimination" (1973). University of British Columbia, Victoria, British Columbia, Canada.

Chapter 6
Figure 12. Biochemical Pathways to the Fake M-State
1. Pomerleau, O. F., Fertig, J. B., Seyler, L. E., and Jaffe, J. H. (1983). Neuroendocrine reactivity to nicotine in smokers. *Psychopharmacology*, 81:61–67.

2. Romano, C., Goldstein, A. (1980). Stereo specific nicotine receptors on rat brain membranes. *Science*, 210:647–649.

3. Henningfeld, J. E., Goldberg, S. R., Miyasato, K., Spealman, R. D., and Jasinski, D. R. (1982). Functional properties of nicotine in monkeys and humans. *Fed. Proc. Fedn. Am. Socs. Exp. Biol.*, 41:7406.

4a. Hutchinson, R. R., Emley, G. S. (1973). Effects of nicotine on avoidance, conditioned suppression, and aggression response measures in animals and man. In *Smoking and Behavior: Motives and Incentives* (ed. W. L. Dunn), pp. 179–196. Washington, D.C.: Winston.

4b. Bernston, G. C., Beattie, M. S., and Walker, J. M. (1976). Effects of nicotinic and muscarinic compounds on biting attack in the cat. *Pharmac. Biochem. and Behav.*, 5:235–239.

5a. Carmichael, F. J., and Israel, Y. (1975). Effects of ethanol on neurotransmitter release by rat brain cortical slices. *J. Pharmacol. Exp. Ther.*, 193:824–834.

5b. Sinclair, J. G., and Lo, G. F. (1978). Acute tolerance to ethanol on the release of acetylcholine from the cat cerebral cortex. *Can. J. Physiol. Pharmacol.*, 56:668–670.

6. Ellis, F. W. (1966). Effect of ethanol on plasma corticosterone levels. *J. Pharmacol. Exp. Ther.*, 153:121–127.

7a. Israel, Y., Videla, L., MacDonald, A., and Bernstein, J. (1973). Metabolic alterations produced in the liver by chronic ethanol administration. *Biochem. J.*, 134:523–529.

7b. Bernstein, J., Videla, L., Israel, Y. (1975). Hormonal influences in the development of the hypermetabolic state of the liver produced by chronic administration of ethanol. *J. Pharmacol. Exp. Ther.*, 192:583–591.

8a. Goodman, L., Gilman, A. (eds.) (1975). *The Pharmacological Basis of Therapeutics, 4th Edition*. London: Macmillan, pp. 291–299.

8b. Ibid., pp. 379–382.

8c. Ibid., pp. 501–505.

8d. Ibid., pp. 299–300.

9. Wise, Roy A. (1984). Neural mechanisms of the reinforcing action of cocaine. In John Grabowski (ed.), *Cocaine: Pharmacology, Effects and Treatment of Abuse*. NIDA Monograph Series. Washington, D.C.: U.S. Government Printing Office.

10. Ibid.

11. Silverstone, T., Goodall, E. (1985). How amphetamine works. In Susan D. Iversen (ed.), *Psychopharmacology: Recent Advances and Future Prospects*. Oxford: Oxford University Press.

13. Mandell, A. J., Knapp, S. (1978). Acute versus chronic effects of psychotropic drugs: Adaptive responses in brain amine systems and their clinical applications. *Psychopharmacol. Bull.*, 22:465–474.

14. Jones, Reese T. (1984). The pharmacology of cocaine. In John Grabowski (ed.), *Cocaine: Pharmacology, Effects and Treatment of Abuse*. NIDA Monograph Series. Washington, D.C.: U.S. Government Printing Office.

15. Campbell, A.M.G., Evans, M., Thomson, J.L.G., William, M. J. (1971). Cerebral atrophy in young cannabis smokers. *Lancet*, 2:1219.

16. Rosenkrantz, H., Miller, A. J., Esber, H. J. (1976). Delta-9 tetrahydrocannabinol suppression of the primary immune response in rats. *J. Toxicol. Environ. Health*, 1:119–125.

17a. Carlini, E. A., Kramer, C. (1965). Effects of cannabis sativa (marihuana) on maze performance of the rat. *Psychopharmacologia*, 7:175.

17b. Tinklenberg, J. R., Melges, F. T., Hollister, L. E., Gillespie, H. K. (1970). Marijuana and immediate memory. *Nature*, 226:1171–1172.

18. Mendelson, J. H., Keuhnle, H., Ellingboe, J., Babor, T. F. (1974). Plasma testosterone levels before, during and after chronic marihuana smoking. *New England Journal of Medicine*, 291:1051.

19. Holtzman, D., Lovell, R. A., Jaffe, J. H., Freedman, D. X. (1969). Tetrahydrocannabinol: neurochemical and behavioral effects. *Science*, 163:1464–1467.

20. Mendelson, J. H. (1970). The biologic concomitants of alcoholism. *New England Journal of Medicine*, 283:24, 71.

21. Wintrobe, M. W., Thorn, G. T., et al. (eds.) (1980). *Harrison's Textbook of Medicine*. New York: McGraw-Hill.

22. Peele, S., Alexander, B. K. (1985). Theories of addiction. In *The Meaning of Addiction*. Lexington: Heath.

23. Peele, S. (1985). Addiction to and experience. In *The Meaning of Addiction*.

24. Morehouse, L. E., Miller, A. T. (1983). *The Physiology of Exercise*. St. Louis: Mosby.

25. Ibid.

26. Ibid.

27. Wurtman, R. J., Wurtman, J. J. (1979). *Nutrition and the Brain, Vol. 4, Toxic Effects of Food Constituents on the Brain*. New York: Raven Press.

28. Ibid.

29. Ibid.

30. Jaffe, J. H. (1975). Narcotic analgesics. In L. S. Goodman, A. Gilman (eds.), *The Pharmacological Basis of Therapeutics, Fourth Edition*. London: Macmillan, pp. 237–272.

31. Ibid.

32. Ibid.

33. Sharpless, S. K. (1975). Hypnotics and sedatives. In *The Pharmacological Basis of Therapeutics*, pp. 98–120.

34. Ibid.

35. Ibid.

INDEX